THE REAL ARCHBISHOP MANNIX
FROM THE SOURCES

JAMES FRANKLIN
GERALD O. NOLAN
MICHAEL GILCHRIST

connorcourt
PUBLISHING

Published in 2015 by Connor Court Publishing Pty Ltd

Copyright © James Franklin, Gerald Nolan, Michael Gilchrist

ALL RIGHTS RESERVED. This book contains material protected under International and Federal Copyright Laws and Treaties. Any unauthorised reprint or use of this material is prohibited. No part of this book may be reproduced or transmitted in any form or by any means, electronic or mechanical, including photocopying, recording, or by any information storage and retrieval system without express written permission from the publisher.

Connor Court Publishing Pty Ltd.
PO Box 224W
Ballarat VIC 3350
sales@connorcourt.com
www.connorcourt.com

ISBN: 9781925138344 (pbk.)

Cover design by Ian James
Cover image: Mannix 1920
© MDHC Catholic Archdiocese of Melbourne

Printed in Australia

CONTENTS

PREFACE ix

First Impressions 1
   First speech in Australia 1

Chapter 1: Conscription and the "ordinary trade war" 9
   Conscription 11
   The "Trade war" episode 13
   Chaplain General 14
   Prime Minister Hughes attacks Mannix 15
   Behind the scenes 16
   "Australia First" speech 18
   The Menace of Mannixism 20

Chapter 2: Irish Troubles viewed from Australia 23
   Have we solved the Land Problem in Ireland? 24
   The Easter rising, Easter Week, 1916 27
   The Great Richmond Racecourse meeting 28
   Speech at St John's College, Sydney University 33

Chapter 3: Arrest on the high seas, 1920 39
   Mannix arrives in America 40
   The address at Madison Square Garden, New York 41
   The British had had enough 54
   Mannix departs from New York 55
   Cabinet considers 57
   The View from Ireland 61
   Arrest at sea 62
   Hughes denounces 68

Chapter 4: Irish Republican icon, 1920–1925 72
    The Bootle affair 73
    Words of farewell: The possibility of peace in Ireland 77
    De Valera letter to Mannix 78
    William T. Cosgrave letter to Mannix 80
    Last visit home, Dublin, 1925 85

Chapter 5: The high tide of sectarianism in Australia 89
    Freemasonry, 'the great tumour' 91
    Protestant attacks 91
    Young Robert Menzies critical of Mannix 93
    The Spanish influenza: No popery 98
    VCs on white chargers 101
    Loyal Orange Lodge protests 104
    Heydon's response to Mannix's 'Australia First' speech 104
    "No Irish need apply": Did Mannix increase employment
    discrimination against Catholics? 108
    A mad dog from Maynooth 111
    Mannix, ecumenist? 111
    Mine enemy grows older: Mannix and Hughes reconciled 112

Chapter 6: Loyal son of the Church? 117
    Mannix on his right to speak 118
    Vatican, Foreign Office and bishops fail to restrain Mannix 118
    Mannix unrepentant again 124
    Archbishop of Dublin? 124
    Mannix meets the Pope 128
    Political action defended 130
    Rebuke from the Apostolic delegate 131

Chapter 7: Mannix as Church leader 135
    The intricacies of Canon Law 136
    Catholics in Australia: Panegyric on Archbishop Carr 139

Catholic principles 143
Mannix's piety 145
Newman College 148
The laity 150
Sex education 152
Vatican II submission 1962 152
State aid: the final victory 156

Chapter 8: Mannix and Labor: the first round 159
Catholic education 160
Catholic interests and the Labor Party 164
Scullin: state aid as electoral poison 166

Chapter 9: Social justice and political action 169
The Church and the workers 171
Capitalism and Depression 175
Women 177
The "Demon drink" 178
Colonialism and Aborigines 178
Jews 180
Communism 181
The interview 182
The Spanish Civil War, 1936 183
Immorality of the Atomic bomb 183
Theory of democracy 185
The Australian Commonwealth and States rights 186
Vietnam 189

Chapter 10: Race suicide and immigration 193
Empty cradles 194
Rural virtue 196
Immigration: 1930s doubts 198
Foreword to *Exit Australia* 199
White Australia 201

Chapter 11: The real Mannix at home 204
    A Maynooth student's view 206
    Rumour of firearms stored at *Raheen* 207
    Dinner at *Raheen* 207
    The daily walks; Maureen 209
    Banter with Fr Hackett, "court jester" 210
    Raheen under the Virgona sisters 212
    What AFL team did Mannix support? 216
    TV comes to *Raheen* 216

Chapter 12: Arthur Calwell, Mannix's man 219
    Calwell reminisces 221
    Young Calwell picked up by Security 221
    Calwell on social justice 224
    Maiden speech on the population problem 225
    Mannix and Calwell in support of Italian internees 227
    Gilroy's reception of the red hat 230
    Immigration succeeds with Eastern Europeans 233
    The White Australia policy 235
    'What the Popes have said on capitalism'
    and Mannix on nationalisation 237
    Santamaria and Calwell fall out 238
    Calwell "hurt" by Mannix 239

Chapter 13: Santamaria and the Movement 243
    Mannix makes an offer 244
    The Communist Party dissolution debate 246
    Santamaria reports to Mannix on the Movement's aim
    to transform Australia 248
    Does Calwell deserve absolution? 251
    The Pope acts against Mannix and Santamaria 251
    Mannix despondent 255
    Mannix and Evatt clash: the 1958 election 255
    Santamaria at the death of Mannix 257

Chapter 14: Death and transformation into legend 260
    Mannicdotes 263
    Hardy's *Power without Glory* 264
    Oakley's *The Feet of Daniel Mannix* 265
    The next generations 268

Afterword: Back of house 271

Acknowledgements

The authors are grateful to Patrick Morgan for valuable advice, to Rachel Naughton of the Melbourne Diocesan Historical Commission for archival assistance, to Danny Cusack for research in Ireland, and to Peter Barrett and others who helped with proofreading.

Preface

There have been twelve books written about Mannix, a count rivalled only by that other Irish-Australian troublemaker, Ned Kelly. That is good evidence that the subject is still far from exhausted, especially given that the existing interpretations range from the adulatory to the scathing.[1] It is time to let the man speak for himself.

Archbishop Mannix missed by a few months becoming Australia's most famous centenarian. He was undoubtedly Australia's most famous ecclesiastic, its most famous Irishman, most prominent tribal leader and most vigorous mixer of those two volatile ingredients, religion and politics. Though his fifty-years in Melbourne (1913 to 1963) is now a long time ago, he cast a long shadow forward over church and state. His younger admirers B.A. Santamaria and Arthur Calwell directed Australian history into new channels. In the next generation, Cardinal Pell and Tony Abbott even now maintain some of the directions set when the new coadjutor Archbishop arrived at Spencer Street Station just before Easter, 1913. Mannix is not just a figure of the distant past.

Appreciating Mannix is a special pleasure since he was a man notably gifted at speaking for himself. He was one of the great Australian orators, in a style uniquely sardonic and mockingly patrician.

The classic Mannix speech has the audience laughing every few sentences at the follies and self-contradictions of his opponents. Audience participation was essential, as in this extract from an anti-conscriptionist speech chosen for inclusion in a book of Australia's most notable speeches:[2]

You will be appealed to as if everything depended on what Australia does or leaves undone. *[Laughter]* Now Australians are – have proved themselves to be – the bravest of the brave. *[Applause]* But if every man of them were as brave as Hector – *['They are!']* – a hundred thousand of them, more or less, would not count for much when 15 million men are said to be engaged . . .

They talk loudly about the 'last man'. They talk in a more subdued tone about the 'last shilling'. But when it comes to raising the taxes, these people are ready enough to pass the burden to others . . . [*Cheers*]

Everyone was enjoying themselves.

He could, with that verbal magic, elevate agreement into sheer joy, the ecstasy aroused by exact expression wonderfully achieved, and he could transform opposition into the frenzy of powerlessness induced by overwhelming mastery of words' weapons.[3]

It was entertainment, but entertainment with a purpose. To understand the point of Mannix, it is necessary to remember that in early twentieth century Australia most Catholics were at the bottom of the social heap. And in those early industrial times, the bottom of the heap was an overworked, dirty, dangerous and deprived place to be, a place very hard to get out of. If their reaction was resentment, there was a lot to resent.

Cardinal Pell, who stands in the tradition of Mannix and grew up in a world suffused by his influence, explains the need felt by the poor Catholics of early 20th century Melbourne for a leader in the self-confident and regal style of Mannix:[4]

These people, many of Irish extraction, without too many of this world's goods, felt that they had a social and religious champion, a leader, someone who would defend their rights, preserve their faith and help them win a place in the sun for their children . . . Mannix, in particular, sparked the confidence and determination of the Catholic community not to be treated as second-rate citizens . . . to gain a full place in Australian society without jettisoning their Catholic baggage.

If from this distance one wonders if "getting on" is really the point of Christianity, that is to forget what it was like to see one's children in poverty and without opportunities. Mannix's long campaigns over education were focussed on the way out for his flock.

We give space not only to Mannix himself but to his associates and opponents. Mannix was not a direct political actor, but his followers Calwell and Santamaria were. They too were masters of forceful English prose.

Mannix's opponents, from Prime Minister Billy Hughes down, delivered a stream of colourful abuse which makes interesting reading – in small doses. Their words shine a light onto an old sectarian Australia, a scene of bitter feuds now forgotten – and forgotten, in part, because of the success of postwar multicultural immigration, a project foreshadowed by Mannix and implemented by Calwell.

This is a book of documents, not a connected biography. Unlike a biography, it does not need to cover everything. It can confine itself just to the interesting, well-expressed and self-revelatory pieces. In the case of Mannix, that constitutes a great deal.

The essentials of Mannix's life, sufficient to organise the following material, are laid out in this timeline:

1864	Birth in Charleville, County Cork, Ireland
1890	Ordained priest at St Patrick's College, Maynooth
1901	Paper on the Irish land question
1903	President of Maynooth
1913	Arrival in Melbourne as Coadjutor Archbishop
1914	Failed attempt to influence Labor policy through Catholic Federation
1916	Anti-conscription speeches before first conscription referendum
1917	Archbishop of Melbourne on death of Archbishop Carr, purchase of *Raheen*
	Opposition to second conscription referendum and Richmond speech for Irish nationalism
1918	Opening of Newman College at Melbourne University and St Kevin's College
1919	Controversy over offer of nurses during Spanish flu epidemic
1920	US tour and Madison Square Garden Irish nationalist speech
	Arrested off Ireland by British destroyer
1921	Interview with Pope Benedict XV on Irish questions
1923	Foundation of Corpus Christi seminary, Werribee
1925	Last visit to Ireland, speeches in favour of Irish Republicanism
1934	Rebuke from Rome for Irish Republican utterances
1936	Encouragement of B.A. Santamaria to found *Catholic Worker*
1937	National Secretariat for Catholic Action set up to coordinate political activities
1940	Calwell's maiden speech on population and child endowment
1947	First Eastern European Displaced Persons in Calwell's immigration program
1955	Support for Santamaria in Labor party split
1961	ABC television interview at the age of 97
1963	Death at *Raheen* at age 99

[1] Arranged in approximate order from hagiographic to critical, they are: Cyril Bryan, *Archbishop Mannix: Champion of Australian Democracy*, Advocate Press, Melbourne, 1918; Walter A. Ebsworth, *Archbishop Mannix*, H.H. Stephenson, Armadale, 1977; Frank Murphy, *Daniel Mannix, Archbishop of* , Advocate Press, Melbourne, 1948 updated in Polding Press, Melbourne, 1972; E. J. Brady, *Doctor Mannix: Archbishop of Melbourne*, Library of National Biography, 1934; B. A. Santamaria, Daniel Mannix: The quality of leadership, Melbourne University Press, Carlton, 1989; Michael Gilchrist, *Daniel Mannix: Priest & patriot*, Dove Communications, Melbourne, 1982, updated in *Daniel Mannix: Wit and wisdom*, Freedom Publications, North Melbourne, 2004; Colm Kiernan, *Daniel Mannix and Ireland*, Alella Books, Morwell, 1984; Niall Brennan, *Dr Mannix*, Rigby, Adelaide, 1964; Patrick Mannix, *The Belligerent Prelate: An alliance between Archbishop Daniel Mannix and Eamon de Valera*, Cambridge Scholars Publishing, Newcastle upon Tyne, 2013; James Griffin with Paul Ormonde, *Daniel Mannix: Beyond the myths*, Garratt Publishing, Mulgrave, 2012. To appear are the book from the Daniel Mannix: His Legacy conference of 2013 and Brenda Niall's biography. Patrick Morgan's *Melbourne Before Mannix*, Connor Court, Ballan, 2012, is partly about Mannix.

[2] Speech on the second conscription referendum at the Stadium, Melbourne, Oct 1917, repr. in *Well May We Say: The speeches that made Australia*, ed. Sally Warhaft, Black Inc, Melbourne, 2004, pp. 235-8; also in L. Lloyd Robson, *Australia and the Great War, 1914-1918*, Macmillan, Melbourne, 1969, pp. 934.

[3] Patrick O'Farrell, Santamaria's Mannix, *Quadrant* 22 (9), Sept 1978, 24-27.

[4] George Pell, Review of Michael Gilchrist, *Daniel Mannix: Priest and Patriot*, *Australasian Catholic Record* 60 (1983), 211-5.

First Impressions

Coadjutor Archbishop Mannix shortly after his arrival in Australia in March 1913[1]

First Speech in Australia

On Easter Sunday, 23 March 1913, Dr Daniel Mannix arrived in Melbourne from Dublin as Coadjutor to Archbishop Carr. On that day he read his first speech in Australia at St Patrick's Cathedral before an audience of 5000. He had carefully prepared a speech which raised issues he was to pursue for fifty years – justice in education, the independence of Ireland, the hopes and demands of Catholic Australians. We give the speech in full.[2]

Very Reverend and Dear Fathers and my Dear Friends, – I am deeply touched by your kind words, and by the warm and generous welcome with which you have greeted my arrival at my new home. From a full heart I thank you. For, having travelled far, it is a grateful thing to find oneself still among trusty and warm-hearted friends.

"This event is an epoch-making one, we are welcoming a new energy, a new light, and a new force"

Dean Hegarty of Kyneton

In spite of your kindly and too generous references to me, I cannot but feel that to most of you I come as a stranger, untried and unknown. I, therefore, recognise in the cordiality of the reception you offer me a pledge of your undivided loyalty, first to the Father of all the Faithfull by whom I was sent, and then to your own illustrious and beloved Chief Pastor, whose labours I have come to share.

For, with me you hope and pray that his Grace the Archbishop, now relieved by my coming of some part of the burden which he has borne for more than a quarter century, will husband his energies, and so continue for many years to rule this diocese with that conspicuous ability to which you have paid rightful tribute in your addresses and by which the Metropolitan See of Melbourne has been raised to undisputed pride of place among the great dioceses of the Church of God.

Ireland and Australia

It is a long way from Ireland to Australia, from Maynooth to Melbourne. And, if I may confess the truth, it was a great sorrow and a great wrench to turn my face away from my own dear country and from my own kindred. A hundred bonds stronger than steel bound me to the dear old land, from which so many of you, like myself have come.

With congenial work and kind friends around me in the cloisters of Maynooth,

> "... I have come to another Ireland over the sea ..."

I might have hoped to look out for years to come from my peaceful and happy seclusion upon the increasing prosperity of Ireland, at length the mistress – as I hope she soon will be – of her own destiny;* but if this was not to be, and if the burden of the episcopal office was to be laid upon me, then I am free to confess, with equal sincerity and candour, that the Holy Father could have laid no more pleasing and acceptable command upon me than that to join the priests of the Archdiocese of Melbourne in their loyal and devoted service to their revered Archbishop. No words can express my gratitude to the priests of the Archdiocese for the warmth and loyalty of their welcome. I am proud to be a worker in their ranks, and the years to come will prove how deeply I feel my indebtedness to them.

"Youngest Daughter of the Church"

I am assured, and I know, that in coming to Australia I am to be associated with the youngest the fairest and the most promising daughter of the Church.

For God's hand is not shortened, and He will surely finish the grand imposing edifice whose foundations He has well and truly laid by your hands and those who went before you in the fair Australian land. I know that I have been sent to minister to a noble-hearted, generous, faithful Catholic people, who in the span of a lifetime have built up an organisation and raised monuments of faith and piety, that claim the admiration and wonder of all those who have watched the progress of the Church in Australia. I know that in this diocese I am privileged to work with a clergy learned, pious, zealous, and self sacrificing, loyal to their Archbishop and loved and trusted by the people. I know, in fine, that I have been honoured by the Holy Father with the commission to serve with an Archbishop whose rare gifts of mind and heart have won the esteem and affection, not merely of his own flock, but even of those who do not worship within his fold – a prelate whose voice and pen have conferred distinction, not upon Melbourne only, but upon the whole Church in Australia.

> "... Australia ... the youngest, the fairest and the most promising daughter of the Church"

Yes my dear friends, I left Ireland with natural regret and not without misgivings for my own shortcomings. But, assuredly I am not without compensation and hope. I have come to another Ireland over the sea, rich in the best gifts for which I love my own land and my own people, rich beyond all comparison in the wide and

---
* The Irish Home Rule Bill passed the House of Commons for the third time on 25 May 1913.

fertile field that it offers to the husbandmen of the Lord. I share your confidence and your hope that a great future lies before the Church in Australia, and I pray God to hasten the day when this fair land may be truly said to be conquered for His Kingdom.

THE EDUCATION QUESTION.

It is not without reason that you have touched upon the Education question in your pregnant and stimulating addresses. That question is always with you. I know its urgency, how much it presses upon you and hampers your progress.

> *... the unequal treatment meted out to you in the schools is ... the one great stain upon the statute books of this free and progressive land"*

From the Catholic standpoint, the unequal treatment meted out to you in the schools is, as far as I can judge, the one great stain upon the statute books of this free and progressive land. Long before I ever thought that the Education question of Australia would have for me the practical interest that it has to-day, I wondered that a problem that has been solved with greater or less success, in many of the old countries had found no satisfactory solution – no attempt even at a solution – in any of the States of this great democratic land, in which freedom and fair play for every good citizen are claimed to be the very life breath of the Constitution. With just pride you have reminded me that the open handed generosity of the Catholic people of Australia, and heroic sacrifices of the teaching Sisters and Brothers, have enabled the pastors of the Church to meet a situation otherwise intolerable, without violence to the Catholic conscience. I am fully aware of the facts, and I know, too, that even in Australia, Victoria stands without a rival for generosity in the cause of Catholic principle. I am proud to be associated with a people who give such an example to the fidelity of their faith. But the heroic sacrifices of the Catholic body are no palliation for a crying public wrong. From this day I claim to be – and as time goes on I hope to justify my claim to be considered – a good Australian, jealous of the interests and of the good name of my adopted country. But, as a citizen of Victoria and of the Commonwealth, it will be to me as it must be to all fair-minded people who value the fair fame of Australia, a source of genuine regret that the Catholic body – good patriotic citizens – should suffer for conscience sake, and be forced to buy twice over with their hard-won, money and with the heroic and ill-requited labour of their teaching Sisterhoods and Brotherhoods, the right to educate their children according to the dictates of their consciences. Catholics, do not expect the impossible. They only want fair play from any statesman or party who will come out to meet them, and to treat with them on the borderland of reason and just concession.

Higher Education.

You have been good enough to refer to my connection with higher education in Ireland, and to express the hope that my interest in that question may be continued in my new sphere of work. You look forward, no doubt, to the time when the Catholics of Australia will avail themselves even more fully than they do now of the culture and learning and other advantages which the Universities place within their reach. The progress and development of the Commonwealth, and its place and standing among the nations is bound up with the work of the Universities. If Australia is to prosper, and to grow and develop along national and staple lines, if it is to use to lasting advantage its great natural wealth and resources, it must spare no effort to raise the standard and efficiency of the Universities, and bring the advantages of higher education within the reach of all those who are fitted to profit by it. I am aware that Australia is alive to this, and that the different States have done much to provide adequate endowment and the most perfect equipment for the State Universities.

Now, in a community in which religious interests are at variance and educational ideas conflicting, Catholics cannot always secure that type of University education which they should desire. There must be a certain amount of adjustment of rival claims. There will inevitably be difficulties to be surmounted and dangers to be guarded against. But in a progressive age, and especially in a new and progressive country like yours, probably the greatest danger of all would be if Catholics were to stand aloof from the Universities, to contribute nothing to the atmosphere which the coming men of Australia are breathing in the formative period of their lives – to exercise no influence in shaping the thought and ideals of the Universities – to accept the status of an inferior caste in their own land. In the natural course, the men who will make their mark for good or ill in Australian life will come from its Universities. Exceptions there will be for whom no rule can provide. But, for the most part, the leaders of thought and action, the captains of industry, the heads of the learned professions, the men that will control the press, the scientists who will claim to extend the confines of knowledge and make war or peace with religion, the leaders of public

"... probably the greatest danger of all would be if Catholics were to stand aloof from the Universities, to contribute nothing to the atmosphere which the coming men of Australia are breathing in the formative period of their lives..."

life who will make or mar the wellbeing of the Commonwealth – all these will pass through the halls of the Universities. And hence, I am in full agreement with you when you convey the hope that every inducement should be held out to Catholics to take their proper place in the Universities, with all due and sufficient safeguards for their faith and for the practice of their religion. They will, at the Universities, form those youthful friendships that often count for so much in the struggle for success in after life.

> "... *Catholics might justly hope to secure without fear or favour their due and proportionate share of the good things that Australia has to offer in public and private life*"

They will have a better opportunity of measuring themselves in early life with those who are later on to be their rivals and competitors for the bigger prizes of life and for that power and influence that will shape the economical, political, and religious destiny of their country. The Universities should profit by the leavening of live, active Catholicism, the Church unobtrusively would obtain a hearing in the seats of learning, and Catholics might justly hope to secure without fear or favour their due and proportionate share of the good things that Australia has to offer in public and private life.

UNIVERSITY DEGREES

I am much gratified to gather from the address of the priests of the Archdiocese that you are fully alive to the desirability of the clergy also securing for themselves the stamp and the hallmark of University degrees. This will be all the more desirable the more the Catholic laity come to avail themselves of University training. And in a mixed community like yours it will be an obvious advantage to have a recognised public test and guarantee of the standard of learning and scholarship required in the Catholic priesthood. In saying so much, my meaning is not that the existing type of clerical education requires to be substantially modified, or the standard raised, but rather that the time is coming, or has come, when the Catholic clergy should, in the interests of the Church and of religion, secure wherever it is possible official recognition from the Universities for the liberal course of studies through which they gain admission to the ranks of the priesthood. At my own college of Maynooth – the Alma Mater of the vast majority of the priests of Ireland – no candidate is allowed to begin his theological studies until he is a University graduate, having taken out all the courses of study and passed all his public examinations prescribed by the University for a degree in arts. I am glad to know that the same is true of other colleges at which students are prepared for the ministry in this Archdiocese.

Your significant references to University education give me hope and encouragement, and I can assure you that, under the wise guidance of the Archbishop, no effort on my part will be wanting to give effect to your enlightened views and to bring the highest available University training within the reach of Catholics – the clergy and the laity – and under conditions that will not expose their faith or their spiritual interests to needless risk.

". . . appointments in the public service have been thrown open to competition by public examination"

I believe that in recent times the appointments in the public service have been thrown open to competition by public examination. It is not too much to hope that the same enlightened policy will be logically extended to the State scholarships, that open the way, especially for the poor man's child, to a University education, and that the last vestige of the discrimination still existing at the portals of the Universities against Catholics and their schools will be speedily removed.

Thanks for Cordial Welcome.

I thank you all again for the cordial welcome you have given me, for the kind words you have spoken, and, above all, for the hearty and loyal co-operation which you are good enough to promise me. On my part, I promise the best that is in me. With God's help, I will ever be at your service in the cause of temperance, of education, and of every good work, spiritual or temporal, in which you, as Catholics, are interested.

"In His own good time He will people the vast solitudes of this fertile land"

Already I am an Australian in this, that, like you, I am a true believer in the great future of Australia. I can feel around me the buoyancy of youth and of hope, the promise of big achievement. The earth is the Lord's, and the fullness thereof. In His own good time He will people the vast solitudes of this fertile land. He will unlock the treasures of the earth and bid His sunshine minister to the needs and to the pleasure of a teeming population. God grant that in that day Australia may be true to her call. God grant that Australia, awakened and arisen, may send up from her young heart the praise of true worship to Him who fashioned her in beauty and waited through all the years for the homage of her love. And, gathered here in the noble Cathedral of our Archdiocese, while we pray in all humility that we, all of us, may do our allotted parts for the material and spiritual expansion of our country, we may also fittingly and reverently ask God to bless this fair city by the Southern Sea, that the fidelity of its Catholic people may ever be the fitting complement of its marvellous beauty, and that it may never yield that proud pre-eminence which so largely enhances the greeting offered to me on this auspicious Easter day.

---

[1] From a very old image supplied by Michael Gilchrist.

[2] Cyril Bryan, *Archnishop Mannix: Champion of Australian Democracy*, Chapter II, The First Speech in Australia, The Advocate Press, Melbourne, 1918, pp. 16-22.

Chapter 1: Conscription and the "ordinary trade war"

The third war year, 1916, saw increasingly grim news from the Western front. Among the industrial-scale carnage of the Battle of the Somme, with its million casualties, were Australians in numbers that people at home had never imagined. On the night of 19-20 July 1916, a botched attack on German trenches at Fromelles resulted in 5,533 Australian casualties including nearly 2,000 dead. It was the worst twenty-four hours in Australian military history.

Over the next two weeks, there were 23,000 Australian casualties at Pozières.

Recruitment at home fell drastically. The Prime Minister, Billy Hughes, wished to introduce conscription as in most belligerent nations, including Britain (but not Ireland). Only conscription could supply the numbers needed if Australia was to keep up its contribution to the Empire's task. He announced a referendum for 28 October 1916, aiming to give the government a mandate to introduce conscription.

Almost all leaders of society urged a vote for conscription, to give the troops overseas the help they needed and eliminate the advantages of "shirking". Protestant clergymen in particular were almost all strong supporters – Protestants often saw the British Empire as sacred and support for it a religious as well as a civic duty.[2]

Billy Hughes addresses a crowd in Sydney's Martin Place during the first conscription campaign, 1916[1]

On the other hand ... should even more men be sacrificed when the contribution of a small country to a distant war was unlikely to make any real difference to the outcome? Perhaps Australia had done enough? The Irish in Australia were sceptical of the British Empire's claim to be the embodiment of freedom, memories of centuries of British oppression in Ireland having been revived by the British execution of leaders of the Easter Rising in Dublin in 1916. In the pro-war atmosphere of the time, very few public figures came forward to express these misgivings – indeed, only two at the highest level of public prominence, the Catholic Labor premier of Queensland T.J. Ryan, and Archbishop Mannix.

Mannix gave a few restrained speeches on the reasons for opposing conscription – at public meetings, not from the pulpit as Protestant ministers often did. The referendum was narrowly defeated. Loyalists blamed Mannix, though his degree of influence on the vote was unclear.

The war news was just as bad through 1917, with massive Australian casualties at Bullecourt and in Flanders, again without victory being apparently any closer. Hughes determined to try again and a second referendum was announced for 20 December 1917.

Catholic opinion moved against conscription during the second referendum debate. As the Pope pointed out, it was conscription in Europe that had made the slaughter of the war so much greater than it would have been otherwise. "Conscription," Benedict XV wrote in 1917, "has been the real cause of many of the evils for now more than a century; in the mutual simultaneous abolition of conscription lies the sole remedy."[3] In addition, Hughes's proposal did not exempt teaching brothers and seminarians, intruding on religious prerogatives.[4]

Passions ran high as Mannix again attacked conscription, connected it with Irish issues, advocated "Australia before the Empire", and went so far as to describe the War as an "ordinary trade war". Irish Catholics in general and Mannix in particular were widely attacked as disloyalists and traitors.

Hughes himself denounced Mannix vigorously and blamed him for the defeat of the second referendum. He encouraged action against alleged Sinn Fein traitors by the Counter Espionage Bureau, Australia's first secret service, which was run from the Governor-General's office in Melbourne by his official secretary, George Steward.[5] The spies intercepted some of Mannix's correspondence but discovered nothing more sinister that a "plot" to import Irish priests by appointing them as troop ship chaplains, and Mannix's efforts to take over the *Advocate* newspaper.[6]

Hughes, the Governor-General, and the Imperial government in London corresponded in unrestrained terms on Mannix's faults, while Protestant organs in Australia warned their readers of "the menace of Mannixism".

Conscription

Mannix recalled much later the reasons why he became involved in the conscription referendum campaigns of 1916-1917.[9]

I really couldn't say now whether I had made up my mind that I would make any public intervention in the conscription issue until I read in the newspapers that the Anglican Archbishop at the time in St. Paul's Cathedral, from the pulpit, came out definitely – as he was quite entitled to do – in favour of conscription and if I hadn't been thinking already, that put me to thinking. I was not in favour of conscription, and I was greatly afraid that conscription put to the people at that time might possibly have succeeded. The whole press of Australia was in its favour, a strong section of the people was in favour of conscription because the Government, under Mr. Hughes, was in favour, and I had the idea that with the wave of enthusiasm, almost hysteria, conscription would be carried.

When opening a bazaar held in the Albert Hall, Clifton Hill, in aid of the funds of St. John's Roman Catholic parish, Clifton Hill, on 16 September 1916, Archbishop Mannix gave an anti-conscriptionist speech. The tone was measured and reasonable by later standards:[10]

I am as anxious as anyone can be for a successful issue and for an honourable peace. I hope and believe that that peace can be secured without conscription. (Applause.) For conscription is a hateful thing, and it is almost certain to bring evil in its train. (Applause.)

I have been under the impression, and I still retain the conviction, that Australia has done her full share – I am inclined to say more than her full share – in this war. (Applause.)

Her loyalty to the Empire has been lauded to the skies, and the bravery of her sons has won the admiration of friend and foe alike. (Applause.) There may be in the Commonwealth those who have not borne their fair share of the common burden, but I think their number is comparatively small. It seems, therefore, truly regrettable that Australia should be plunged into the turmoil of a struggle about conscription, which is certain to be bitter, and which will give joy to Australia's enemies. (Applause.)

Australians, brave as they have proved themselves to be in the field, are a peace loving people. They will not easily give conscription a foothold in this country. (Applause.) The Prime Minister has very wisely ignored evil counsel and allowed the people to decide for themselves. (Applause.) He has promised them full freedom of discussion. I hope the discussion will be conducted with as little heat and friction as the circumstances permit. I trust that the voice of the people will be heard, and that it will prevail. (Applause.) We can only give both sides a patient hearing, and then vote according to our judgment. There will be differences among Catholics, for Catholics do not think or vote in platoons (applause) and on most questions there is room for divergence of opinion. But, for myself, it will take a good deal to convince me that conscription in Australia would not cause more evil than it would avert. (Applause.) I honestly believe that Australia has done her full share and more, and that she cannot reasonably be expected to bear the financial strain and the drain upon her manhood that conscription would involve. (Applause.) If conscription were adopted I should expect to find later on that many who are now its loudest advocates would be the first to rise up against the taxation necessary to redeem our obligations to the returned soldiers or to their widows or orphans or dependants in case the soldiers gave their lives on the battlefield. I think I can say that I have read most of the appeals that have been made for conscription in Australia. But in spite of these eloquent and impassioned appeals my common sense will not allow me to believe that the addition of 100,000 or 200,000 conscript Australians to the 15,000,000 of fighting men that the Allies have at their disposal could be a deciding factor or even a substantial factor in the issue of the war. However, the people must decide for themselves. The vast majority of the voters at the referendum will, of course, be persons who could not be called to serve in a conscript army. But still, I think that even they, or a majority of them, will prefer to rely on the voluntary system and make it more efficient, if they can, rather than to force the men of Australia, married and single, to face enemy guns in Europe. That is what conscription, in many cases, would mean, and I incline to believe that those who propose it have misjudged the temper of the Australian people in the mass and their passionate love for freedom. (Loud applause.) I notice that certain authorities of the Anglican Church have given their public support to conscription. They are, of course, quite within their rights in doing so. We all have equal right to contribute to the discussion, and in the exercise of that right I have spoken to-night. (Prolonged applause.)

> "... *Australia has done her full share and more*"

The referendum of 28 October 1916 was narrowly defeated with 1,087,557 in favour and 1,160,033 against.[11] Victoria was one of the three states to vote YES.

The "Trade War" Episode

In an address delivered at Brunswick on Sunday 28 January, 1917, Mannix said:[12]

They had heard much about the causes of the war, and about the fight for the small nations. It was fortunate for them that they were fighting on the side of small nations.

"... like most wars – just an ordinary trade war"

But, when all was said, and all concessions made, the war was like most wars – just an ordinary trade war. (Applause.) As long as they could remember, Germany was capturing more of the world's trade than other nations thought to be her due. The other nations, or some of them, had equal opportunities, but they could not, or they did not, achieve the same success. Trade jealousy on both sides had seemed for many years

Melbourne, Vic. c. 1945. Archbishop Daniel Mannix, Catholic Chaplain General of the Australian Army with three unidentified representatives from the Australian Army Nursing Service (AANS), Women's Royal Australian Army Corps and the Women's Royal Australian Naval Service in the garden at the Archbishop's residence Raheen. The visitors were completing a moral leadership course for Catholic personnel during a special visit to Raheen (Donor J. Morgan)[7]

past to make a great war inevitable. How it would come about was a matter of accident. The invasion of Belgium was the spark that lighted the fire in Great Britain. But it was useless to shut one's eyes to all that went before. (Applause.) Trade jealousy was long leading to a trade war, and the war came. Even now, people were arranging how the vanquished nations – when they were vanquished – were to be crippled in their future trade. They told us that the victory would be a barren victory, and all the bloodshed vain, if the enemy were to retain after the war a chance of again beating in trade the rivals whom they failed to beat in war. Whatever else may be involved, it was just a truism that the war was a trade war. (Applause.) But, like many truisms, it was likely to startle those who take all their views from the daily press. (Applause.)

Early editions of the *Argus* of 29 January 1917 reported that Mannix had actually said "sordid trade war", but it seems unlikely that was true.[13] The *Argus* led the attack, as it was to lead many attacks on the Archbishop in the coming years. It replied with this editorial:[14]

"Argus" Leader, 31/1/1917.

The speech delivered on Sunday last, at the opening of the new Roman Catholic school at Brunswick, was, perhaps, the most wicked and mischievous of an extremely unpleasant series of speeches designed to outrage the loyal feelings of the great mass of the people … It would be vain to attempt to argue with one who outrages decency by his monstrous perversions as Dr. Mannix does, with apparent enjoyment of the pain he inflicts.

Chaplain General

Indignation naturally ensued when in 1917 Archbishop Carr died and Mannix, as Archbishop of the capital city, assumed the title of Catholic "Chaplain General of the Armed Forces".

The protest was led by the Reverend Henry Worrall,* who will appear again.[8]

While lesser rebels were beaten in our streets by angry women using umbrellas as weapons of chastisement, and the Courts inflicted heavy fines, Dr Mannix was rewarded with a commission in an army that was, according to his pious or impious judgement, engaged in a "sordid trade war". The whole situation had grown from the grotesque to the monstrous. The Roman Catholic Church had a perfect right to nominate a candidate for

"*. . . While lesser rebels were beaten in our streets by angry women using umbrellas as weapons . . .*"

---
* Rev Henry ("Wowser") Worrall, Methodist minister, scourge of drinkers, gamblers, shirkers, disloyalists and Roman Catholics; later grand master of the Loyal Orange Lodge of Victoria.

the position of Chaplain-General but no loyal Government, returned to win the war, had any right to dishonour the army and to disgrace itself by presenting a commission and an officer's uniform to a man who had publicly declared, "If I am a Sinn Feiner[†] I have nothing to apologise for." If it were not derogatory to the dignity of a Sinn Feiner to fire the nation's flag, to stain his hands with the blood of inoffensive women and children, to wreck property and to lead insurrections, it ought to be repellent to any self respecting section of the British Empire to see such a man strut through the ranks of British and Australian heroes clothed in the King's uniform. Any valiant Australian soldier who refused to salute Chaplain-General Mannix might be court-martialled!

PRIME MINISTER HUGHES ATTACKS MANNIX

Hughes split the Labor Party, but led a Nationalist Party to victory in the election of May 1917. He soon determined to try again for conscription and set down a second referendum for 20 December 1917. The contest was more bitter than in 1916. Opening the campaign in the Sydney Town Hall, Hughes violently attacked all those undermining the war effort, especially "a certain ecclesiastic".[15]

A VITAL QUESTION

Will the Favourite Fall, and let the Imported Outsider Win?[16]

. . . Recruiting did not fail because of a shortage of men, nor for want of work, nor want of money, nor because the Government held up the spectre of compulsion to frighten the people. It failed because there has been these months past in our midst, propaganda preached by various sections, having, per-

---

[†] Mannix's Irish nationalism is dealt with in the next chapter.

haps, nothing in common with one another, expressing hatred of all that we have, hatred of the British and hatred of all those things Australia and loyal citizens value, spragging the wheel of voluntary recruiting. It failed, as did the Russian army, as did the Italian army, because of the treachery in our midst.

SINN FEINERS CENSURED

I say deliberately that there is a section of men in our midst, in addition to the I.W.W., Syndicalists,* and reckless extremists – a band of men whose one foremost desire is to hinder England and do her harm. (Applause.) They are followers of that society known as Sinn Fein. I say that it is vile that a certain ecclesiastic should declare:

Voices: Why don't you intern him? Kick him out of Australia.

[Mr Hughes passed over the interjections and went on]

This ecclesiastic insulted the whole Australian people vilely. More than any other section, he insulted those loyal Irish Australians who have gone out to die for these men, who put Australia first. (Cheers and voices: Intern him.) This man and those who follow Sinn Fein are prepared to offer up Australia on the altars of something obtainable only by the disintegration of the Empire. (Applause.)

A voice: You made him Chaplain-general of the Australian forces.

At this stage a woman in the front seats stood up and cried, 'Why don't you deal with him?' (Applause and dissent.)

Continuing, Mr. Hughes repeated that what Sinn Fein desired could only be brought about by disintegration of the British Empire.

Whether you be English or Irish, show that man and those who stand with him that you do put Australia first. (Thunderous applause. Hundreds stood up and waved their hats.) I say to you, Irish Australians, that if you want to prove your loyalty to Australia, do not desert these gallant men – these gallant Irish. (Cheers.)

BEHIND THE SCENES

Intelligence gathering in Australia began in earnest in January 1916 at the behest of MI5 in London, there having been no nationwide organisation for this purpose before then. Major George Steward, appointed head of the Australian Counter-Espionage Bureau, reported:[17]

---

* Industrial Workers of the World and Syndicalists: revolutionary socialist organizations with small followings in Australia.

I attribute the defeat [of the referendums] almost entirely to the Roman Catholic element resident in this country; particularly do I attach the greatest blame to Dr. Mannix ... That Dr. Mannix should have been allowed to act as he did during the referendum campaign without being stopped by the authorities will constitute for me one of the most inexplicable things with which I have ... come in contact ... He has been the most disturbing element this country has ever seen; clever, cunning, and untrustworthy in anything and everything which concerned the rights of the Empire ...

The Governor-General, Sir Ronald Munro Ferguson,‡ wrote to the Colonial Office in September 1917:[18]

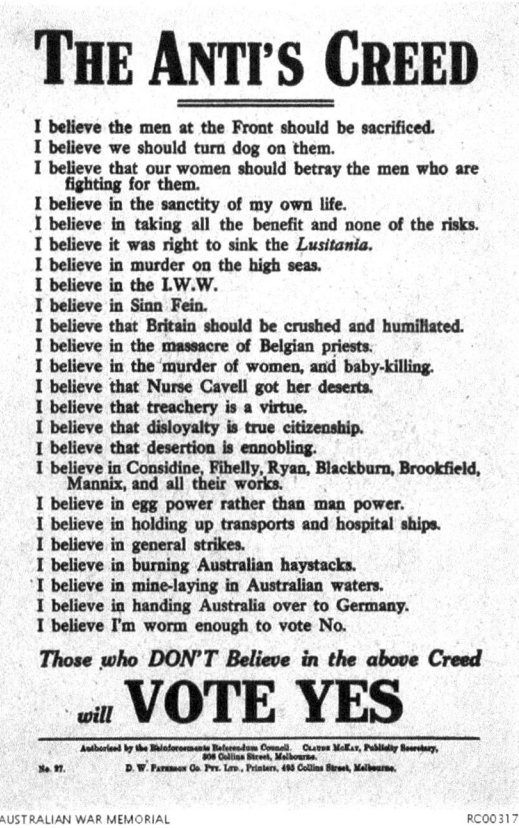

AUSTRALIAN WAR MEMORIAL   RC00317

This person is engaged in stirring up strife sectarian industrial class *(?sic)*. His attitude towards the war may be manifest from his reference to it as "a sordid trade war". He sympathises openly with Sinn Fein and is himself its protagonist although in his speech on the subject he said "he would not say whether he was a Sinn Feiner or not." He was one of the most blatant opponents of Conscription. He said on Saturday last that he and those who voted with him were the saviours of the country. He vehemently supports the Pope's peace proposals mainly because they seem to hit Great Britain and help Germany. Men on strike receive his support not because he believes in the cause of labour but because he sees that such eulogy tends to hamper recruiting and by stirring up class feeling prevents the despatch of food, etc., shipping to Britain and her Allies. He is not Australian having been here only about twelve months before the war and he looks at everything through Sinn Fein glasses. Upon the decease

---

‡ Sir Ronald Munro Ferguson, later 1st Viscount Novar, the last Governor-General of Australia to be actively involved in political affairs on a day to day basis.

of Archbishop Carr the Roman Catholic Church was asked to recommend a successor as Chaplain General and recommending this person the Government had no option but to appoint him. It is now considering dismissing him from his post. He is a dangerous man.

The British government agreed with Munro Ferguson's view of the seriousness of the Mannix threat. Arthur Balfour, the Foreign Secretary,§ wrote to Count de Salis, head of Britain's Special Delegation to the Holy See, in July 1918:[19]

". . . cannot permit his activities to continue"

The Australian Government have treated him with the utmost consideration, but they cannot permit his [Mannix's] activities to continue. They will be forced to allow the law to take its course unless the Vatican recall him. He is liable to arrest at any moment and I need not emphasize that scandal would ensue if the Australian Government were compelled to take such action.

(We will see in chapter 6 the results of further efforts by the British Government and the Vatican to contain the Mannix problem.)

Hughes' office supplied the British with a memorandum on "Sinn Fein in Australia", whose "acknowledged leader" was "still at large":[20]

". . . Had anyone else dared to say the things he has said, he would have been interned or deported . . ."

This man declared that "he was a Sinn Feiner and was proud of the fact." His name is Daniel Mannix and he is Archbishop of Melbourne, and head of the Roman Catholic Church in Victoria. Because he holds that position he is still at large in Australia. Had anyone else dared to say the things he has said, he would have been interned or deported long ago.

"AUSTRALIA FIRST" SPEECH

In March 1918, Archbishop Mannix used the slogan "Australia First", with the suggestion that loyalty to Australia was an alternative to Imperial loyalty.[21]

Many Australians are prepared, apparently, to place Australia below the Empire in their affections. These imperialists, in the abundance of their alleged loyalty to the Empire, are ready to sacrifice Australia politically and economically. They are not ashamed to put the Empire first and Australia second. Now, whether it comes from the pulpit, from the

---

§ Arthur Balfour, 1st Earl of Balfour, philosopher, British Prime Minister 1902-05, Foreign Secretary 1916-19 and responsible for the Balfour Declaration promising the Jews a national home in Palestine.

bench or from the bar, it is a very silly thing, as well as an unpatriotic thing, to say that Australians should put the Empire before their country.

We tax British products coming into our country. That may be good economics or bad. But, whatever else it is, it means that Australia puts Australia first and the Empire second. Just now our shop windows display the legend 'Made in Australia' and it is supposed to be a passport to a decided preference for things Australian. It will make no appeal to the patriots who put the Empire first and Australia second. The sun never sets upon the Empire, with its many-coloured races. But we, a handful of whites in a huge continent, insist on a White Australia policy. Our coloured fellow-citizens of the Empire ask for an entry. But no, not even for the Empire's sake do we lift the embargo.

Australia is first, and the Empire, with its coloured people, and its allies, have to fall into a second place. Certain people say I am a disloyal and seditious person, and that I ought to be deported or interned for putting Australia first. They know nothing about the Constitution under which they are living; or, if they do, they want to hide its nature from the Australian people.

When the Australian Constitution was being drawn up, and when the relations between the Commonwealth and London were being defined, Australia demanded that no appeal should lie from Australia to the King-in-Council. It was a demand that no colony had previously made to England. But it was a demand that Australia was perfectly justified in making. But I wonder was it putting Australia behind the Empire.

It was rightly putting Australia first and the Empire in its proper place.

> "... *rightly putting Australia first and the Empire in its proper place*"

The English authorities raised all manner of objections; Australia was ungrateful to the Motherland, and wanting in respect to the Throne, and disloyal to the Empire. However, the Premiers of Australia at that time had more backbone than some in office today. They went to London and fought the matter out. The result was a compromise; Australia succeeded in preventing any appeal to the King-in-Council unless with the permission of the Supreme Court of Australia. In other words Australia kept the ultimate and supreme power in its own Supreme Court. Yet some people who ought to know the law better than I do, say we have to put, and ought to put, the Empire before Australia. It is a nonsensical statement, an unpatriotic statement, whether it comes from the pulpit or the bench, and it will not be accepted by the people of Australia.

The Menace of Mannixism

Protestant opinion added its weight against Mannix's "disloyalty". At a public meeting in March 1918 at the Albert Hall, Hobart, under the auspices of the Baptist Union, the President (Rev H. H. Jeffs) delivered an address entitled 'The Menace of Mannixism':[22]

I do not propose to attack the religious practices of any other persuasion. As a matter of fact Baptists are fervent believers in perfect freedom of conscience and worship. We are also, however, loyal subjects of the King and resolutely desire to be faithful to constituted government. At a time like this we regard it as most necessary that the Empire in all its parts should be maintained in perfect unity and concord.

> "... the efforts ... by Dr Mannix to introduce sedition and sow the seeds of discord and disloyalty ..."

It is with sincere concern as patriots that we perceive the efforts that are being made by Dr Mannix to introduce sedition and sow the seeds of discord and disloyalty among our people. Observe that it is not against Dr Mannix as a Roman Catholic that we are seeking to direct what influence we may have. If he were a member of any other Church we should take the same stand and Dr Mannix himself has asked us to accept his utterances as those of a citizen and not as an Archbishop. At the same time, we cannot but recognise that his high ecclesiastical rank, added to the authority with which Roman Catholics are taught to receive the teachings of their priests, gives the influence of Dr Mannix an extraordinary peril ...

But does this disloyalty accord with the attitude of the Vatican toward the Empire because if so, the menace is a very grave one. Is it true or is it not that a curse was pronounced by the Vatican on the British Protestant throne in the time of Queen Elizabeth? If so has it ever been revoked? I am not aware of any revocation. Was not the head of the Russian Greek Church under the curse of the Vatican? Is not the French Republic under the curse of the Vatican and is not King Immanuel of Italy regarded by the Vatican as a usurper? Does not all this mean that the curse of the Vatican rests upon the cause of the Allies? If so one can understand why we listened in vain for some word of disapproval when Belgium was so sadly wronged, and when the Lusitania was sent to the bottom with its women and children. It is highly urgent that some League of Loyalty be formed in Tasmania so that we can get into line with the other States in our relationship with the Mother Country and upon our liberty here. If we do not defend our heritage which has been given us at such great cost we shall have reason before long to execrate our lethargy.

Similar came from the Rev T. E. Ruth's pamphlet 'Mannixisms', which also emphasised how different Mannix's disloyalty was from the Protestant view of the sacred nature of the War:[23]

We are not attacking him. We are rather resisting his attacks upon this British community. As patriots, not as Protestants-I repeat, not as Protestants, but as patriots-we are defending British integrity against this "defamer of Empire."

But this defence, let it be understood, is an integral part of our religious faith. Our patriotism is not a party political pastime, but a religious passion. It is not an art union affair to be bought and sold at a religious bazaar, neither can it become the subject of bargaining with party political bosses. It is our British birthright, and if we barter it away we cease to be Britishers, and become bastards. And in the Providence of God the time has come for patriots to say, "Now neither is Liberalism anything nor Labour but the British Empire and our common humanity."

---

[1] Australian War Memorial: http://www.awm.gov.au/collection/A03376/

[2] Alan D. Gilbert, Protestants, Catholics and loyalty: An aspect of the conscription controversies, 1916–17, *Politics* 6 (1971), pp. 15-25; Michael McKernan, *Australian Churches at War: Attitudes and activities of the major churches, 1914-1918*, Catholic Theological Faculty/Australian War Memorial, Sydney/Canberra, 1980; Neville Meaney, Australian Irish Catholics and Britishness: The problem of British "Loyalty" and "Identity" from the Conscription Crisis to the end of the Anglo-Irish War, *Journal of the Australian Catholic Historical Society* 34 (2013), 28-43; James Franklin, *Corrupting the Youth: A history of philosophy in Australia*, Macleay Press, Sydney, 2003, pp. 121-6.

[3] Pope Benedict XV, *The Pope's Peace Note*, Catholic Social Guild, London: 1917, discussed in Glenn Calderwood, A question of loyalty: Archbishop Daniel Mannix, the Australian Government and the Papacy, 1914-18, *Australian Studies* (London) 17 (2002), pp. 55-94, repr. in *Footprints* 22 (1) (2005), pp. 13-48; 'Dr Mannix: The Pope and conscription', *Argus* 15/12/1917, http://trove.nla.gov.au/ndp/del/article/1670114.

[4] Jeff Kildea, Australian Catholics and conscription in the Great War, *Journal of Religious History* 26 (2002), pp. 298-313.

[5] Chris Cunneen, Steward, Sir George Charles Thomas (1865–1920), *Australian Dictionary of Biography* 12 (1990), http://adb.anu.edu.au/biography/steward-sir-george-charles-thomas-8657.

[6] Frank Cain, *The Origins of Political Surveillance in Australia*, Angus & Robertson, Sydney, 1983, pp. 26-31.

[7] This image is in the public domain: http://www.awm.gov.au/collection/P03081.001/?image=1

[9] *Argus*, 23 July 1917, p. 6.

[9] Frank Murphy, *Daniel Mannix: Archbishop of Melbourne 1917-1963*, Melbourne: The Polding Press, 1972, pp: 253-4.

[10] *Argus*, 18 September 1916, p. 6: http://trove.nla.gov.au/ndp/del/article/1606798

[11] National Archives of Australia: http://www.naa.gov.au/collection/fact-sheets/fs161.aspx

12. Cyril Bryan, *Archbishop Mannix: Champion of Australian Democracy*, Chapter XII, The "Trade war" episode, pp. 68-72.
13. Bryan, *Archbishop Mannix*, Chapter XII, The "Trade war" episode, Appendix pp. 232-235. *Argus* 29 January 1917. *The Catholic Advocate*, 3 February 1917 gave a more moderate version, namely 'The war was just like any other war – just an ordinary trade war'. Michael Gilchrist, *Daniel Mannix, Priest and Patriot* (Blackburn, Vic: Dove Communications, 1982), p. 39. *Sydney Morning Herald*, 25 April 1917, p. 12; another view in Griffin, *Daniel Mannix*, p. 162.
14. Bryan, *Archbishop Mannix, pp. 68-72*
15. *Daily Telegraph, 15 November 1917, W. M. Hughes Opening the Second Conscription Referendum Campaign in the Sydney Town Hall.*
16. *Punch* (Melbourne), 13 December 1917.
17. Calderwood, A question of loyalty, p. 28, n. 82, quoting Steward to Hall, 30 Jan. 1918, in NAA A891 1/240, Reverend Dr D Mannix (Anti Conscription and Anti-British Utterances: Sinn Feiner).
18. Calderwood, A question of loyalty, p. 12, n. 1 quoting National Archives (UK), FO 38014 1917, Foreign Office: Legation, Vatican: General Correspondence, Paraphrase of telegram, Governor General of Australia to Secretary of State for the Colonies, 4 Sept. 1917.
19. Calderwood, A question of loyalty, p. 23, n. 62, quoting Balfour to de Salis, 26 July 1918, in National Archives, FO 380 17 1918 Foreign Office: Legation, Vatican: General Correspondence.
20. Calderwood, A question of loyalty, p. 24, n. 65, quoting National Archives, FO 380 17 1918 Foreign Office: Legation, Vatican: General Correspondence. Correspondence Received I. Sinn Fein in Australia, 23 July 1918.
21. Walter A. Ebsworth, *Archbishop Mannix*, H. H. Stephenson, Armadale, 1977, pp. 193-194.
22. *Mercury*, 20 March 1918, p. 4, http://trove.nla.gov.au/ndp/del/article/11386473
23. Rev T. E. Ruth, *Mannixisms*, Critchley Parker, Melbourne, 1916, p. 3; on the author see John Garrett, 'Ruth, Thomas Elias', *Australian Dictionary of Biography*, vol. 11 (1988).

The young Mannix poses for the camera

RE RUMOUR OF ARMS STORED AT "RAHEEN"

On 9.5.18 I visited Mrs Davies, 19 Yarra Street, South Yarra, who informed me that she had got the information from a Mrs Cashmore of 12 Yarra Street, South Yarra. I then paid Mrs Cashmore a visit and she stated that she had heard the rumour from her daughter, who then appeared.

Miss Cashmore stated she had heard it from a girl, a small child at school, who in turn had got the information from her sister who works at a Factory, the sister having got it from another factory girl who had got the information from her father, who had got it from a carpenter who had worked at Raheen when the alterations and improvements were being made before Christmas.

From Miss Cashmore's demeanour and evident desire that I should not proceed further with the enquiry, I came to the conclusion that this rumour was nothing more than idle gossip which had gathered importance in its travels.

Hurley
10/5/18

Report of intelligence investigators on the rumour of arms stowed in Raheen, 1918 (NAA, A8911, 240: Reverend Dr D Mannix (Anti-Conscription and Anti-British Utterances: Sinn Feiner): pp: 66-72)

R.M.S. Baltic on which Archbishop Mannix sailed for Ireland in August 1920 but was forbidden to land (National Library of Australia image: nla.pic-vn4507431-v)

Archbishop Mannix in full regalia for the Ecclesiastical Congress in December 1934 (The Advocate, Ecclesiastical Congress Number, 6 December 1934, p. 61)

Raheen in recent times (Wikipedia: http://en.wikipedia.org/wiki/Raheen_%28estate%29)

The Split, as imagined by Chris Grosz (Copyright *The Monthly* magazine, October 2008)

Statue of Archbishop Mannix, St Patrick's Cathedral, Melbourne © MDHC Catholic Archdiocese of Melbourne

Replica of the Cross of Cong, similar to one gifted to Mannix (National Museum of Australia)

Chapter 2: Irish Troubles viewed from Australia

To all appearances, the Mannix who left Ireland was a respectable upholder of received political ideas. As rector of Maynooth seminary, he had politely received King Edward VII and George V. He said himself in 1917, "I do not remember that up to the time I came to Australia I ever took part in controversy of any sort or description."[1]

The Mannix who arrived in Melbourne was a rabble-rousing tribal leader ready to make trouble. In the first instance, that concerned the rights of the Catholic community to education and positions in society, as in his first speech in Melbourne. Then from 1916 on, his attention increasingly turned to Irish nationalism, and soon to the most extreme forms of it. The reasons for this sudden about-face remain unknown.

Part of the reason for sectarian tensions in Australia was that Irish Catholic immigrants brought to Australia fundamentally different memories of British rule from British immigrants. For the British, the Empire was the guardian of liberty and the rule of law; it was desirable that Australian democracy reproduce that as far as possible, with loyalty to the British Crown. The Catholic Irish remembered instead the harsh penal laws of the eighteenth century, the niggardly British government help at the time of the Potato Famine of the 1840s, and the oppressed conditions of tenant farmers. Occasional outbreaks of violence and their suppression confirmed Irish in their hatred of British rule and British in their view of Irish as fanatical and priest-ridden potential terrorists.

In the early years of the twentieth century, peace seemed likely to break out because of the near-success of the Home Rule movement led by John Redmond, which achieved the passage of a Home Rule Bill through the British Parliament in 1914. It would have granted Ireland a semi-independent status within the British Empire similar to the Dominion status enjoyed by Australia.

It was not to be. Implementation of Home Rule was suspended for the duration of the War, and in any case the Ulster Unionists had made it clear already that they would use force to avoid incorporation in a Catholic-dominated Irish State. Then in 1916 came the Easter Rising, in which some thousand Irish Republicans, with minor assistance from Germany, unexpectedly staged a revolution in Dublin. It was put down and fifteen surviving revolutionaries were shot, including the overall leader, Patrick Pearse.[2] British and Australian opinion was angered at such a stab in the back during the War, but over time much of Irish and Irish-Australian opinion, including that of Mannix, came to see the executed leaders as martyrs. During the conscription debates, British reaction to the Rising reminded Catholic Irish Australians of their doubts as to whether the Empire was on the side of liberty.[3]

Towards the end of the War, Irish nationalist feeling ran strong in Australia and Mannix gave two of his most celebrated speeches on the theme, the one at Richmond racecourse in 1917 being probably his largest audience in Australia.

Justice for the Irish was the one controversial issue on which Mannix had expressed an opinion before his arrival in Australia, albeit in a restrained academic style rather than platform polemics. His 1901 paper on the "land question" (that is, the justice of relations between landlords, law and poor tenant farmers) is interesting for several reasons. Mannix never wrote a book, nor in Australia did he write any extended article. This paper is his only extended analysis in an academic style. It also has interest as evidence of an analytic approach to questions of social justice that would lie behind his later statements on those issues in Australia.

Have we solved the Land Problem in Ireland?

Mannix wrote only one full serious article. It is interesting for showing an early interest in two themes prominent in his later speeches in Melbourne – the troubles of Ireland and an approach to questions of social justice through abstract moral principles. The following are extracts from the full speech at the Maynooth Union 1901:[4]

We have often had the Land Question settled for us in Ireland. But yet the population of this agricultural country has been reduced by one half in fifty years. The arable land is annually shrinking, and the tide of emigration does not cease . . .

If the landlord system of land tenure were to be satisfactory, or even tolerable, two things should have been secured. The conditions of the land market should have enabled the tenant to obtain the use of the land at a fair rent; and, secondly, the tenant, who in Ireland made practically all the improvements, should have been secured against the confiscation of improvements effected by the expenditure of his labour or capital. These two conditions, however, were conspicuously absent. The law gave the landlord an absolute legal title to improvements on which he had not spent one penny. And, owing to the fierce competition and hunger for land, the tenants' rent was in too many instances fixed, not by the value of the land but by the tenant's ability to pay. What was nominally charged as a rent was in reality a tax upon the tenant or upon his sons, who worked as farm labourers in England, or upon the wages of his daughters in New York or San Francisco.

Until very recent times in Ireland, there was very little attempt to define what constitutes a fair rent. There was a vague idea that the rent was fair, when it left a living for himself and his family. But of course it is obvious that rent cannot be estimated on such a basis. If we look at the matter from the point of view of the economist, we see that the tiller of the soil has a right, in the first place, to normal wages for his labour, and for the management, and superintendence of his farm, as well as for the normal return on capital judiciously expended in the cultivation and improvement of his land . . .

Now, this legislation has been denounced in unmeasured terms, as an attack on the rights of property: a violation of the sanctity of contract; an organised system of legal plunder. True, it is a perilous thing to tamper with the rights of property, and undue interference will usually bring its own punishment. But the rights of property are not absolute, and it is a wise and a fundamental principle of English law that no man is deemed to have an absolute ownership in the land.

Landlord and tenant had been hitherto allowed to fix the rent by what was called free contract. But the result had proved disastrous. Free contract was impossible. Under threat of eviction, and under the pressure of the hunger for land, the tenant was forced to promise a rent which was in most cases exorbitant, and often impossible. So-called free trade in land had, therefore, been tried and failed. We have all been witnesses of the fact that it landed the country in an angry War of classes; that, in default of legal redress, it goaded the tenants to methods of defence which were unjust and demoralising. The legal right of the landlord to confiscate the tenant's improvements, by screwing up the rent and by the process of eviction, was morally indefensible, and could not stand the scrutiny of an electorate that was beginning to question the traditional interpretation of the rights of property. The right and freedom of contract is a sacred thing; for it is at the root of all commerce.

It should be jealously guarded; for it is a frail thing that does not stand unskilful

> "... when contracts are free only in name ... it is the right and the duty of the state to protect those who are not able to protect themselves"

handling. But there is something more sacred than the untrammelled right of contract. And when contracts are free only in name – when, in the name of free contract one class systematically seizes what belongs to their neighbours – it is the right and the duty of the state to protect those who are not able to protect themselves ...

I do not, of course, undertake to say that individual landlords did not suffer severely, and in some cases, perhaps unfairly, by the reduction in their rents, and generally through the recent land legislation. But a great social revolution can scarcely be brought about without dealing roughly with individuals ...

The only question, therefore, is whether the existing system of land tenure should be gradually replaced by voluntary purchase, or whether it is not better, once for all, to grapple with the system boldly by a scheme of compulsory purchase. For my part, though in itself I dislike compulsion, I am strongly of opinion that, in existing circumstances, compulsory purchase would be found the easiest as it is the only immediate adequate remedy for the evils of the existing system ...

I am old-fashioned enough to think that the benefits of Free Trade, even to England, have been greatly exaggerated. She has built up great manufacturing centres, and her wealth and population have increased enormously. But, even in England, the land is going out of cultivation, and her virile, stalwart peasantry are disappearing. I am tempted to think that England might be really a greater and more powerful nation today if she had not sacrificed her peasantry in order to push her manufactures. Already England has had to take anxious thought for her food supply in the event of war: she has reason to regret the strong, vigorous tillers of the fields, the strength of her armies in war, and the sires of a virile, healthy people. But, however that may be, Free Trade has been the ruin of Ireland's staple industry.

The report of the speech continues with comments afterwards:

The Most Rev. Dr. Dunne, Bishop of Wilcannia, [New South Wales] said he spoke as a stranger; but he had not ceased to have an interest in his native land. He agreed with the previous speakers in their hearty congratulations to Dr. Mannix for his able and interesting lecture.

In Australia, that principle was acted upon, and in portions of Australia large estates could be broken up in the neighbourhood of cities and towns in order that they might be sub-divided, and the people placed in homes near a market or town.[*]

---

[*] The Land Acts of the 1860s encouraged selection of small holdings by poorer farmers. The Irish-born John Dunne was the first Bishop of Wilcannia, 1887-1916.

Mannix with Queen Mary and Cardinal Logue during the royal visit to Maynooth in 1911[5]

THE EASTER RISING, EASTER WEEK, 1916

Mannix, like others, took an initially cautious view of the Easter Rising, very different from the Irish Republican view of the rebels as heroic martyrs:[6]

It is needless for me to say how deeply pained I am by what has just happened in Ireland, and how grieved I am for the lives that are lost. The Archbishop has already spoken on this matter, and I am sure that he has truly voiced the feelings of the Catholic body here. This outbreak is truly deplorable. But we must not lose sight of the facts of the situation. Both must expect to reap what they sow. And knowing, as I do, what has been going on in Ireland before and since the outbreak of the war, I am not altogether surprised at the lamentable things that have occurred. They are the natural regrettable sequel and response, as it were, to the campaign of armed resistance and civil war which the Carsonites† have been allowed to preach

---

† Sir Edward Carson, leader of the Protestant Ulster Unionists, threatened civil war if Ulster were included in an independent Ireland. He was First Lord of the Admiralty in the British Cabinet in 1916-17.

and prepare for within the past few years. The Carsonites, of course, had no opportunity of coming into collision with the forces of the Crown. They got a free hand, though some of them boasted that they were intriguing with the German enemy.‡ They were assured, on the authority of Mr. Asquith, that the British army would never point a gun at them; their leader, instead of being sent into prison, was taken into the British Cabinet. The hot-blooded young men who have now taken up arms began, I suppose, to ask themselves how Ireland was to stand when this war in defence of small nations was over. To truckle with treason is never safe for any government. I am quite clear in my own mind that the British Government, by its failure to deal with the treason of the Carsonites, and by its shifty policy in regard to Home Rule, has, unwittingly I suppose, led up to the result which we must all deplore. I hope the immediate trouble is already over, or that it soon will be over; and I hope, too, that those who are already calling out for executions will first try to fix the responsibility for this outbreak. Before condemning the misguided leaders of this movement to be shot, they should remember that leaders of another movement were taken into the Cabinet.

THE GREAT RICHMOND RACECOURSE MEETING

5 NOVEMBER 1917

With tensions rising in Ireland, the Young Ireland Society in Melbourne hired the Exhibition Building in Melbourne for a rally, announced for the eve of Melbourne Cup day, 1917. A deputation representing the Loyal Orange Institution and the Protestant Alliance Friendly Society called on the Premier "to tell him Protestants were apprehensive that the peace of the community would be seriously disturbed". The trustees of the Exhibition Building backed down and cancelled the meeting. Mannix gave his scathing views on the trustees:[7]

It is a wonderful thing that while we could discuss the affairs of every other nation under the sun – Belgium, Syria, Greece, Montenegro, and a number of other places that would be difficult to find on the map – we are not allowed to discuss the affairs of the Irish nation. We are asked to hurry forward in thousands – Catholics and non-Catholics – to go to the rescue of Belgium and other small nations, but we are not allowed to

---

‡ Carson sat at lunch with the Kaiser in 1913 and the Ulster Unionists received a large shipment of arms from Hamburg in April 1914. It is speculated that Carson's threat of civil war encouraged the Germans to believe Britain would be too preoccupied to go to war. Unlike the Republicans, the Unionists did not intrigue with the Germans during the War. See Tim Pat Coogan, *Ireland In The 20th Century*, Arrow Books, Random House, London, 2004, chapter 1.

meet in Melbourne to talk of the wrongs of a country more dear to many of us than even Syria or Belgium. (Applause) The Exhibition trustees, in solemn conclave, came to the wise, sapient conclusion that to hold the proposed meeting would lead to great bitterness. Some of those who were so anxious to avoid bitterness (there were two on that list) gave the use of the Town Hall recently to the Protestant Federation one of whose planks is to exclude every Catholic from Parliament and every public position . . . Of course, the meeting will be held. (Applause) If the decision of the trustees is a fair sample of their intelligence, they are not fit to be trustees of a Punch and Judy show. (Laughter) From some of them I did not expect anything else, as they are either Orangemen or well-known sympathisers with Orangemen. However, there are others who do not pose as Orangemen or sympathisers with Orangemen.

But I regret to say that some of these have just as much backbone as a stick of boiled asparagus. (Laughter) The trustees have done a silly and futile thing, and when the meeting is over they will look even sillier than they do now.

". . . as much backbone as a stick of boiled asparagus. (Laughter)"

It strikes me as very peculiar that, from the time the meeting was talked of in the Exhibition, the public would get in the Argus every morning what they had not got previously – a special cablegram about those awful Sinn Feiners. (Laughter) When special cable messages are required, they seem to be readily available. When Conscription was the objective, the papers told of smashing defeats at the Front. The Empire was doubling up. But a week later, perhaps, they forgot all they had said, the great offensive was pushing on to Berlin, and there were scarcely any casualties, unless among the enemy, who had suffered frightful slaughter . . . How far the message comes or who sends it I do not know; but the fact is, it comes when it is wanted. (Laughter) Persistently, systematically, and virulently, the Argus has misrepresented me and everything I have said. (Applause)

The refusal to allow the use of the Exhibition Building was perfect publicity for a huge replacement rally at Richmond Racecourse, kindly made available by its owner, John Wren.

The meeting was held on Monday 5 November 1917, and perhaps 100,000 attended, probably Mannix's largest audience in Australia. Foot and mounted police cleared a way for the Archbishop through the roaring crowd. We give the speech in full:[8]

Men and women of Australia and friends of Ireland every one. (Applause) We are here tonight for a double purpose. First of all, we are here to vindicate in Australia the right of free speech.

"Men and women of Australia and friends of Ireland every one"

(Applause) There is a faction here, just as there is a faction in Ireland, which for political purposes would be glad to stifle every opinion but their own. And you, men and women of Australia, have given your answer to that faction tonight. (Applause) . . . We are here for another purpose – the original purpose – to stand behind one of the small nations. (Voices, Ireland) Yes, it is sympathy with Ireland that has brought over 100,000 Australians to this meeting tonight. (Applause)

We have over and over again in this war been called upon to rush to the rescue of the small nations, and I am not the one to object to that call, as long as it stops short of compulsion. But apparently, there is one small nation for which no hand must be lifted, whose wrongs we must not even discuss, if that political party to which I have just referred is to have its way. (Applause) Within the last week, these cowardly political despots have used a certain committee here in Melbourne as their tool, and through their sinister influence you, the men and women of Australia, have been denied the use of the Exhibition building. We have our revenge. We have here a gathering that would fill the Exhibition twice over, and we have the vault of Heaven as a cover for our meeting-place. (Applause)

We have been asked – young men and even old men – to rush to Europe to avenge the wrongs of Belgium and the other small nations, and the call has not gone unheeded. (Cheers) But there is a nation whose scars are deeper than Belgium's scars. (Cheers) Her daughters have been ill-treated, and her shrines and churches have been laid in ruins - and that not by Turks or Austrians or Germans. (Cheers) There is a nation which, we fear, may still remain in slavery when a peace conference has righted the wrongs of Belgium and of Poland, and that is the reason we are here tonight. (Applause)

We are here for Ireland's sake. But we can claim that we are here for the sake of the Empire, of which Ireland, fortunately or unfortunately, is a part. For, admittedly, the present condition of Ireland is a reproach and a standing disgrace to the whole British Empire, wherever it is to be found. It has made England and the Empire, I might say, the laughing-stock of the nations; even the Russians themselves, on a notable occasion, were able to cast the stone at their British allies. (Applause) We are here, therefore, to stand by Ireland; but we can claim to be here also to wipe out the stain from the Empire to which we Australians belong. (Applause)

And what is this Empire, of which we hear so much? Does the Empire belong to England alone? Or to Scotland alone? Or does any part of it, any part of its achievement, belong to Ireland and the Irish people? (Applause) Now I am not going to answer that question in my own words. I answer it in the words of a man of longer, wider, and greater experience than I can presume to have – one of Nature's gentlemen, and one of the most gallant soldiers that ever wore a British uniform – an Irishman, of course (laughter) – the late Sir William Butler,§ with whom I had the privilege of being personally acquainted. If England had listened to Sir William Butler at the proper time, England would have escaped the series of disasters that befell her armies and lowered her prestige in the South African war. Sir William Butler is dead, but his words on the Empire are worth quoting for you tonight. Speaking of the British Empire, in which some of us are supposed to have no claim, General Butler used words which seem to me to be very true and very significant. I came across them today, and I have written them down.

He said: 'If it had not been for the blood and brain and brawn which Ireland had given for England, neither England nor her Empire would be what they are today. I doubt, indeed, if the Empire, as distinct from England would have any existence at all'. (Applause) Those are his words, and Sir William Butler wore the King's uniform – though I do not. (Laughter) Sir William then goes on to say, and we echo this: 'Ireland has seldom been thanked for her work'. He said in the course of the same lecture, 'It is time for Ireland to think of giving service to herself'. Cheers)

We are told, however, that we should not just now raise strife in Australia, should give the British Government time. (Laughter) After hundreds of years, they want just a few days more. (Laughter) Everything will be well one of these days, these plausible people tell us, and our present hopes ought to be very rosy. (Laughter) In the words of a great Englishman, they say, we ought to 'wait and see'. (Laughter) If only we would keep quiet until after the war, everything will be well for Ireland. (Laughter)

Now, first of all, I say that Ireland and Irishmen, and men and women of Irish extraction, are tired and weary of this waiting. (Applause) The time has passed in which we could wait with patience. During the years through which we have been waiting, Ireland has been depopulated; her harbours have been emptied; her trade has been ruined; her people have been scattered; drip by drip her life-blood has been ebbing away. And still these plausible people tell us to wait and see. (Loud Applause) I myself have a strong conviction that some of those – I do not say all – who are now entreating us to wait and see are the very people who have always been opposed to Home Rule for Ireland, who are opposed to Home Rule now, and who, when the war is over, will snap their fingers at the Irish people. (Applause)

> *"Now, my advice, if I could give it to the Irish people . . . would be to say, Now or never"*

Now, my advice, if I could give it to the Irish people – I can, at all events, whisper it to you – would be to say, Now or never. (Applause) They have the opportunity now which they are not likely to have again, and which they will certainly have forfeited when the war is over. If they are not able to get

---

§ Sir William Butler (1838-1910), British army officer and writer, briefly Commander-in-Chief in South Africa.

Home Rule during the war, then I think they will have very faint hope of getting it when England has got out of her present difficulties. (Applause)

But, it is said, is not a Convention¶ sitting in Ireland? Is not the Convention going to settle the Irish question, and are not the members of the Convention Irishmen? We are here tonight, not to hinder, but to help, the Convention. (Cheers) But we know what that Convention is. We know very well, in the first place, that the Convention is a sign of the bankruptcy of British statesmanship. (Applause) British politicians have been peddling with the Irish question for years, and they have failed to solve it. And, because they were afraid to face, as they should have faced, one little corner of Ireland in the north-east with which we are familiar; because they were afraid, or unwilling, to enforce the Act of their own Parliament, they have sent the Irish contending parties into a Convention to settle amongst themselves the form that Home Rule ought to take.

The English politicians who sent Irishmen into this Convention, had, I think, a very shrewd suspicion that no agreement would be come to, and they knew the reason why. (Applause) They would never have called the Convention at all if it had not been for the President of the United States and the Irish people in America. (Applause) That Convention, such as it is, is the price, or part of the price, that America made them pay for coming into the war. (Applause) I hope against hope that the President of the United States and the American people will see Home Rule through to the end. (Applause) At all events, we want to give them any help that we can from Australia, and that is why you and I are here tonight. (Applause)

But we must realise that this Convention does not really represent Ireland. As a matter of fact, the driving power of the Convention is not within the walls round the Convention, but out in the country, on the hillsides of Ireland. (Applause) That will be branded Sinn Feinism. Here in Australia people talk about the Sinn Fein movement without having the least idea of what the Sinn Fein movement is. The Sinn Feiners would, I have no doubt, say with Parnell that no man 'can set bounds to the march or a nation'. But theirs is that Ireland should be ruled by Irishmen according to Irish ideas, and in the interests of Ireland. (Applause) They determined that Ireland shall be ruled no longer by Englishmen, after English ideas and in the interests of England. The men of Ireland today are determined that the first and paramount consideration in judging every question will be, 'Does it, or does it not, serve Ireland?' (Applause) The Empire will have to take second place. That policy holds in Australia as well as in Ireland.

You here in Australia are Sinn Feiners, though you do not call yourselves by that name. (Applause) With you here in Australia, with all good Australians I mean it is Australia first and the Empire second, if there is a conflict of interests. (Applause) I know

---

¶ The Irish Convention met in Dublin from July 1917 until March 1918; its report was ignored.

right well that a great many people will say that this is sedition, and that in making this assertion I am absolutely disloyal. I am very glad indeed that my type of loyalty is different from theirs. (Applause) I am very glad that my loyalty to the Empire, such as it is, does not prevent me from being loyal in the first place to Australia, my adopted country, and to Ireland, the land of my birth. (Prolonged applause) And you Australians, being Sinn Feiners in the sense which I have explained, can sympathise with those in Ireland, who are determined at last to do what they can to wrest from English hands the government of their own country, and to set up in Ireland a government with Irish ideals and for Irish interests. (Applause)

Ireland stands as she has stood for many a day. The tragedy of Easter Week has not been all loss to Ireland. She lost some of her bravest, best, most brilliant sons. She has knelt over their graves, though their bodies are buried in prison yards. She has wept over the loss of the heroic dead; but, as she wept, a new soul has entered into her body. (Applause) She stands erect, more self-reliant, more nation-like than before. (Applause) She claims that the ashes of her brave sons should be given back to her. (Applause) She claims that Ireland should not be thrown on the dissecting-table of the British Parliament; that the Dark Rosaleen** of all the years should not be hacked and cut up into sections in order to please an unworthy and disloyal faction in the North of Ireland.

> *"You here in Australia are Sinn Feiners, though you do not call yourselves by that name"*

Finally, she asks that when the Peace Conference assembles, she should be allowed, like the other small nations, if she has not been satisfied in the meantime, to plead her own case, and to provide for her own participation in the benefits the freedom and the peace to come. (Prolonged cheering).

SPEECH AT ST JOHN'S COLLEGE, SYDNEY UNIVERSITY

*Dr. Mannix addressing the gathering at St. John's College, Sydney.*⁹

** Personification of Ireland

Mannix travelled to Sydney for the laying of the foundation stone for additions to St John's College, Sydney University, on 9 Mar 1918. Crowds of people greeted his train at almost every station en route. A large crowd assembled, estimated at 10,000 (*The Argus*) or 40,000 (*Daily Telegraph*). The university academics, Catholic and Protestant, absented themselves, and there was disquiet from the more peaceable elements in Sydney Catholicism, including Archbishop Kelly.[10] *The Freeman's Journal* gave a full report.[11]

The rising of the Archbishop was the signal for a spontaneous outburst of cheering that must have been heard for miles around. For minutes it continued, and then the assemblage broke into "For He's a Jolly Good Fellow!"

When silence reigned, his Grace said that his first words would be of heartfelt thanks for the magnificent reception they had given his name and himself. (A Voice: "You deserve it.")

It reminded him of an incident at the beginning of the first Conscription campaign, when someone wrote to him from Sydney, saying that the whole or Australia was laughing at him because he ventured to tell Australian people what he intended doing.

As he was busy at the time, his Grace said that he did not reply to the letter. The people of Australia gave an answer, which they subsequently repeated with emphasis. (Applause.) I hope this interesting friend of mine is here to-day," continued the Archbishop. "He has found out that, while I make no claim to infallibility that sometimes I happen to be right. (Applause.) I must confess it does hearten a man like me to see so many friends and to receive such an enthusiastic reception, because I think I am recognised as a rather cold blooded individual. I am not altogether devoid of feeling, although, perhaps, with one exception, I am the best abused man in Australia.

"... I am recognised as a rather cold blooded individual. I am not altogether devoid of feeling, although, perhaps, with one exception, I am the best abused man in Australia"

Of course there is a difference between us. He deserved what he got and more, but I have not deserved anything. (Laughter.) In the abuse hurled at my head they have sometimes searched the dictionary for names to describe me. I have been called every opprobrious name – (A Voice: "Even an Irishman.") (Laughter.) "Yes," continued his Grace, "even an Irishman. In fact, they have called me everything except a Bolshevik. (Laughter.) Perhaps before I leave Sydney someone may so designate me. These people, however, got their answer from Australia in a most emphatic form: (Applause.) There was once a meeting in Ireland which it was said would not be forgotten by all who were there and those who were not. (Laughter.) This meeting at all events, will be a memorable one in the minds of those present, and I hope it will be a lesson to those who are not."

THE REASONS FOR HIS VISIT

Continuing, his Grace said that he came to Sydney for three things. Firstly, to return with his Excellency the Apostolic Delegate to Melbourne to honour St. Patrick's Day celebrations with his presence, and to bless Newman College. Victoria endeavoured to follow in the footsteps of New South Wales in regard to a Catholic University. St. John's College had been endowed, and as a stimulus a generous offering was made to Melbourne of £30,000, providing they raised an equal sum. At the first meeting held to raise that amount over £40,000 was secured, of which only £20 came from a Protestant friend, and altogether over £100,000 was contributed by the generous Catholics. (Applause.) Another reason for his trip was to help the distinguished Rector of the College.††

"I have known him a long time," said his Grace, "and I esteem him as much as anyone knowing him can. (Laughter) But I know that if I wanted anyone to make a pun or a poem, or money, I need not go beyond Father O'Reilly. (Hear, hear.) He has not always been as successful with his poems as I would like (laughter), and has sometimes been unfortunate in the choice of his subjects (laughter), but I hope in the matter of making money there will be no mistake. Any assistance I can give him, small as it is, I will do it from my heart." (Applause.)

> *"I have known [the Rector] a long time, and I esteem him as much as anyone knowing him can, (Laughter)"*

His Grace went on to explain why they were so anxious to erect such buildings as St. John's, and said that unless the Catholics were trained and prepared in such places they could hardly hope to attain their proper place in the Commonwealth. In the war the value of education has been brought home to them in a terrible way. The war, he was afraid, began long ago in the schools of Germany. Those people know the value of education and how to spend their money. He did not say that they made good use of the power acquired. The Allies were now seriously realising that in the course of the present war. He hoped that Australia would realise the value of education. He only did his duty as a Bishop when he helped forward the cause of education in its highest form.

CATHOLICS AND THEIR PROPER PLACES

He was also anxious that the Catholics would find their proper places within the University. As far as the Melbourne University was concerned, the positions of emolument

---

†† Dr Maurice O'Reilly, Rector of St John's College 1915-33, Irishman, opponent of conscription and defender of Mannix.

> "... *the positions of emolument held by Catholics could be counted on the fingers of one hand*"

held by Catholics could be counted on the fingers of one hand. (Father O'Reilly: "It is exactly the same here.")

They were badly in need of the Catholics of Australia, not so much in the professions and communal life but in public life. He was afraid that in Victoria and in New South Wales they would search long for a Catholic man of standing with a University education in the front rank of politics or public life who had not denied the faith in which he was brought up, or the country to which he or his forefathers belonged. They wanted to remedy that state of things. "We do not want those Catholics," continued his Grace, "who are – how shall I describe them?" (A Voice: "Shoneens."‡) "No, I do not know any such people. We want Catholics not of the type who are more Catholic than the Pope, and more loyal than the King. We know these people well. (Applause.) We know of their loyalty on certain occasions. I remember the time in Ireland when certain persons said that they would kick the Crown into the Boyne. I know the class of people who supported them then, and I know the class of people who support them now. (Hear, hear.) These are the people who call me disloyal to the Empire, these who are more Catholic than the Pope, and are able to instruct their Bishops.

We never heard from them, when there was a campaign of sectarianism throughout Australia the like of which was never seen outside the country. We never heard from those people one word of protest when the Archbishops, Bishops and priests and Catholics down to the man who sweeps the streets were vilified.

> "*We never heard from them, when there was a campaign of sectarianism throughout Australia the like of which was never seen outside the country*"

We have been told that the Empire to which we belong – and I suppose we ought to be proud to belong – with France, Italy and Russia had pledged themselves never to allow the Pope to have a hand or part in making peace in Europe.§§ (Shame.) We were told that the different Emperors, Kings, Prime Ministers and prominent statesmen, were sending plausible letters to the Pope, thanking him for what he had done for the prisoners, and in minimising, as far as possible the horrors of war, and his endeavours to bring about peace. Yet, at the same time, they would not consent to the Pope turning Europe into a peaceful country. (Shame.) Why was it that these people, more Catholic than the Pope, never uttered a word of protest against this. No, there is only one thing which appeals

---
‡ Derogatory Irish term for those who prefer English attitudes and customs to Irish.
§§ Pope Benedict XV's peace plan of August 1917 was rejected by the Allied powers.

to them, and that is the Empire. I am reminded of their attitude by the headlights of a motor car, which, when facing one, obscures everything else. When these people see the Empire they cannot discern anything else." (Laughter.)

Australia's freedom

His Grace said that he had been accused of various misdemeanours. He was guilty from the point of view of various people who made the charges and saw nothing beyond the Empire. They travelled the country with spurious loyalty to the Empire, and wanted to make Australia commit political and economic suicide. (Hear, hear.) These people got their answer on December 20.[¶] (Applause.)

He contended, and said that time would prove, that the Catholic people had done their duty from the beginning of the war, and while he said that his vote would at the same time be cast always against sending any man to the front to face death. *(sic) (Applause.)*

A man who was once great had said that when the time came for Australia to be defended by Conscription, then it would not be worthwhile defending. "I endorse these sentiments," added his Grace, "but I believe that man has since abandoned those ideas, but I am going to stick to them." (Applause.) His Grace contended that there should be perfect freedom of speech as long as the laws of God and men were observed. He had never taken a hand in the matter of Conscription until the Bishops of another Church in solemn convention assembled, dressed in all the ecclesiastical robes they could put their hands on, passed a resolution in favour of Conscription.

> *"A man who was once great had said that when the time came for Australia to be defended by Conscription, then it would not be worthwhile defending. I endorse these sentiments"*

His Grace did not agree with that, and was foolish enough to think that being Catholic Archbishop he had the right to say so in a paddock, while the others had their say in the church. "I expressed my views as a citizen of Australia," said the Archbishop, "not as an Archbishop, and it turned out that my views were endorsed by the greater part of the people of Australia. (Applause.)

[¶] Date of the second conscription referendum, 1917.

1. Quoted in Patrick Morgan, *Melbourne Before Mannix*, Connor Court, Ballan, 2012, pp. 149-50; account of the royal visits to Maynooth in Griffin, *Daniel Mannix*, pp. 103-5.
2. A standard account in Tim Pat Coogan, *1916: The Easter Rising*, Cassell, London, 2001.
3. Alan D. Gilbert, The conscription referenda, 1916–17: The impact of the Irish crisis, *Historical Studies* 14 (1969), 54-72.
4. Daniel Mannix, Have we solved the Land Problem in Ireland? *Record of the Maynooth Union*, 1901, pp 55-69, sourced by Danny Cusack, June 2013.
5. Photo News Ltd NPX91573.
6. *Argus*, 1 May 1916, p. 7
7. *Argus*, 5 November 1917, p. 6
8. Walter A. Ebsworth *Archbishop Mannix*, H. H. Stephenson, Armadale, 1977, pp. 188-193.
9. *Freeman's Journal*, 14 March 1918, p. 1.
10. Michael McKernan, Catholics, conscription and Archbishop Mannix, *Historical Studies* 17:68 (1977), 299-314.
11. *Freeman's Journal*, 14 March 1918, pp. 20-1; Cyril Bryan, *Archbishop Mannix: Champion of Australian Democracy*, Advocate Press, Melbourne, 1918, pp. 172-3.

Chapter 3: Arrest on the High Seas, 1920

Mannix's chief claim to fame on the world stage was his extraordinary stunt of 1920. With an inflammatory speaking tour of the United States, he constituted himself such a dangerous Irish Republican figure that the British Cabinet determined it was unsafe to allow him to set foot in Ireland. A destroyer was sent to arrest him on the high seas.

After World War I ended, it became clear that Britain would not grant Home Rule to Ireland. The Republican party, Sinn Féin, won a landslide victory in the election of December 1918 (except in Ulster, of course). Violence gradually worsened through 1919 and early 1920, with no outright war but more and more acts of violence on both sides. About 300 had been killed up to late 1920. Winston Churchill recruited in England the notorious Black and Tans to assist the security forces in Ireland; they conducted reprisals against civilians which increased support for the Republican cause both in Ireland and among Irish overseas.[1]

In this worsening atmosphere, Mannix used the opportunity of his official visit to the Pope to travel via the US and give rousing speeches to large crowds of Irish-Americans on the evils of British rule in Ireland. There he met Éamon de Valera, one of the leaders of the Easter Rising who had narrowly escaped being shot. Then President of the assembly of Sinn Féin MPs that claimed to be the true government of Ireland, he was on a mission to gain American financial and political support. Mannix, rarely close to any other person, was deeply impressed by de Valera and became, and remained, a close friend and ally for life.[2] De Valera and his allies welcomed Mannix's support as the bishops in Ireland resolutely refused to support violent confrontation.

Archbishop Mannix's tour across America culminated on 18 July 1920, when he and de Valera were guests at a rally at Madison Square Garden. Mannix had

Mannix prepares to leave for overseas, 1920³

by now aligned himself completely with de Valera's extreme republican position.⁴

Amid wild scenes on the dock, he boarded the SS *Baltic* on July 31, 1920, bound for Queenstown near Cork. The military situation in Cork was extremely tense, made more so by anticipation of Mannix's arrival. The British Cabinet had considered the problem several times and decided it was too dangerous to allow him to land. A destroyer was sent which stopped the *Baltic*. Mannix was formally arrested and landed in Cornwall.

The farce of arresting a cleric by destroyer handed a propaganda victory to Mannix and the Republicans.

Mannix arrives in America

ARCHBISHOP MANNIX.
ABUSE OF ENGLAND
NEW YORK, July 15. ⁶

A report from Plattsburg states that Archbishop Mannix, addressing Cliffhaven Catholic Summer School, declared himself a Sinn Feiner. He said Australian Catholics were solid for De Valera.

". . . the English were the enemy of the United States, and always would be"

He affirmed that England was the greatest hypocrite in the world. He hoped Ireland would fight England the same as the Americans did. Ireland was the most decent and respectable of all nations. He declared that, British denunciation of his attitude had been an excellent advertisement. He roundly abused all things British. He declared that the English were the enemy of the United States, and always would be.

Archbishop Mannix arrives with his party at San Francisco[5]

THE ADDRESS AT MADISON SQUARE GARDEN, NEW YORK

Archbishop Mannix's tour across America culminated on 18 July 1920, when he and *Sinn Fein* President Eamon de Valera were guests at a rally at Madison Square Garden hosted by New York's Archbishop, Patrick Hayes. Mannix, the principal speaker, was introduced by de Valera as "a champion, a true champion of the plain people, and of Ireland's mission in the world today."

David Fitzpatrick quotes from the diary of the Irish revolutionary Harry Boland, who was present at the rally, that 15,000 people attended to hear Mannix deliver a wonderful speech.[7] It is Mannix's headline speech, a model of rhetoric and organisation as it builds to an emotional conclusion. We therefore give it in full despite its length.

It is a long way from Melbourne to New York, but if it were ten times as long, I should have travelled every step of it in order to have the opportunity of looking upon this magnificent assembly and witnessing the demonstration of love and affection that you have made for the President of the Irish Republic.

Ireland is a small nation, but it has a very long arm. Evidently, it reaches to New York, and I can assure you that it reaches to Melbourne also; and though you have given so warm a welcome to the President of the Irish Republic, I can assure him from my own knowledge that your welcome is not more enthusiastic or more warm than the welcome he will get in Melbourne if he ever reaches there. Ireland has a long arm, as I say, but so has England (hisses and boos) (A voice: Cut it off). (A voice: Down with England). She has here amongst you her English propagandists, and she herself has her ear to the ground in London. I hope they have heard your cheers already.

Now, I should be hard to please if I were not proud of the reception that I have got tonight in the capital of the United States of America. I have been welcomed warmly by your beloved archbishop, and though I have not been personally acquainted with him for long, I can say that Ireland has no more loyal son than Archbishop Hayes of New York. He was good enough to say that he hoped I would go away with the impression that I should have been a fortunate man if I were Archbishop of New York. Now, I am a man of small ambitions (A voice: we will make you cardinal before you go back) It has been delicately suggested by some of your friends and mine that I may now be allowed to land on British soil (A Voice: Yes, you will). (Another voice: Go to Ireland) (Another voice: You will on the Irish Republic, though). I have no intention of trying to land on British soil. I am going to land on the soil of the Irish Republic.

But if by any chance I were unable to land there, and unwilling to land or remain on British soil, then possibly I may make my way back to New York and if the archbishop by reason of his promotion or other cause requires an assistant bishop I will try to cooperate with you in getting him all the help that we can. But I have not merely been welcomed by your archbishop and by the clergy, but I feel also that I have the welcome here of two republics. No doubt I have got no welcome from the President of the United States, but I have got a welcome from those who made him president and who may make him president again. Then I have got a welcome also from another republic and I have got it from one who certainly is entitled to give it and that is President de Valera, president of the Irish Republic. This welcome has come to me in New York as a fitting answer to those who thought that I should not land in the United States. I hope that some of their representatives are here tonight. They have got for me in my progress from the Golden Gate in San Francisco over here, they have obtained for me what is a veritable triumphal march through the United States of America. I am therefore thankful to them and publicly make my acknowledgements (laughter).

Now, ladies and gentlemen, President de Valera told you that your welcome to him was not to be taken as a personal welcome. I feel equally that your welcome to me is not a personal welcome, but rather, as he rightly said, the welcome given to him and to me is given to him because he is the chosen leader of the Irish people and to me because I have said a word in season to help a righteous cause. You and I, ladies and gentlemen, are not here because we are the enemies of any people or the enemies of any nation. We are not here by reason of any hate that we bear to the British people. No – we are here not from hate; we are here from love of Ireland.

We are here because we love freedom and we hate oppression. We are here because we are not hypocrites who say one thing and mean another. We are here because you and I believed in the principles so nobly enunciated by the President of the United States, because we sincerely held these principles and because we are consistent. We are here because we have no favourites amongst the tyrants of the world. And because, as a consequence, we want to apply President Wilson's principles to England and Ireland as well as to Germany and Belgium.

> *"We are here from love of Ireland. We are here because we love freedom and we hate oppression"*

You have not forgotten why it was that you went into the war. You have not forgotten what it was that your brave American soldiers died for. You are not unmindful of what these men fought for who have come home crippled and maimed, to spend the remnant of their lives in homes that might have been so happy. You remember that these boys died and that other boys risked their lives in order that there should be an end of all wars – in order that the world should be free for democracy, not for hypocrisy, as somebody said. You fought in order that there should be a reduction of armaments over the world, that there should be open diplomacy, and that the nations, great and small, should every one of them be allowed to carve out its own destiny and shape its own fate.

> *"... that the nations, great and small, should every one of them be allowed to carve out its own destiny and shape its own fate"*

These were the principles for which America went into the war. You did not go into the war for more trade, as some people did, probably. You did not go into the war for more territory, or for annexations. You had, I hope, no secret treaties to try and get fulfilled. No, the American people went into the war for noble ideals. They went into it with clean hands. They came out of it with a victory that other people were not able to achieve, and now, when the war is over, in parts, that is to say, when the war is over, there are people who expect President De Valera and you and me to forget the lofty principles, nobly expressed during the war, when there were people with their backs to the wall who were calling for America's men to help them.

I do not say that the president of America has forgotten his principles. Far be it from me to say anything disparaging of him. I shall always honour the president of America. Although his achievement fall far short of what I should like the words, at all events that he spoke, when the whole world listened to him, were words that enshrined the great eternal principles, and they were nobly expressed by him. Therefore, I honour the president of America. But if he had forgotten his principles and his words, and if America had forgotten them, President de Valera remembers them and so does Ireland. It was your own president who said – and I have taken down his words because I am anxious to do him no injustice – it was he who said: 'We were fighting, you and those associated with you, were fighting that there should be the reign of law based everywhere upon the consent of the governed.' That is an eternal principle that was not invented by President Wilson, though he put it in terse and beautiful language. No, it is an eternal principle founded upon God's law and enshrined as well in your own Declaration of Independence. On the 4th of July I had an opportunity of hearing that Declaration of Independence read, and the following words, I thought, were very pertinent to the Irish cause. Those who put their names to that declaration said: 'We hold that all men are created equal and that they are endowed by their creator with certain inalienable rights; that among those rights are life, liberty and the pursuit of happiness, and that to secure those rights governments are instituted, deriving their just power from the consent of the governed.' President Wilson, therefore, was on very safe ground. He based himself upon the Declaration of Independence, and upon the eternal law of God himself. Whoever else forgets the eternal law, we are not amongst them, and whoever could forget the Declaration of Independence, American citizens will never believe. But, these principles were not merely the principles of President Wilson. They were accepted, all his 14 points were accepted, by all the belligerents on your side, because at the time they wanted your help, and they had no notion then of abiding by the principles. But whatever their intention was, they accepted the 14 principles, and they would have at the time accepted 400 principles. It is late in the day for them now to think of throwing all these fine principles over-board. Ireland bases her claim also upon these same principles enunciated by President Wilson. President Wilson did not give Ireland her right to be free – no. Ireland was a nation before President Wilson was ever heard of (Cheers and applause; cries of 'Long Live Ireland!'). Ireland did not get her right to nationhood either at Paris or at Washington, and it is not in the power either of Washington or Paris to take it away. (Cries of 'Hear, hear!').

". . . if only our enemy had been Germany, then Ireland . . . would have her freedom acknowledged"

But I often have cause to regret that Ireland, instead of having to fight for her liberty against England, had not to fight for it against Germany. I wish – it may seem a strange thing to say – but I wish that the invader had been the German invader. And I will tell you why, not that I wanted any invader; but if there were to be an invader, I think I might have chosen the German, and I will tell you why.

Not exactly because under German rule Ireland might have increased in population and in trade, as Alsace Lorraine did under German rule. That, however, is not the reason. But, if only our enemy had been Germany, then Ireland at the present moment would have her freedom acknowledged before all the nations of the world. I have been putting the case in this way to every audience that I have had the privilege of addressing since I came to America. If our president here, President de Valera – if he had gone over to the Paris conference and if he had knocked at the door of the conference where these great plenipotentiaries were assembled in secret conclave, to give us open covenants – if he knocked at the door there and said that he was anxious to plead Ireland's cause, and if he had been asked, against whom Ireland had a complaint – if he were fortunate enough to be able to answer that Ireland's grievance was against Germany, the doors would have been flung open to him, he would have been invited into the secret conclave, he would have been invited to take a chair at the head of the table, next to your own president, perhaps, or between Clemenceau and Lloyd George, and when they had made him at home and comfortable, they would ask him to state briefly his case against Germany.

Now, suppose that President de Valera could have addressed that conference and said, 'I come here to represent an ancient nation. I come to represent a nation older than most of those now existing, a nation that has its own proud history, a nation that I hope has its own great future, and that nation of mine,' if he could say, 'small though it is, that nation of mine has its own language, its own race, its own blood and ideals, its own needs and its own opportunities. But unfortunately many hundreds of years ago the blight of alien German oppression invaded that fertile and beautiful island and during the 750 years that they have been there these Germans have maintained in Ireland their German rule based not on the will of the people but on bayonets – German bayonets – and within even 100 years or less, the population of my little country, a small nation,' and he might look round to the walls because they were all talking of the little nations, they had an interest in them all, the little nations were the pets and darlings of the commission, he might have said to them, 'my little nation, small as it was, in 50 or 60 years has lost half its population.

'It had a population of eight or nine millions. Now it is down to four,' and they would all have turned up the whites of their eyes, and they would have asked him what became of the other millions, and President de Valera would tearfully but truthfully tell them that they had been sent over the seas, some of them in coffin ships, and never reached their destination, others went to America and Australia, and they are all over the world, and those that remained at home or tried to live at home, hundreds of thousands of them, millions of them I might say, were buried, starved men and women, in paupers' graves, and all that under ruthless German rule in Ireland. (Voice from the audience: Saxon rule.)

We will come to that in a moment (laughter). De Valera would say that not merely had she lost her population, but the Germans had contrived that her trade would be practically extinguished, that her harbours, which once were full, would now be empty, that a ring had been made around Ireland and she was cut off from direct communication with any country in the whole world except England. If he were able to say that the Germans had tried to trample the Irish language out of the mouths of the Irish people and to trample their Catholic religion out of their hearts; if he were able to say that Germany had taken the parliament, or what stood for a parliament in Ireland 100 years ago, that they had taken that parliament from them by bribery and corruption of which anybody but a German would be ashamed; if he were able to say to them that in the last 100 years every new generation had brought its own uprising against German rule in Ireland and the last of these uprisings was that in 1916 in which he himself played a part; if he were able to tell them that since that uprising the Irish people had set up their own government; that their government was governing or trying to govern the country, but was everywhere hampered by German bayonets, 100,000 of them, perhaps 200,000, with their machine guns and their tanks and all the rest – what would be the reply to President De Valera? Remember, he is sitting at the conference in Paris. President Clemenceau is at the head of the table; your own president is sitting somewhere near, with Mr Lloyd George and others whose names I do not know, and do not remember – what answer would they give? Why, they would not have listened to him as long as you have listened to me. They would tell him, 'Cut short that litany of Irish grievances against Germany: 'the German Hun' – they would surely call him a Hun – 'the German Hun will never again rule Ireland, or attempt to rule it. We will give you the charter of Ireland's liberty, write it out and we will all sign it on the spot.' They would ask him what were the boundaries of this new republic, and President de Valera would be able to say to them that God's own finger had drawn the boundary of Ireland. And, when he had written out the charter of his country's liberty, they would come, every one of them if necessary on his knees, and sign the charter of Ireland's liberty, and put an end in Ireland to the reign and rule of the German Hun.

And if we may make an exception for Mr Lloyd George – I would like to give him a special commemoration. When he came to sign it, I have always thought that Mr Lloyd George, the famous Welsh attorney, who was at the head of the British Empire, when he came to sign his name, he would have turned up the white of his eyes and thanked God that God had spared him to see the day in which he could liberate this poor oppressed aggrieved little nation, Ireland, from the blighting rule of the Hun, and he would have dropped – I think I could see him – he would have dropped a hot salt tear upon his signature, and he would have blessed God that he, a poor humble Welsh attorney, had it in his power once to do this great noble thing, to liberate once for all this ancient little nation from the thraldom and enslavery of the Germans.

Now, perhaps, ladies and gentlemen, you can see, perhaps now you can see what you did not see before – that I regret that Ireland's case is not against Germany rather than against England. If it were against Germany, what I have related to you would have been verified in every iota and Ireland at the present moment would be not merely a free and independent republic but it would be acknowledged by all the nations in the world under the sign and seal of the Paris Conference. But unfortunately for President de Valera and for Ireland, his case was not against Germany, which was not represented at the conference, but his case was against England, who had a representative at the head of the table, and that is the reason that President de Valera or his representatives, instead if being brought comfortably to the top of the table, were kept outside the door, and soon after some of them were sent into a British jail. The only difference is that the case was against England and not against Germany.

Now, I know there are people who say: 'All this is beside the mark. The Paris conference could not have heard the Irish case. They were there only to settle the questions arising out of the war, to arrange for the partition of the belligerent nations that had been beaten.'

Well, there may have been a technical difficulty, but these gentlemen had no difficulty whatever in getting over technicalities whenever it suited them to do so. And we all know that Russia was dealt with by the Peace Conference, though Russia was not one of the final belligerent nations, and if they could have dealt with Russia, apparently they could have dealt also with Ireland. But I am not concerned with the matter. I do not care whether they could have dealt with it consistently or not. Whether or not Ireland's case was heard at the peace conference, the peace conference is not able to bar Ireland from making her case before the nations of the world. She has made it and the verdict has been already given. And mind, it is no use for anybody who was at that conference, whether he be the President of the United States or any other, it is no use to say that all these fine sentiments that were spoken during the war, that all these had reference only to those who were engaged in the war, and that Ireland was not one of these. No, ladies and gentlemen, as I told you already and as you know, these principles on which Ireland relies are not principles that were first enunciated in the Declaration if American Independence. They are eternal principles of justice, and therefore the peace conference, or any other conference may not set them aside. Hence it is that when Ireland makes her case before the world, Ireland's case is heard and the verdict is given in Ireland's favour by all those who consistently hold to the principles that we thought everybody held when we were going into the war.

Then you may say to me, if all the nations are in sympathy with Ireland, why is it that Ireland is making a special appeal, and the first appeal, to America? Well, I think you ought to be proud that Ireland appeals to you in the first instance. Ireland might appeal to you because America owes a great deal to Ireland. Ireland might appeal to you because the United States is the greatest democracy of the world, because during the war America was recognized as the champion of the nations, and especially of the small nations.

Therefore, on all those grounds, Ireland might reasonably appeal to you, and appeal to you in the first instance. But it is not for any one of these, nor all of these reasons, that Ireland appeals to America.

"Ireland appeals to America on the eternal principles of justice . . ."

Ireland appeals to America on the eternal principles of justice that I have already referred to, and she appeals to America, first and above all others, because America is the one nation in all the world that is freest to stand by Ireland without having to fear anything for herself. Ireland appeals to you, but she knows that you can give what she is asking without exposing yourselves to any national risk whatever. You are big enough and great enough to take any risk that will come; and don't you let anybody prevail on you to think that if you were to give recognition to the Irish Republic – I mean formal recognition from America – don't let anybody try to persuade you that there is danger of war between America and England. I know right well that you are not much afraid, most of you, of war between England and America; but I am in the fortunate position in this case of being able to speak for the British Empire. It is a singular privilege which I am glad to exercise, and I can give you absolute assurance that if you tried to go to war with England at the present moment you could not. There must be two people to a contest, and England is not going to take on a battle with the United States at the present moment. She would probably want your money to fight you. Therefore, you don't listen to anybody who tells you that you are being asked for something that might lead to war. No, you are not being asked for something that might lead to war with England. Mind, I am not able to give you a guarantee, I want to guard myself cautiously, I am not able to give you any guarantee that in the distant future there may not be war between England and America. They were at war before, and they may be at war again.

But, for the present at all events, there is no question of war. You are asked to do something which does not imperil your national existence, or even expose you to the risk of conflict. You are asked simply to formally recognize the Irish Republic, legitimately established in Ireland by the deliberate will of the Irish people – a government functioning today in Ireland and represented here tonight by President de Valera.

"You are asked simply to formally recognize the Irish Republic . . ."

I am not able to talk for American politicians or American conventions; but, having travelled through every part of America, and seen more of it than a great many Americans, I think I have some just ground for saying that if a plebiscite were taken tomorrow in America as to whether or not America should give recognition to the Irish Republic, my own personal belief is that, by an overwhelming majority, the people of America would vote for formal recognition by America of the Irish Republic. And why do I say that? I say it because I have experience in going through the various cities, but also because I have too much respect for the American people to think that they will go back upon the lofty professions made in America's name only so recently. I believe the Americans were sincere, I believe the Americans are consistent, and therefore when they said they were fighting for the reign of law to be established all the world over, they meant what they said, and therefore if they were to be asked whether or not they would recognize the republic in Ireland, all the difficulty they would have would be to ask themselves, 'Does that Irish Republic or does it not stand upon the consent of the governed, that is the Irish people? If it does we are bound to recognize it. If it does not then we will have no more to say to it.' Mind, there are two authorities in Ireland at the present moment, they are both trying to rule Ireland and neither of them unfortunately is able (laughter). The British Government is notable because British rule has ceased in Ireland forever. The government of the Irish Republic is not able to exercise its functions freely, because it is hampered at every step by the presence of British bayonets, in their country, but the two authorities are there. We know what they are, we have the British authority, or pretended authority; we have the Irish authority. We know the basis on which they stand, both of them. British authority in Ireland is based on brute force. It stands upon the point of 100 British bayonets. The authority of the Irish Republic stands not upon bayonets, not upon force, but it stands upon the freely expressed, deliberately determined, will of the Irish people themselves.

Now, put all the politicians out of court. Put them all aside for the moment, and let the American people, as honest men and women, face that question and answer it. Are they going to give their recognition to the authority based on brute force, or to that which is based upon the will of the people. There ought to be no difficulty about the answer, and, as I said, I have too high respect for the common sense and the sincerity and consistency of the American people to think that they could give any answer but one, and that answer would be that they would give their recognition to President de Valera, who derived his authority from the will of his own people, and that they give the back of their hands to that authority who has usurped power in Ireland now for 750 years. Yes, America has lost a great deal in the war. America has lost, like Australia, 60,000 of her bravest men. She has lost practically a great many others who have come back and who can never again be what they might have been and what they would have been only for being drawn into the vortex of the war. America has lost her men, she has squandered her money. But there is one thing that America has not lost, there is one thing America is not going to lose, and that is her honour.

The American people were sincere and they are consistent. They know best themselves – it is not for me to suggest to them and I would not if I could – they know best how this formal recognition is to be brought about. But it is bound up with America's honour. America's honour, as it were, is in the scale until that formal recognition is given; and if I can judge the temper of this meeting, and if I can be any judge of the atmosphere in which I find myself in America, the American people will make their politicians toe the line, and will make them, even though they be unwilling, make them sooner or later – and I hope sooner – give to Ireland the formal recognition that she is justly entitled to according to President Wilson's principles, according to the Declaration of Independence, and according to the laws of eternal right and justice. Don't be afraid of falling out with a friendly nation. People will tell you that I am going to ask you, or that President de Valera would ask you, to fall out with the friendly English nation. Now, I know right well that you have your finger on the pulse of England. You know what England thinks of you. She thinks that you are a very valuable ally in a war in which she is weakened, but when she does not want you what does she think of you? Was she ever friendly when she did not want your help? Never, and never will be.

The only way to make her friendly is to do without her and let her see that you are going to walk the path of rectitude and justice no matter what she thinks about it. And I promise you like every other bully she will come after a while and fawn upon you again. Do not be therefore disturbed by this talk about a friendly nation. You were at war before and you may be again. England is looking at you at the present moment with a very jealous eye. You are building up a great navy, and she is asking for what. You are building up a mercantile marine, I understand, and she is trembling for her trade.

"She is fearing perhaps that you are going to take the place from which she thought she had dethroned the German . . ."

She is fearing perhaps that you are going to take the place from which she thought she had dethroned the German, and that having cast down the German she has only put the American in his place so far as trade goes and their control of the world.

Now you may be perfectly sure that if you want England to be a friendly nation, in my opinion, you are going the wrong way about it. I do not want you to change your policy but I say if you are building up a big navy and building up a mercantile marine, and if more and more you are going to take the trade of the world, then you are going the very worst way to cultivate friendship with England. Now, therefore, I say, and take it for granted, that you have made up your minds and that you are going to pursue your course in spite of any warning I say to you, and therefore I say do not rely on the friendliness of the friendly nation which was never friendly, which was never more unfriendly than she is now in her heart.

The future will have to look after itself. Do not listen to them when they talk to you about the outrages that are going on in Ireland. That is the only argument they have now. Mind, I know much about Ireland and you know as much almost as I do. Now, what do we all know about it. We know this, that if England and England's agents in Ireland are not fermenting and fostering outrage in Ireland at the present moment, then this is the first time in their history that they did not do it. As a matter of fact, we know that they are doing it, and many of these so-called outrages are perpetuated by their own agents, but suppose that Ireland were a crime-ridden country; suppose that it were steeped in all the crime that they allege against the Irish people. Would that be a reason for continuing English rule in Ireland? I do not believe it would be. To me it seems the argument is quite the other way. This is the way I put it: 'You say Ireland is ridden with crime, steeped in iniquity of all kinds. My answer to that would be, you have been there 750 years, and if that is the result of your labours, then it is time for you to clear out and let somebody else take a hand.' They will tell you that Ireland does not know what she wants; there is no unity in Ireland. Yes, there is no unity in Ireland; the Irish people are not united in their national demands. I wonder where could you find unity all the world over? But do not take it on my authority. Just before I came out, I stumbled on a quotation from an eminent man whose name I have already mentioned with your approval. It is Mr Lloyd George himself (laughter and hisses). Now, listen to what he says: on this occasion, at all events, there is no equivocation: 'If,' he said, 'we asked Ireland what they wanted' – I suppose he meant if we asked the Irish people what they wanted – 'they would overwhelmingly say they wanted independence and the Irish Republic.'

Now, I don't want to call any other witness. I don't think it necessary even to cross-examine him. We will let him go. He knows, and all the world knows, that Ireland is united, and that the Irish people as a whole are overwhelmingly in favour of the Irish Republic established since 1916. Don't let them talk to you about the want of unity, and don't listen to them if they talk about Ireland's uneconomic position. They tell you that Ireland could not pay her way. They are anxious to go on paying her way for her. The fact, of course, is, and mind you, here again I am not giving you my own words, but I am giving you the findings of a Royal Commission appointed by the British Government to inquire into the financial relation between Ireland and England. What do they say? They said, 20 years ago or more, that Ireland had been robbed systematically and deliberately by England of between 2,000,000 and 3,000,000 dollars a year, and that over a long period, and that report has since remained in their pigeonholes and they have gone on robbing Ireland not at the same rate but at a greater rate. And yet they say that they want to make Ireland economic and financial. You know the answer to give them. You know that Ireland is prepared to take the risk, that she does not want any more fondling from the fairy grandmother and godmother; but that she wants to be allowed to make her own bed and to lie on it. She is perfectly satisfied to take all the risks and wherever else she goes to look for help, she won't look to the sister isle. They tell you sometimes that if Ireland were a republic, how could she get on without the English markets? You would think they were going to close their markets the day that Ireland became a republic. Why, the suggestion of course is that they have been buying Ireland's beef and butter for Ireland's good and not for their own. Of course, the fact is that they have been buying, not for Ireland's good, but for their own good, and the profit in it is that whenever they could get anything one farthing in the pound cheaper from Canada or California or any other place, they left the Irish goods to rot in Ireland and they bought the cheaper goods from over the sea; and yet the fairy god-mother would want you to believe that England's markets would be closed, and that Ireland would never be able to pay her way. Her markets will be as open as ever they were, and Ireland will have the same right to send her goods there, and Ireland's goods will get the same welcome they have always got, if they are better and cheaper than can be bought elsewhere.

There is just one other thing and it is the last that I will mention: They will say, 'Oh, well, Ireland might be a free and independent nation, for all we are concerned!' They pretend, in their 'moral' way, that they have no interest in it; that they are very sick of it. They say 'It could be free if only it were 1000 miles away from us!' That is what they call 'the strategic reason'. The meaning of that is Ireland is so near that they require it in order to protect their own coasts, and because they require it, they are going to hold it, whether they have a right to it or not. Well, I can understand that argument; it is a splendid British argument (laughter). In fact, it is the only argument that they have. It is a good, down-right British argument. But what does it come to when you take off its clothes? It comes to the naked fact that might is right when the might is in British bayonets and when the right is in Ireland or in Ireland's cause. Then might is right, and, as long as they are able to, they will hold Ireland, even though they have no right whatever to it.

But, mind you, if proximity to their coasts gives them a right to it, they ought to seize the coast of France as well. In fact, they have a greater right to it, because it is nearer to them than Ireland, and if they want Ireland, then they want France, as well, and I have no doubt that in their hearts, they would be very glad to be able to take it. As a matter of fact, of course, they did take it, and they did hold it as long as they could, and they gave it up when they couldn't help it (laughter). That very same thing is going to happen with Ireland. They took Ireland also, and they hold and they will hold it as long as they are able, but they will give it up when they can't help it, and that will be soon.

Now, ladies and gentlemen, I have trespassed at great length upon you; but I want to be able to say, when I get over to Ireland – because I am going there direct from New York – want to be able to say to them in Ireland that I have tested the pulse of the Irish-American people, and of other Americans, too. I want to be able to tell them that there is not merely barren sympathy here in America for Ireland, but there is a desire to give all the practical help to Ireland that America can possibly give. There is going to be no war, I hope, in Ireland; there certainly will be no war between America and England; but America can do, and ought to do for Ireland what no other nation can do so easily, no other nation, perhaps, can do without exposing herself to a risk that America has not to face.

I am going to Ireland, at all events, and I am going to kneel at the graves of those men who, in Easter week gave up their lives for Ireland. When they gave their lives, British politicians and British people thought that the Irish nation was extinguished; that the Irish spirit was buried in their graves under British quicklime. But they were never more mistaken; they were never guilty of greater folly. They did not know the Irish nation. Ireland was prostrate for a moment upon the tombs of those murdered men, but Ireland rose from their graves, another nation! Their spirit has brooded not merely over Ireland, but over the sea-divided Gael, wherever they are to be found. Ireland at home and abroad is not the Ireland of 1915, and England need never flatter herself that she will find the same Ireland that she had then.

> *". . . I am going to kneel at the graves of those men who, in Easter week gave up their lives for Ireland"*

Now, Ireland is a regenerated nation. Ireland has taken her stand. Ireland has nailed her flag to the mast. She is looking expectantly for help from America. She is hoping that America will be true to herself; that America will not dishonour herself.

> *". . . God will, at last, remember his nation, and will give to that nation that has always been true to him the freedom that Ireland deserves . . . "*

But whether America's help comes or not, Ireland has taken her stand upon her own hearth; she puts her trust in God and in the right hands of her own sons and daughters, and she hopes that almighty God, who has allowed her to suffer so long, God almighty who has allowed her to be martyred through these centuries, that God will, at last, remember his nation, and will give to that nation that has always been true to him the freedom that Ireland deserves, the freedom that will enable her to take her place among the nations, and to work out the destiny that God himself intended for her.

When I kneel at these graves, I will think of America and of Australia. I will speak, as it were, to the spirits of those great departed dead, and tell them of the spirit that is in Australia and America; tell them of the sympathy that is deep down in your hearts; tell them that their lives have not been given in vain, and that they have created another Ireland, and will ask the God who saw them murdered by brutal British bullets, to bless the cause for which they died, to bless Ireland now and in the future, and to bless all those who now, in the day of her need, will give her a helping hand, and, among them, I hope, will be the American people. (Loud applause and cheers.)

MANNIX RELAXING IN NEW YORK

Archbishop Daniel Mannix with Mayor J.F. Hylan of New York, 19 July[8]

Australian Archbishop Daniel Mannix throwing the first ball for the Yankee-White Sox doubleheader at Polo Grounds, New York, in July 1920[9]

THE BRITISH HAD HAD ENOUGH

After weeks of reading reports of Mannix's speeches across America, culminating in the highly inflammatory speech at Plattsburg on 15 July and Mannix's *tour de force* at Madison Square Garden on 19 July, the British decided that 'enough was enough!'

On 23 July 1920, a conference of Ministers of the British Parliament decided that Archbishop Mannix would not be permitted to land in Ireland, a decision which resulted in the following VERY URGENT cipher telegram to be sent to Mr Armstrong* in the New York consulate.

```
Cypher telegram to Mr. Armstrong (New York)
        Foreign Office.   23rd July 1920   7 p.m.
No. 153  (R)    VERY URGENT.


             His Majesty's Government have decided that
in view of his attitude and speeches, Archbishop
Mannix who is believed to be about to sail from New
York for the United Kingdom, cannot be permitted
to land in Ireland.  Please take steps to acquaint
him with this decision before he sails.
         Repeated to Washington No. 616.
```

Later meetings of the Cabinet of the British Parliament went further into actual details of how Archbishop Mannix would be prevented from landing in Ireland.

Mannix departs from New York

MANNIX SAILS IN BALTIC[10]

A CRYPTIC MESSAGE: SCENES AT THE WHARF

(Elec. Tel. Copyright United Press Assn.)

LONDON, JULY 31

It is reported that a large number of the crew of the Baltic declared that they would not man the ship if Dr. Mannix were permitted to board, the firemen, who are mostly of Irish descent, declaring that they would not fire the ship if Dr. Mannix were not permitted to sail.

There were many dissensions among the crew of the Baltic. One faction said that Dr. Mannix would travel as an honored guest, but an equal number insisted that he should not travel on a ship under the British flag. Both threatened to strike, and union

---

* Sir Harry Gloster Armstrong, British Consul General in New York 1920-31, active in infiltrating Irish-American secret societies.

meetings were held. The ship officials urged the malcontents to leave the question to the British Government.

There were the wildest scenes on the pier. Men shouted and waved flags of the Irish Republic. Women screamed hysterically. The entire force of pier guards, plus the police reserves, got Dr. Mannix aboard, and prevented a stampede for the gangway by admiring thousands.

The National Catholic War Council has announced that it is rumored in Rome that Dr. Mannix will be made a Cardinal and probably transferred to Dublin.

DR MANNIX'S DEPARTURE FROM NEW YORK.[11]
(From the New York Sun and Herald)

. . . only one really serious incident occurred during the day. Joseph Shaw, a coal merchant, whose home town is Leeds, England, standing beside his wife on the deck above the main gangway facing a sea of Irish faces and Irish flags on the pier below, suddenly conceived a particularly messy way of attempting suicide.

Possibly Shaw thought he was safe, being once more on a British ship, but at any rate, as policemen wrenched the prelate from the grasp of the crowd and got him on to the gang plank leading aboard, Shaw began booing and hissing with might and main. At the first boo, longshoremen who were watching the spectacle from the upper deck of the ship and from the dock, swarmed up the gang planks and up the side of the ship like monkeys. Within an instant he was the centre of a mob of infuriated men.

Shaw, who is a dapper little man seemed somewhat bewildered by the sudden eruption of enraged men, but tried to fight. He was almost killed by the pressure with which men came from all sides, 25 at least, came in on him. For a moment it seemed as if he could hardly escape without serious injuries. He was thrashed severely.

"Kill the lime-juicers!" shouted one assailant.

At the first move four of the police detectives got busy. They dashed up the gangway and to the upper deck, hastily transferring their revolvers from their back pockets to a shooting position inside their coats. Fortunately only Mrs Shaw had intervened to save her husband, and one ship's officer was shouting to the dock for "constables." The fighting therefore had not become general, and the detectives were able to get their guns against the longshoremen and back them off, growling and ready to spring even in the face of the weapons.

Meanwhile Archbishop Mannix had also been escorted upstairs and reached the scene of the conflict.

"Stop it! Behave yourself!" he commanded and the longshoremen reluctantly drew away, muttering threats and assuring the prelate they would see no one bother him.

Demonstration at Chelsea Pier, New York as Archbishop Mannix sailed on R.M.S. Baltic, 31 July 1920[12]

CABINET CONSIDERS

CONCLUSIONS of a Meeting of the Cabinet, held at 10 Downing Street, S.W. on Monday, 2nd August 1920 at 12 Noon. Agenda item concerning prohibition of Mannix to Ireland.

> (1) With reference to a Conference of Ministers held on July 23, 1920, the question was raised of the arrival of Archbishop Mannix in this country. The Cabinet was informed that instructions had already been issued to stop Atlantic liners calling at Queenstown, so that the Archbishop, when he arrived, would probably land at Southampton. It was stated that, although all possible precautions would be taken, it was impossible to give an absolute guarantee that the police could prevent the Archbishop escaping their vigilance and crossing to Ireland. If such an attempt was successful, it was suggested that the whole authority of the Crown should be used to effect his arrest and deportation. It was pointed out, however, that this might involve bloodshed. A suggestion was made that the seditious speeches already delivered by the Archbishop might be an offence against the Crown for which he could be arrested immediately on his arrival in this country. Doubts as to the wisdom of such a course were expressed, however, owing to — (a) the fact that the Archbishop would be able to obtain bail, and (b) that a long-drawn-out trial would be the inevitable result.
>
> The Cabinet agreed —
>
> (a) That, should Archbishop Mannix succeed in landing in Ireland, the Irish Executive should take any step necessary to arrest and deport him;
>
> (b) That the Home Secretary should take steps formally to warn Archbishop Mannix, through the Chief Officer of the "BALTIC", that he would not be allowed to land in Ireland;
>
> (c) That the Law Officers of the Crown should examine the speeches of Archbishop Mannix and ascertain whether they contained anything of a nature which would admit of his prosecution in this country or by the Australian Government.

A subsequent meeting two days later concluded that the *Baltic* would be diverted to a port somewhere in the south of England.

British Parliament: CONCLUSIONS of a Meeting of the Cabinet, held at 10 Downing Street, S.W. on Wednesday, 4th August 1920 at 11.30 am:

ARCHBISHOP
MANNIX.

    (6) With reference to Cabinet 44 (20), Conclusion 1.

    Cabinet authorised —

        The Home Secretary to arrange with the White Star Company for the diversion of the S.S. "BALTIC", conveying Archbishop Mannix, from Liverpool to a port on the South Coast, Southampton or Plymouth being suggested as suitable

It was decided later that Archbishop Mannix would be arrested at sea and removed from the *Baltic* to be detained on *HMS Wivern* until he could be landed, which resulted in a Defence of the Realm radio message to the *Baltic*.

                2nd August, 1920.

Dear Sir,

    As a result of a Cabinet decision this morning the Home Secretary wishes the following message sent by wireless to Archbishop Mannix on the SS "Baltic":-

    "An order has been made under Number 14 of the Defence of the Realm Regulations by the General Officer Commanding-in-Chief, Ireland, prohibiting you from residing in or entering Ireland. Should you enter Ireland in contravention of this order the military authorities have instructions to take steps immediately with a view to your removal."

              Secretary of State
                  for Home Affairs."

    Will the Admiralty kindly arrange to send off this message and let the Home Secretary know when it has been done.

              Yours faithfully,

The Duty Captain,
    ADMIRALTY.

Aboard the *Baltic*, Mannix said a mass for world peace.[13]

Below is a facsimile of the letter from H.M.'s Principal Secretary of State for Foreign Affairs, Foreign Office, London, to the British Consulate General, New York, dated 4 August 1920.

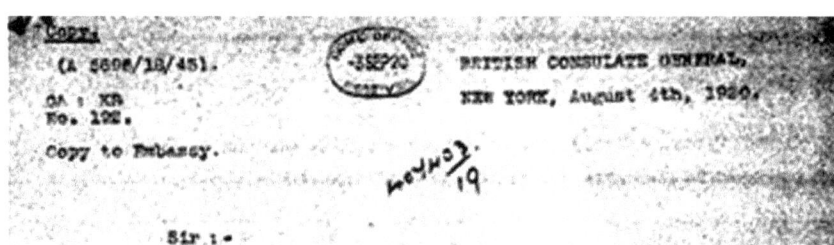

> has been done probably in order to convey the impression
> that has resulted, but possibly in anticipation of his
> intention of leaving here at an early date.
>
> I have, etc.,
>
> (Signed) O. Armstrong,
>
> H.M.'s Consul General.

"A report has been circulated that Dr. Mannix did not sail on the "Baltic", his place being taken by a man disguised to represent him"

HMS Wivern, *the British destroyer that met the* RMS Baltic *at sea, and to which Mannix was removed and taken to Penzance*[14]

THE VIEW FROM IRELAND

As the *Baltic* approached Queenstown (Cobh), tensions on shore heightened as the Archbishop's arrival seemed imminent. Some enthusiasts proposed to rename the town "Port Mannix". An I.R.A. leader in Cork, Seamus Fitzgerald, recalled the scene:[15]

> On August 8th, 1920, the Cameron Highlander
> Battalion took complete charge of the streets of Cobh,
> which were packed with people awaiting the disembarkation
> of Archbishop Mannix from the liner 'Baltic'. They placed

machine-gun posts at both ends of the town, and armed patrols kept moving constantly along the principal streets.

The projected visit of Archbishop Mannix had received tremendous publicity, and bonfires had been arranged on the headlands and a great welcome had been assured him.

I was ready, as the Chairman of the Local Council, to present him with an address of welcome, and special Dáil Éireann representatives had been delegated to welcome him.

When the ship was five miles outside the port, British agents went on board, placed the archbishop under arrest, transferred him to a destroyer which carried him to England, while the British Government forbade him to visit Ireland, Manchester or Liverpool. That night in Cobh, I organised a large number of our men, ostensibly as civilian stewards, to maintain order and prevent incidents. The situation was so tense, wanted men walking side by side with Crown Forces, and everyone felt that any untoward incident might lead to considerable trouble and disturbance. Our men, however, and the people co-operated successfully, and everything passed off without incident. Later, when Archbishop Mannix was able to come to Ireland, I had the honour of presenting him with the original address of welcome at Cork station.

Arrest at Sea

The destroyer *Wivern* intercepted the *Baltic*. Mannix's secretary Fr Vaughan provides a vivid account of what ensued:[16]

We were off Queenstown and could see the lights of the city. We could clearly distinguish the huge bonfires along the coast and on every hilltop, which admiring fellow-countrymen had lit as a 'welcome home' to Erin's great son and fearless patriot, the Archbishop of Melbourne. It was a never-to-be-forgotten sight. But my mind was too busy speculating to allow me to appreciate the scene. 'What is going to happen?' everyone was asking. Soon we had the answer.

Lights winked off from Destroyer No 66. They flashed the message from the Navy calling on the *Baltic* to stop. Gradually we slowed down and the searchlights of the war vessels flashed hither and thither over the waters – now resting on our ship – now searching the sea – now directed on the nearby coast. A boat is lowered from the Destroyer. There were several aboard. As she nears the Baltic a cheer goes up from the English on board. I retired to a quiet spot and lit my pipe, and alone watched the historical event unfold itself . . . as a Naval Lieutenant and two attired as civilians (they were detectives from Scotland Yard, I later ascertained) ascended the gangway lowered for them.

Soon the Archbishop is summoned to the Captain's room. What is happening there, I wonder. Minutes pass and then the Purser comes round looking for 'Father Vaughan'. 'The Archbishop's compliments, Sir, and will you kindly join him in the Captain's room'.

I knock the ashes from my pipe and realise that I'm taking a hand in the making of history . . . Well, I slouched along through the ranks of gaping passengers and members of the ship's crew. I entered the room. The Archbishop was seated, and opposite him, standing, were the two John Hops, one of them holding a formidable looking document . . . I was told that the 'Government of His Britannic Majesty' had seen fit to deny to Archbishop Mannix the right to land in Ireland, or to go to Liverpool, Manchester or Glasgow. (The Irish are strong in those places). The Government was willing to allow his secretary to accompany him. Was I willing to go? I'm not going to repeat here what I then said. But I can assure you that in the heat of my anger I told those agents of the Government what I thought of their masters! Go! Of course I would go. And I went out with His Grace to prepare. We took our time in getting ready for the transhipment. When quite ready we went to the deck, where the gangplank was let down to the waiting pinnace with its crew of British Jack Tars. The Archbishop then quietly and deliberately said: 'I refuse to leave this vessel', thereupon throwing the onus for his removal entirely on the British Government. One of the Scotland Yard men then placed his hand on the Archbishop's shoulder, which amounted to a technical arrest.

Many years later a priest met the destroyer's captain at Lourdes. He had a message for Mannix:[17]

About three years ago a priest was commissioned by a man to give a message to Archbishop Mannix. The message was, 'Tell him from me that you met at Lourdes the captain of the *Wyvern* (sic).[18] That was the destroyer which conveyed Dr. Mannix off his boat, the *Baltic*, when, in 1920, he was forbidden to land in Ireland. I would like him to know that, of all the nasty jobs I ever had to do, there was none I disliked more heartily. I often wished to be able to tell him. I shall be very glad if you do it for me. And you may add that I speak also on behalf of the entire crew. Everyone of us hated having to do it.'

Inspector Ernest Mole, the police officer who arrested the Archbishop on board the *Wivern*, reported:

> **METROPOLITAN POLICE.**
>
> Special Branch,
> Metropolitan Police,
> Scotland House,
>
> 10th day of August, 1920
>
> I beg to report that, accompanied by Sergeant Passmore, I left London by the 9.5 p.m. train, 6th inst., for Pembroke Docks, where we embarked on H.M.S. "Wivern" at 7.30 a.m., 7th inst., and proceeded to sea.
>
> At 12.30 a.m. 9th instant we boarded the R.M.S. "Baltic" at Ringabella Bay, Queenstown. I served on Archbishop Mannix a copy of the attached orders made under Regulation 14 Defence of the Realm Act. In addition, I read to him paragraphs 47 and 48 D.R.R., and explained to him that as the "Baltic" was going to Liverpool, he could not proceed by her without committing a breach of the Order. I also told him that he must leave the ship and accompany me aboard H.M.S. "Wivern", from which he would be landed at an English Port.

The Archbishop said, "I strongly protest against this high handed action by the Authorities and refuse to leave the 'Baltic'". I then told him that if he persisted in his refusal to leave I should be compelled to use force, and appealed to him to leave voluntarily, which he did subsequently, accompanied by his secretary, Father Vaughan. He was placed in the Captain's cabin on board the H.M.S. "Wivern" - which proceeded to Penzance - where we disembarked about 4 p.m., 9th instant.

The Archbishop then drove to the Railway Station, where I had his baggage examined by H.M. Customs, in which was found a quantity of literature, copies/

copies of which I herewith submit. Subsequently he drove to the residence of Canon Wade, Roselevan Road, Penzance, where he stayed until he returned to the Railway Station.

We left Penzance at 7 p.m. and arrived Paddington 6.10 a.m. to-day.

At Penzance and Plymouth Archbishop Mannix received Press representatives and gave them particulars of what had happened on board the "Baltic" and H.M.S. "Wivern".

Ernest Mole.
Inspector

SUPERINTENDENT

Shane Leslie,[†] who had not set eyes on Dr Mannix since the latter departed from Maynooth seven years earlier, was shocked at the toll taken by his episcopal responsibilities and public involvement in Australia:[19]

> I felt shocked when I saw an old and war-weary man. Instead of the spruce college President, enshrined in its success and armoured with his books, stood a battered old man, his flesh worn away, his skin shrunk upon the framework of bones which upheld his purple biretta. His hair had changed and turned a light grey, his eyes were sunk into their sockets and every year of life in Australia seemed to have left a deep chevron across his face.

"Since the Jutland battle, the British Navy has not scored a success comparable to the capture of the Archbishop of Melbourne ..."

Interviewed later in London, Archbishop Mannix declared that he stood by 'every syllable' he had uttered in America, adding:[20]

> Since the Jutland battle,[‡] the British Navy has not scored a success comparable to the capture of the Archbishop of Melbourne, and not a single British sailor had lost his life. It has rendered the British Government the laughing stock of the world. I still claim the right to go to Ireland and intend to press the claim by any means in my power.

Very soon after his arrival in London, Mannix wrote to the Irish people via a handwritten letter which appeared on the front page of the Dublin *Freeman Journal* with a photograph of him writing it:[21]

> I appeal to the Irish people to be calm and firm under the insult offered to them and to me. Ireland can afford to be patient. For, though she is suffering much, her cause is almost won. The recent "English naval victory" has but added fuel to the flame which it was meant to extinguish.

[†] Irish politician and writer, cousin of Winston Churchill, Catholic convert.
[‡] Battle of Jutland, 1916, the major naval battle of WWI.

Among a barrage of comment on all sides, G. K. Chesterton's column in the *New York Times* got to the point of the farce:[22]

CHESTERTON DECRIES FLURRY OVER MANNIX

British Novelist Thinks His Government Acted Foolishly in What He Calls a Gigantic Farce.

Copyright. 1920 by Cross Atlantic Newspaper Service.

LONDON. Aug. 13.–G. K. Chesterton has written the following comment on " the Mannix affair " :

" The whole Mannix affair is a gigantic farce in which the British Government has played an extraordinary part. What surprises me most is that the newspapers, except the labor papers, have applauded and backed the Government's amazing example.

" Anyhow, why worry about Archbishop Mannix? What harm is one man going to do in Ireland? Denounce the British Government to a million Irishmen? Why, those million Irishmen are spending all their time denouncing the British Government to the rest of the world.

" The only point that could be raised is against the Archbishop's moral theories. How could he stand in the pulpit and plead in support of murder and cold-blooded assassination?

" Meanwhile the British Government has acted a sort of miracle play to the intense amusement of the rest of the world, playing Herod to Mannix's John the Baptist. Such a thing could never have happened in the eighteenth century, when, had Mannix lived, he might easily have been hanged or assassinated or something equally horrible happened to him, which would never have been advertised.

" Most of the Irish Roman Catholics take little interest in the political opinions of their priests; therefore let Mannix alone. His cordial reception in America was due partly to the large number of Irish Americans, whose welcome was naturally vociferous, and partly because the average American is brought up to believe that England is a tyrant. This idea needs removing to foster the Anglo-American brotherhood.

" There are many reasons why there should be such a brotherhood. Chief among them is the fact that America and England understand liberty in the same way. Prussia doesn't and never will. But all talk of Anglo-American unity being the chief tie between the countries is twaddle.

" It will take time to make America believe that England is not a tyrant, but it call be done, though history has nasty things against England, and history is strengthened by the tyrannical treatment of Archbishop Mannix. "

Hughes denounces

Back home in Australia, Mannix's doings had not escaped attention either. Billy Hughes, still Prime Minister, addressed a meeting of the National Federation in the Bendigo Town Hall on Sunday 25 July 1920, while Mannix was still in America.

DR. MANNIX DENOUNCED.
SPEECH BY MR. HUGHES.[23]
High Commissioner to be Appointed.

[. . .] Referring to the obstructionist tactics in Parliament of the Caucus party, which, he declared had been a criminal waste of time and had sought by every means in its power to prevent Parliament from doing the work it had been elected to do, Mr Hughes said that that party to-day was the hack of the disloyalists and extremists of the Commonwealth. "I do not condemn at all," he said, "the rank and file outside. I know how hard it is for them to break the ties that the years have woven between them and their party.

> "... he pulled the strings of this great machine, and made these marionettes dance at his bidding"

It is their leaders who have changed and who are taking them in the opposite direction to that which the party took in the days which are gone. Who is their leader now? Dr Mannix is their leader – not their titular leader but their real leader.

He boasted of it, and if he had been silent everyone would have known that he pulled the strings of this great machine, and made these marionettes dance at his bidding. Why is it that when I say this it whips them as if they had been struck with lashes of steel? It is because it is true. Some of them it cuts to the heart. They are not all of that kidney. They have been entangled in this infernal web and dare not break loose. You will understand, if you ask what manner of man he is, why, by every means in their power his followers seek to hurl me to destruction. Everywhere we see the British Empire surrounded by enemies. Bolshevism and Sinn Fein are among them. We in Australia are where we are by the grace of God, and the fact that we are part of the British Empire. This is a matter that goes to the very root of our existence. United, we are unconquerable. When we see in our midst men who would plunge a dagger into the heart of the Empire we can only say that they are traitors to us and to their country. I care not what they think of England as England. I am concerned for the safety of Australia. The division of the Empire means death to us and because of that I shall smite them hip and thigh. (Cheers) These men are so envenomed with age long hatred of England that they are prepared to destroy us if they can only aim a blow at England. Take Dr Mannix. At one time he cooed like a sucking dove, at other times not so softly. (Laughter) I want you to contrast the words now and during the war, in order that you and the American people may understand. I want the American people to know what manner of man he is, whom he represents and whom he does not represent. Whomever he represents he does not represent Australia. If he says that the sentiments he utters are supported by the people of Australia, he says that which is not true. In 1917, when the war was on, Dr Mannix said:

'Australians are loyal to the Empire, and every reasonable and legitimate demand on their loyalty will be met and ensured.'

It was in some such way as this that the serpent beguiled Eve. (Laughter) In December 1917 he said: 'I do not speak as priest or an archbishop, but simply as an honest true and loyal citizen of Australia.'

As time went on and he thought he saw in the heavens signs that his star was in the ascendant he changed his tone. He came out more openly. He began to speak as he felt.

He made us see more and more plainly as he did feel and what cause he stood for. During these last few years we have been under no illusion at all about him. We knew he had only one objective, the destruction of the Empire, or, at any rate, the achievement of a republic in Ireland.

I have always been a Home Ruler. I am not going to say that Ireland has not had grievances. But while I have always been a Home Ruler, even when it was most unpopular, I am irrevocably opposed to a republic in Ireland. I will fight it tooth and nail by every means in my power. It means the dismemberment of the Empire, and the dismemberment of the Empire means the destruction of Australia. (Cheers)

AT DE VALERA'S RIGHT HAND

'Dr. Mannix went to America', continued Mr. Hughes, 'after having figured very prominently in an election campaign in which he did me the honour to win me a very great number of votes – (Laughter) – and in which he selected as campaign leader Mr. Ryan, an appointment in which we all congratulate him heartily. (Laughter) He says that his tour was not political, but that he was going to the Vatican. If he is going to the Vatican, what is he doing in America? When did that become the shortest way to Italy? He says his mission is not political. What is it? We are not concerned with the Archbishop as such, and our quarrel with him has nothing to do with religion – (hear, hear) – for we have, thank God, many loyal Roman Catholics in our midst, and we are living in peace and harmony with them, as we always lived in peace and harmony until he came. His predecessor was a Christian. (Hear, hear) But this high priest of the Prince of Peace goes to America and says it is his one hope that England and America will be enemies, that Ireland will fight England and

America will fight England. If that hope could be realised we would see a war the like of which had never been seen before. We should see the destruction of the only bulwark of peace that exists. The hope of peace in this world lies not in the League of Nations, but in that firm alliance and understanding that has existed these last hundred years between America and the British Empire, in the closer co-operation of the Anglo-Saxon races.

". . . if we are to choose between the Kaiser and him as to who is the greater criminal, I know whom I should choose"

The man, therefore, who seeks to make bad blood between America and the British Empire is a criminal, and if we are to choose between the Kaiser and him as to who is the greater criminal, I know whom I should choose. The Kaiser was pushed into this, but Dr. Mannix went into it of his own free will. By his own words he stands condemned as a minister of Christ, he stands condemned as a man who said that his mission was not political. Show me in the words he has spoken in America one thing that savours of the doctrine of Christ, one thing that any minister of Christ dare speak from the pulpit. They stamp him as a man who has gone out in the guise of an archbishop to foment war between England and America, as a man whose mission is political in essence.

He is there at the right hand of De Valera, who, during the war, said that Germany was Ireland's friend, and that the only hope for Ireland was a German invasion of England. This is the man whose machinations broke the Labor Party, who stands behind and directs and foments all that cataract of hatred directed against me and those like me who had the courage to decline to be led by such a man as he. The people of Australia have had ample opportunity of judging him from his words and from his works, and they repudiate him. He represents a section in this country that does not even include all the members of his own Church.

Many of them are bitterly incensed that he should speak in this fashion, for they are as loyal to the Empire as the men and women of any other Dominion. (Cheers.) Dr. Mannix goes out for what he is. He is a Sinn Feiner. He is a man who, in the garb of a priest, has carried the baton of a political agitator. He has used his high position for that purpose.

". . . in the garb of a priest, has carried the baton of a political agitator"

Congratulations came from the Prince of Wales, who added the hope that "dear Mr Hughes would not let such a horrid man return to Australia."[24]

1. Michael Hopkinson, *The Irish War of Independence*, McGill-Queens University Press, Montreal, 2002.
2. Patrick Mannix, *The Belligerent Prelate: An alliance between Archbishop Daniel Mannix and Eamon de Valera*, Cambridge Scholars Publishing, Newcastle upon Tyne, 2013.
3. State Library of Victoria.
4. Malcolm Campbell, Mannix in America, *Australian Journal of Irish Studies* 5 (2005), 95-107.
5. Professor Patrick O'Farrell photograph collection: http://trove.nla.gov.au/version/32878986
6. *Sydney Morning Herald*, 19 July 1920, p. 7: http://trove.nla.gov.au/ndp/del/article/15898486
7. Campbell, Mannix in America.
8. Professor Patrick O'Farrell photograph collection: http://trove.nla.gov.au/version/32878096
9. *Advocate*, 4 October 1962: 'Special issue with supplement for Episcopal Golden Jubilee of His Grace Archbishop Mannix, D.D., LL.D. 1912–1962', *p. 5*.
10. *Poverty Bay Herald*, Volume XLVII, Issue 15282, 2 August 1920, p. 3.
11. *Oamaru Mail*, 24 September 1920, p. 8: http://paperspast.natlib.govt.nz/cgi-bin/paperspast?a=d&d=OAM19200924.2.49
12. National Library of Australia image: nla.pic-vn4507431-v
13. Thomas E. Hachey, The quarantine of Archbishop Mannix: A British preventive policy during the Anglo-Irish Troubles, *Irish University Review* 1 (1970), 111-30, a p. 122.
14. Cropped image from: http://www.ekmpowershop1.com/ekmps/shops/jhpictures/hms-wivern-destroyer-ww2-1287-p.asp
15. *Bureau of Military History, 1913-21*, Statement by Witness. Document No. W.S. 1,757. Witness, Seamus Fitzgerald, "Carrigbeg", Summerhill, Cork.
16. Michael Gilchrist, *Daniel Mannix: Wit and Wisdom*, Freedom Publishing, 2nd edition, 2004, pp. 94-95, n. 42, quoted from *Footprints* (Journal of the Melbourne Diocesan Historical Commission), October 1972, in which details from Fr Vaughan's long letter to members of his family are reproduced, pp. 15-21.
17. *The Advocate* (Jubilee supplement) 4 October 1962, p. 15.
18. Lieut. Francis Flynn, a Protestant, but the son of a native of Cork (Ebsworth, *Archbishop Mannix*, p. 237).
19. Gilchrist, *Daniel Mannix*, p. 98, n. 52, quoted from *Tribune*, 2 April 1925.
20. *Argus*, 12 August 1920, p. 7.
21. Ebsworth, *Archbishop Mannix*, p. 240.
22. *New York Times*, 1 August 1920.
23. *Argus*, 26 July 1920, p. 7.
24. C.M.H. Clark, *A History of Australia,* vol. 6, Melbourne University Press, Melbourne, 1987, p. 150; Griffin, *Daniel Mannix,* p. 216.

Chapter 4: Irish Republican icon, 1920-1925

After the high farce of Mannix's arrest at sea, the Irish story darkened. The death toll on both sides in Ireland mounted through the second half of 1920 and into 1921, with a growing spiral of assassinations and reprisals by poorly-disciplined forces.

On arrival in England, Mannix showed no hurry to resume his travel to Rome to call on the Pope. Instead he spent months addressing large gatherings of Irish in England. Though forbidden by the British authorities to visit Liverpool, Manchester and Glasgow (the main centres of Irish concentration), he spoke at many other major cities.[1] No major incidents ensued, although many were threatened.

When the Sinn Féin Lord Mayor of Cork, Terence MacSwiney, died from a hunger strike in London in October 1920, Mannix's expertise in moral theology proved useful in establishing that death in a hunger strike was not suicide (forbidden to Catholics).[2] Mannix led the funeral cortège.

Proceeding to Rome, Mannix met the Pope. Contrary to British hopes for a papal condemnation of him, Mannix persuaded the Pope to issue an "even-handed" statement on Ireland (as described below in chapter 6). His return to Australia was permitted by the Government, despite widespread Protestant opposition.

There was worse to come in Ireland itself. After a ceasefire in the War of Independence, negotiations led to a compromise Anglo-Irish Treaty being signed in December 1921. It provided for the establishment of an Irish Free State in all of Ireland except Ulster, with Dominion status within the Empire similar to Australia's. Peace seemed at hand. But hardline Republicans including de Valera refused to accept the Treaty and provoked a civil war. The brutal war lasted eleven months in 1922–3 and killed more people than the War of Independence. Among the dead was the young Chairman of the Provisional Government, Michael Collins, who was assassinated by the IRA in August 1922. The pro-Treaty forces eventually defeated the IRA and de Valera called on the IRA to stop fighting, but Republicans continued to hope for political victory.[3]

Irish supporters overseas were naturally dismayed by these developments and passionate involvement in Irish affairs waned.

The Catholic Church in Ireland set its face firmly against the violence of Republican fighters and refused them the sacraments. There were a few priests who associated with the rebels, but the Republicans had only one friend at the higher levels of the Church, Archbishop Mannix. Although Mannix never explicitly called for violence, his support for the position of his old friend de Valera was unquestioned and his advocacy of the Republican cause unqualified.[4]

In 1925 Mannix visited Ireland via Rome – his only return home during his long years in Australia. De Valera visited Rome disguised as a priest and discussed politics with Mannix and other allies.[5] Largely shunned by the Irish clergy, he was feted by Republicans (by then in the political wilderness) and gave enthusiastic speeches on their behalf.

The wheel turned. De Valera came to power by peaceful means in 1932 and dominated Irish politics for the next thirty years. He resumed the Republican agenda, enforced Catholic social policies including a ban on divorce and the sale of contraceptives, and launched a trade war with Britain that contributed to Ireland becoming an economic backwater.

During a brief period in opposition, de Valera visited Australia in 1948. His reception in Melbourne was rapturous.[6]

THE BOOTLE AFFAIR

Mannix's speeches in England largely repeat what he had said in America. Instead of taking extracts from them, we look behind the scenes at the fears engendered in Protestant circles and the security authorities by Mannix's progress. By this time events in Ireland had raised tensions further; for example some officers of the Lancashire Fusiliers had been assassinated in Dublin on 21 August 1920.

Bootle, an industrial area on Merseyside, was just outside the zone of Liverpool where Mannix was forbidden to speak. A speech by him was set down for 5 December 1920. The Irish Catholics were not the only ones with a large local following ready to take action. The police received letters from local associations such as the Bootle Constitutional Association, the "Bootle Village True Blues", and the Loyal Orange Institution, in effect threatening mass violence if Mannix were allowed to speak. An example:[7]

LOYAL ORANGE INSTITUTION OF ENGLAND.

BOOTLE PROVINCE – CIRCUIT No 12.

26, Chelsea Road,
Litherland,
Nov. 25th, 1920.

Dear Sir,

It has come to our knowledge that Dr. Mannix (who is prohibited visiting Liverpool), is to visit Bootle and or Seaforth On Sunday, December 5th, 1920, and an outside dialogue demonstration is to take place.

In view of such an event occurring, we are organising with the assistance of other bodies a monstre demonstration in protest, and I feel as loyalists and in justice to you to write you of this our intention not to allow a banned prelate of his known character to insult the loyalist population, without uttering our protest against such a visit.

Yours faithfully,

(S'd) A. F. REANNEY.
Prov. Grand Master,
Bootle.

To Chief Superintendent of Police,
SEAFORTH.

Stamped "Lancashire Police, Seaforth, 26th November, 1920".

The Chief Constables of Lancashire, Liverpool and nearby areas met to consider the threat. They panicked. With a week to go before Mannix's visit, their joint letter begs London to ban Mannix from the whole region to prevent "grave disorder".

```
                    4300
    TELEPHONE No. 2200 CENTRAL
    ~~~~~~~~~~~~~~~~~~~~~~~~~"           CENTRAL POLICE OFFICE.

    Please address your letter                   LIVERPOOL.
            CHIEF
        THE HEAD CONSTABLE,
                                         29th. November, 1920.

    and in your reply quote No                   Your reference No
                                                 ~~~~~~~
```

Sir,

We beg to inform you that, at a Conference of Chief Constables representing the Merseyside Boroughs and the Hundred of West Derby, presided over by the Lord Mayor of Liverpool on this date, it was unanimously agreed that the Secretary of State be requested to take steps to include in the existing order made last August by the Competent Military Authority, London, prohibiting Archbishop Mannix from visiting Liverpool, the Boroughs of Birkenhead, Bootle and Wallasey, and the Hundred of West Derby situated in the County of Lancaster. We desire to point out that if Archbishop Mannix should visit this area as it is contemplated he will do next Sunday, December 5th., organized opposition will be offered and grave disorder will result, particularly in view of recent happenings.

We further request that you make an order under Regulation 9A, Defence of the Realm Regulations, prohibiting the holding of any meeting or procession, as defined in the said Regulation, in the above named area on Saturday and Sunday next, the 4th. and 5th. December, for the same reasons.

We are,
Sir,
Your obedient Servants,

Chief Constable of Lancashire.
Chief Constable, Liverpool
Chief Constable, Birkenhead
Chief Constable, Wallasey.
Chief Constable, Bootle.

The Under Secretary
    of State,
        Home Office,
            Whitehall,
                LONDON, S.W.1.

The letter got immediate action. As requested, Field Marshal Sir Henry Wilson,[*] Chief of the Imperial General Staff, on 1 December 1920, invoked the Defence of the Realm Act to prohibit Mannix from entering the region. The threat of blood on the streets was averted.

It is Mannix, not the Loyal Orange Institution, who is described, by a kind of legal fiction, as acting "in a manner prejudicial to the public safety".

> DEFENCE OF THE REALM.
>
> WHEREAS Archbishop Mannix is suspected of having acted or of being about to act in a manner prejudicial to the public safety and the Defence of the Realm and whereas it appears to me as Competent Military Authority that it is desirable that he should be prohibited from entering not only Liverpool, Glasgow and Manchester, as directed by an Order made by the Competent Military Authority on the 6th August, 1920, but also the Boroughs of Birkenhead, Bootle and Wallasey and the Hundred of West Derby in the County of Lancashire.
>
> NOW, I, Field Marshal Sir Henry Wilson in exercise of the powers conferred on me as Competent Military Authority under Regulation 14 of the Defence of the Realm Regulations and of all other powers enabling me in this behalf and with the consent of the Army Council, do hereby prohibit the said Archbishop Mannix from entering the Boroughs of Birkenhead, Bootle and Wallasey and the Hundred of West Derby in the County of Lancashire.
>
> Dated this 1st day of December, 1920.
>
> Henry Wilson
> Competent Military Authority.

---

[*] Sir Henry Wilson, Chief of the Imperial General Staff, was later elected an Ulster Unionist Member of Parliament. He was assassinated on his doorstep by IRA gunmen in 1922.

Words of farewell: The possibility of peace in Ireland

After visiting the Pope, Mannix departed for Australia via London. His farewell speech at the Cannon Street Hotel on 12 May 1921 sets out his unrepentant (as usual) views on Ireland:[8]

The Government would like the Irish to go on their knees to British politicians, and whine for peace. They have been telling us all along, but they are telling us more and more frequently now, because there is pressure upon them and behind them, that the door is open for negotiation. Yes, the door is open, any time that the Irish wish to negotiate ... I am anxious to preach peace negotiations in the only way peace can be brought about. I would appeal to the Government once more as I have appealed every time: let them withdraw their military forces from Ireland; let them meet the representatives of Ireland face to face; let the two nations confer face to face on a footing of equality. Peace then will be in the offing, but not till then.

> *"Imagination and poetry are gifts that have been denied to me ... but ... I imagined that I was an Englishman"*

Now I have not much imagination, I never attempted to write a poem.

Imagination and poetry are gifts that have been denied to me like a great many others, but on that occasion I made what I may call almost one imaginative flight in my life – I imagined that I was an Englishman. When I say that if I were an Englishman, if I were Mr. Lloyd George the Prime Minister instead of being the Archbishop of Melbourne, that I would have tried perhaps to settle the Irish question in a certain way, it was a great flight of imagination, of course.

I could not really be an Englishman and still less Lloyd George. You remember the speech he made on one occasion when he described himself as standing on the bridge of the ship with a Divine Commission specially chosen by Divine Providence to save the British Empire, and he went on to say that no man should talk to the man at the wheel and that it would be a sacrilege for anyone to attempt to dislodge him; Now I could not occupy any such position, I could not imagine myself, like him a child of Destiny and a vessel of Election; But I tried to imagine myself to be an ordinary Englishman and politician, and I said what I thought I myself might be in that case and this is what I said: "Probably if I were an Englishman I should be very glad to keep Ireland within the British Empire, I should be glad to make Ireland peaceful and contented within the huge boundaries of the great British Commonwealth," and as a consequence of that I said: "If I were an Englishman I should probably set myself to discover how I could make Ireland contented, peaceful and prosperous within the Empire, and if I were to set myself that problem I think I should have come to the conclusion that the only way – the only possible way – (which might be a failure) but the only possible way in which Ireland could be induced to remain a contented part of the British Empire would be to give Ireland full Dominion Home Rule like Australia and the other British Dominions; and then if Ireland were to try for a time it would be my hope, my desire, my prayer as an Englishman, that Ireland would come to be contented." But I went on to say, because I am a consistent man (and even in my imaginative flights I was trying to be consistent) that if Ireland proved on trial to be still dissatisfied, then as an Englishman, though I was not a child of Destiny, at all events I would be an honest and consistent man, and I saw that I was bound in consistency, bound in honesty, to give to Ireland what I had been preaching to be the just right of every nation great and small.

"Ireland can never trust any British politician"

I am going back to Australia with the firm conviction that I brought to England, because I could not bring it to any other place, that *Ireland can never trust any British politician (italics in original).*

DE VALERA LETTER TO MANNIX

Back in Australia, Mannix's welcome was, as usual, "tumultuous". He savoured it to the full.⁹

As I drove up Collins Street on Saturday last, I could not help thinking of the contrast between the lonely ecclesiastic who, at the dead of night, was taken off the Baltic and put aboard a British destroyer with one companion, Fr Vaughan, and the ecclesiastic who rode up Collins St in triumph – amidst the plaudits of better upholders of the British Empire than the British Navy that captured me.

He continued to speak in support of the Republican cause in Ireland, despite the Irish bishops' severe condemnation of the Republicans' violence during the Civil War. Mannix determined to stick by his friend de Valera through thick and thin. De Valera was appreciative, as well he might be given his lack of allies:¹⁰

6 November 1922

Private

His Grace, The Most Rev. Dr. Mannix, Archbishop of Melbourne.

My dear Lord Archbishop:

Since this conflict began, I have often wished but had not the heart to write to you. Long explanations would have been necessary to meet the unrestricted volume of hostile press misrepresentation, and then every explanation would have appeared an excuse or an aspersion on other Irishmen.

I thought it better to risk a possible misunderstanding, and there has been nothing more cheering through all these months than the unerring instinct which enabled Your Grace to appreciate the situation truly, and to read correctly between the lines. I had hoped that Dr. O'Reilly[†] would have shown a similar instinct at Paris, but his judgement there seems to have been warped by the atmosphere in which he suddenly found himself without any personal knowledge of any of us to guide him in sifting the true from the false. I still hope he will yet come to understand how he was misled.

The late Pronouncement of the Hierarchy[‡] here is most unfortunate. Never was charity of judgement so necessary, and apparently so disastrously absent. Ireland and the Church will, I fear, suffer in consequence. The Pope's recent pronouncement on Italian matters is in very marked contrast indeed.

> *"The late Pronouncement of the Hierarchy here is most unfortunate"*

Mr. Barton[§] sent you some time ago, I am told, documents relating to the Peace Delegation. If you have received them, you are in possession of the circumstances prior to, and attending the signing of the Articles of Agreement and the presenting to us of the fait accompli. The tactics subsequently resorted to were still more unworthy and made inevitable the existing situation which, once the document was signed, could have been averted only by the most delicate tact and rigorous straight dealing.

I am convinced that the Free State Agreement must go. It has brought nothing but disaster so far, and promises nothing but disorder and chaos. It gives no hope whatever of ordered stable government. Human nature must be recast before those Irishmen and Irish women, who believe in the national right and the national destiny as in a religion, will consent to acquiesce in the selling of the national birthright for an ignoble mess of pottage, as they regard it. Think then of the prospects of a Government which can only exist by outlawing the most unselfishly patriotic citizens of the State. As Dr. O'Dwyer said, as long as grass grows or water runs, men and women will be found ready to dare and give their lives in the cause of Irish freedom, and will deem the sacrifice virtue and not sin. All these the Free State must now banish, or execute, or murder.

Party feeling is running rather too high now for calm dispassionate thinking, or for

---

[†] Dr Maurice O'Reilly of St John's College, Sydney, chaired the Irish Race Convention in Paris, not always agreeing with de Valera and Sinn Féin.

[‡] On 10 Oct 1922 the Irish Catholic bishops condemned the Republican campaign of violence against the Treaty as "a system of murder and assassination of the National forces without any legitimate authority" and refused the sacraments to Republican forces.

[§] Robert Barton, Sinn Féin member of the Irish Parliament.

real statesmanship to have any opportunity. Still, despite the press which has invariably encouraged the coups that have been attempted, and with the I.R.B. most responsible for the present situation, the people everywhere, young and old, are beginning to realise that the only salvation for the nation now is a return to the old Sinn Féin principle of cleaving to their own institutions, whilst ignoring the authority and the institutions which the foreigner has tried to impose.

Before this reaches Your Grace many things will have happened to determine the future. I cannot but think of the hopes of this time a year ago – the almost certain prospect of a settlement which all could have accepted, or at least acquiesced in, leaving us a united nation with a future to be freely moulded under God by ourselves. It is sad, but chastening to realise how rudely they were all blasted within a month.

I crave Your Grace's blessing, and I assure you of the affection and esteem of all who are striving now that the way may not be closed for those who may be destined to complete the work towards which the hopes of the nation have been set definitely since Easter 1916.

I am,

My dear Lord Archbishop,

Very sincerely yours,

Eamon de Valera

P.S. I enclose you a letter from Mr. Barton to a friend, which will give you an idea of the plight of the prisoners.

William T. Cosgrave letter to Mannix

Not everyone in Ireland was so sure of Mannix's understanding of Irish affairs. His mother, a patriot but no Republican, is reported as saying to a niece, "Poor Dan, if he had been allowed to land in Ireland in 1920 he would have had a different point of view. He did not understand the situation in Ireland."[11] Her opinion was shared by W. T. Cosgrave, President of the Executive Council (in effect Prime Minister) of Ireland from 1922 to 1932. It fell to him to take steps to deal with the rising tide of Republican violence, including imprisoning large numbers of Republicans. Mannix protested from Australia on the treatment of the prisoners. Cosgrave wrote a forceful and direct letter to Mannix on his ignorance of the situation, his propagation of false information, and his support for a campaign of terror. It was a letter which would have given a lesser man – or a better listener – pause.[12]

17 December 1923

My Lord Archbishop,

I have hesitated to answer Your Grace's cablegrams addressed to me and supplied to the Press in Ireland and abroad regarding those persons whom the Irish Government have found it necessary in the interest of the public safety to detain in custody. I have also refrained from addressing Your Grace in regard to certain statements which have been attributed to you by the Australian Press and quoted in the papers here. In this I have been actuated by a desire to avoid the appearance of a controversy which might, in the then existing conditions of prison revolt here, have been calculated to embitter rather than to assuage feeling in the country. I had also cherished the hope that with the passage of time Your Grace would come into possession of more accurate information as to events in Ireland than the propagandist falsehoods which have been acciduously [sic] circulated by a group of malcontents and mischief-makers.

I have, however, decided that it is due to Your Grace as well as to the Government and the people of Saorstat Éireann that I should correct certain misapprehensions which appear to have influenced Your Grace's view upon current events in Ireland, and I will at the same time endeavour to indicate in general terms the Government policy in regard to those persons still in custody.

In order to prevent misunderstanding it may be well to review briefly the circumstances in which it became necessary for the Government to imprison upwards of 13,000 persons. Following the acceptance of the Treaty by Dáil Éireann in January 1922, a number of men holding officer rank in the Army with the connivance and the instigation of the minority representatives engaged in a conspiracy to prevent the majority decision from being carried into effect. They organised mutiny in every locality in the country. They armed themselves in various methods. They acquired a large supply of munitions from the State by undertakings treacherously given at a time when their intentions were not manifest to be treacherously broken as soon as they thought they could do so with impunity. By collusion with the departing British armed forces they possessed themselves of further large quantities of arms and munitions with which to wage war upon their own people. They utilised funds subscribed by Irishmen abroad for humanitarian purposes to purchase weapons of offence, and they secured by various ruses and deceptions possession of barracks and strongholds in different parts of the country.

"Every day brought its crop of robberies, murders, burnings" It was only the forbearance of the Government that prevented an outbreak of hostilities on several occasions during the period March to June 1922. Every possible step that could be taken to prevent recourse to arms was taken by the Government, but they were met by the steady determination that there would be no accommodation, that the people of Ireland would be compelled to swallow the view of the minority or else take the consequences. Every day brought its crop of robberies, murders, burnings, seizures of land and property, until the country was fast becoming a byword for outrage and crime.¶

[Omitted are several paragraphs dealing with the apprehension, trial, imprisonment and sometimes execution of the mutinous troops]

Following the continued outrages by the marauding troops, the Government demanded the evacuation of the Four Courts building, which was being used as rebel headquarters for the more than 10,000 men in arms against the Government, most of whom took part in the national struggle. This demand was refused so action was taken. However, as soon as the National Army had succeeded in defeating these forces, the remnants formed themselves into small bands and continued their outrages, generally striking terror into the unarmed populace. As they were rounded up, the number of outrages grew smaller. Although it was difficult to bring the guilt home to the actual culprits, the crimes had been committed, and to this the recent graves and ruined homes scattered throughout the country bear sad and silent testimony.

The Government did not want to detain in custody any prisoner against whom there was no definite charge and, provided his release would not imperil the safety of the State, any prisoner who was prepared to not take arms against the people's Government, was set free. However, some violated their undertakings and were subsequently recaptured and a few suffered the death penalty.

The Government made repeated attempts to release every prisoner who could with safety be allowed freedom, with the result that, when the general hunger-strike started, the number of prisoners had been reduced to about 8,000 and releases were increasing daily. However, the 7,600 prisoners who refused to take food, had the effect of stopping all releases for about three weeks. Notwithstanding this the number detained in custody was reduced to about 1,200 shortly after . . .

I should perhaps be omitting a very important and relevant fact in connection with the detention of prisoners, if I failed to inform Your Grace that the Government have over and over again offered to release the prisoners provided the arms and explosives

---

¶ Among those assassinated by the Republicans was Cosgrave's uncle.

which they and their associates without having secreted were handed over to the State. No response has been received to these offers.

I have observed with very sincere regret that on a few recent occasions Your Grace has been induced by misleading and inaccurate information to give publicity to statements which are calculated to produce an impression entirely contrary to fact. The "Irish Independent" of 23rd October last, quoting from the "Catholic Press" of Australia, attributes to Your Grace the following statement:

> "If they took these 63 men who have been returned to support the Free State and put opposite them all those on the opposite side, they would find 90 in that camp against 63 to support the Free State Government".

Your Grace will perhaps permit me to say that the implication contained in this statement that the 15 Farmer deputies, the 14 Labor deputies and the 14 Independents returned at the Election were associated with the 44 soi-distant Republicans in their hostility to the Free State is one which is an absolute perversion of fact and which will be very strongly resented by the gentlemen in question. So far from this being the case, there are very few, if indeed there is a single one, of those deputies who, in their Election Addresses and in their speeches, have not definitely and repeatedly declared their adherence to the Treaty and their very definite disapproval and reprobation of the tactics of the irregulars. The best possible proof of their sincerity in this regard may be found in the fact that the Government have met the Parliament of the country in Session and continues to enjoy its confidence.

My attention has also been drawn to a further utterance by Your Grace quoted in the "Irish Independent" of 6th December, again on the authority of the "Catholic Press". It runs as follows:

> "Not long ago a Bill in regard to the Mercantile Marine had been prepared by the Free State Cabinet, who, before submitting it to the Irish Parliament, sent it privately and surreptitiously for the approval or otherwise of certain people in London. A reply was received that the proposal was not in accordance with the customs of any other part of the Empire, and that there was no reason for its adoption. Now the matter was quietly dropped without giving the Irish Parliament an opportunity to decide whether its provisions were in the best interests of Ireland."

I take it that Your Grace's remarks are based upon a bogus Despatch which was printed in an Irregular sheet called "Eire" early in August 1923 and quoted in the "Belfast Newsletter" of August 10. The facts are that no such projected measure of legislation was ever drafted, that it could not therefore have been submitted for the approval of certain people in London either surreptitiously or otherwise, and that naturally no such reply was received. It is unfortunate that while the original lie was brought to Your Grace's notice, the categorical and detailed repudiation issued by the Government on

> "... the implication contained in this statement ... is an absolute perversion of fact ..."

14th August did not meet Your Grace's eye. If it had it would have prevented the publication on Your Grace's authority of a statement which is absolutely without foundation and which is calculated to mislead those of our friends and people abroad who, in the absence of reliable information, may be led by the high authority on which, unwittingly no doubt, the falsehood is propagated, to accept it without further enquiry as a correct exposition of the measure of Ireland's present status.

The source from which this falsehood emanated is exactly the same source which produced the heart-rending description of the conditions under which Irish prisoners were being detained by the Irish Government, and these descriptions contained just as much truth and just as much falsehood as the references to the bogus despatch. Fortunately, the statements regarding the prison conditions were subjected to examination by an independent investigator detailed by the International Committee of the Red Cross and his report upon his visit to the camps and prisons is available to all who desire to obtain accurate information in the matter. He expressed himself satisfied that the treatment accorded to these prisoners so far from contravening international humanitarian conventions was very much better that that usually accorded to prisoners of war.

> "... the publication on Your Grace's authority of a statement which is absolutely without foundation ..."

I have written to Your Grace at great length, and if I have appeared unduly severe upon those who have spent their energies from March of last year in directing a campaign of destruction against their own people, I pray Your Grace to believe that I do so only because it is clear from Your Grace's utterances that the truth regarding events in Ireland has not yet covered the seven thousand miles which lie between us.

Neither my colleagues nor myself desire, or have at any time so desired, to do or say anything which could tend to prevent those of our misguided fellow countrymen who have attempted to set themselves up as the dictators of the Irish nation from renouncing their destructive policy and undertaking the duties and responsibilities of citizenship. May I venture to express the hope that our task will not be rendered more difficult by injudicious and inaccurate pronouncements, however well intentioned, circulated amongst those of our far-flung race whose distance from their native land makes it impossible for them to receive correct impressions of the day to day happenings here.

I remain,

Your Grace's obedient servant,

W. T. Cosgrave

Last visit home, Dublin, 1925

Mannix's visit to Ireland in 1925, his only return to his native country during his years in Australia, was a mixed success. With Ireland settling down under the Treaty and the Free State gaining strength, the extreme Republicanism of de Valera and Mannix was beginning to look out of date. Mannix was shunned by the hierarchy and most priests and politicians. But Republican true believers still turned out for him in large numbers and expected fiery speeches. They were not disappointed. On 22 October 1925, presented with the freedom of the city in the Pillar Room of the Rotunda, Mannix said,[13]

> [. . .] I have not become a politician, fallible or infallible I came, therefore, with, more or less, an open mind. When the unfortunate Treaty, to which reference has been made, was signed, I made up my mind about it; and one thing that helped me very much to make up my mind was that, right from the start, every enemy that Ireland had was ranged on the side of the Treaty. (Loud applause) That is not a convincing argument, of course, but it has its own weight, because it would be hard for me to believe, as evidently it is hard for you to believe, that, once in their lives, those people were anxious to do the right thing for Ireland. I came to see what reality was behind all that I had heard about this Treaty being a stepping-stone to Ireland's ideals. I am too old, I suppose, now, to be in a hurry, and if it were sure that we should be able to go step by step on the road we wanted to go, well, I think I would be able to bide my time. But I was anxious to know what the stepping-stones were like, and where they were leading, and what was happening. And I have been keeping my eyes open and my ears also. And what do I find? I find that there are two classes of people in Ireland who are quite satisfied with this Treaty, and, I suppose, with the stepping-stones; and these two classes are those whom we call Imperialists or Britishers – and they know their own business well – and the second class are those who, under this present arrangement, have secured for themselves and for their relatives good positions. (Applause and laughter) These two classes are enthusiastically in favour of the present regime. But it is no exaggeration for me to say – and I say it with absolute conviction and sincerity, weighing every word – that, speaking of the people generally, the present state of things, outside these two classes that I have named, has no friends. It may be that they do not know what is going to happen next. They do not know how they would substitute something better. But this, at all events, is absolutely certain – that the present state of things has no defenders, and those who are thick-and-thin supporters of this Treaty have no political friends on their own merits.

Treaty Prosperity

That may be a strange thing perhaps, because we have been hearing, from people who ought to know, that, under this Treaty, industries are reviving, trade is flourishing – (laughter) – and if we only have a little patience: everything will be all right. Yes, and if we could only draw cheques upon the optimism of some of these politicians, we would be very wealthy. If only the promissory notes of these politicians could he cashed at sight, there would be no unemployment in Ireland and industry would be booming. But you know as well as I know that there is hollowness in all these bold assertions. And, mind, even if trade were booming, and if industry were reviving, would that settle the Irish question? Not at all. Not at all. When Patrick Pearse** and those who came after him, when the men, in 1918 and later, swore allegiance to Dark Rosaleen, did they ask whether trade was flourishing under British rule? Did they base their demand upon unemployment? Did they ask whether the Shannon was running idly down to the sea? Not at all. Materially, industrially, everything might have been right, and yet Patrick Pearse would have done what he did and the men of 1918, and since would have done and sworn what they did and what they swore. Therefore, I say, while all these things are, of course, important, very important, while it is very important that we should have industries flourishing and trade reviving and that the Shannon should be turned to good account, if it be good account – while all these things are important, they are really beside the main vital question. The main vital question is still what it was in 1916 and 1918. Patrick Pearse was satisfied when he knew that there was a representative of England's King over in the Phoenix Park, and when he knew that there was an oath taken by Irishmen in the British House of Commons. These things were enough for him. He did not want to know any more about Irish industry or about the Shannon flowing down to the sea. And these things are there still. The Phoenix Park has still got a King's representative there – (applause) – and there is oath taken, not in the British House of Commons, but in some institution here in your historic city, and every man up and down the country who holds office under the present Government, is bound, I understand, to take an oath of a similar character. As long as these things are so, it would not matter to me how trade was going, or whether industry was flourishing or was not. I would keep industry flourishing and trade booming, but I would also endeavour to free Ireland, my native country. (Loud applause)

> *". . . when the men, in 1918 and later, swore allegiance to Dark Rosaleen, did they ask whether trade was flourishing under British rule?"*

** Leader of the Easter Rising of 1916.

Take up the work

Let us pray, then, that God's hand may be stretched over Ireland. Let us try to forget, as far as we can, the dreadful things that have torn us asunder. Ireland is too small to be partitioned: Irishmen are too few to be fighting amongst themselves. They never succeeded in anything, and they never will, until they stand shoulder to shoulder. When they stood shoulder to shoulder they defeated the British Government and its Conscription campaign, inflicting one of the greatest defeats that Government ever sustained.[††] And Irishmen did that without shedding one drop of blood. Priests and laymen, gentle and simple, they stood together, and, standing together, they were invincible. There is no use in going over the things that we deplore. We must try to forget as much as we can and take the problem where we find it. And I think, with proper guidance and light from those from whom we should expect it, we ought to be able to devise some means by which all real Irishmen and women would stand upon a common platform. They might not agree perhaps in every way, but at all events they would stand upon a common platform which would not then remain for these Imperialists and Britishers. These are the real enemies – I am speaking, of course, in a political sense – these are the real enemies and the only enemies that we ought to mind. And until we stand together, these people will be dragging us where they dragged us at the recent Senate election. They will be dragging us not towards a free and independent Ireland; they will be dragging us back into the heart of the British Empire, trying to persuade us that there, and there alone, we will get peace and contentment.

I have to thank you all once again for the great compliment that has been paid me, a compliment I shall never forget. If I have said any word that could be the least offensive to anybody here, if I have said anything that might seem to be offensive, I hope that my sufficient excuse will be that I claim to be only a very fallible Irishman coming thirteen thousand miles over the sea to plant my foot again on Irish soil, regretting that I am not able to see that Ireland as free as I thought she would be when I attempted, but failed, five years ago to reach her shores.

But there are better times coming, and when I come again, if I do come, I hope that Ireland will be really free, and that those who are standing together to-night and those who are now divided will be joined like brothers, and that those who stand for Britain as against Ireland will have been put in their proper place. There is a place for them, and they ought to face the fact in time, and I hope that Ireland will not be the Free State, but that Ireland will be simply Ireland. (Prolonged applause).

". . . when I come again, if I do come, I hope that Ireland will be really free . . ."

[††] The British Government's attempt to introduce conscription in Ireland in 1918 failed after intense opposition from nationalists, unionists and Catholic clergy.

[1] John Dunleavy, A great Irishman and a fine Christian gentleman: Archbishop Mannix in England 1920-21, *Footprints* 26 (2) (2009), 3-15.

[2] Archbishop Mannix in London, *Freeman's Journal* 11/11/20, http://trove.nla.gov.au/ndp/del/article/115601907

[3] Accounts in Peter Cottrell, *The Irish Civil War, Osprey*, Oxford, 2008; Tim Pat Coogan, *Ireland in the Twentieth Century*, Palgrave Macmillan, New York, 2004, ch. 2.

[4] Patrick Mannix, *The Belligerent Prelate: An Alliance Between Archbishop Daniel Mannix and Eamon de Valera*, Cambridge Scholars, Newcastle upon Tyne, 2012; Joe Broderick, De Valera and Archbishop Daniel Mannix, *History Ireland* 2 (3) (1994), 37-42.

[5] Patrick Mannix, *Belligerent Prelate*, p. 108; Coogan, Ireland in the Twentieth Century, ch. 3.

[6] Patrick O'Farrell, Irish Australia at an end: the Australian League for an Undivided Ireland, 1948-54, *Papers and Proceedings: Tasmanian Historical Research Association*, 21 (4) (1974), pp. 142-60.

[7] All images are from the National Archives of Australia records file titled 'Archbishop Mannix': citation: NAA: A1606, F42/1: http://recordsearch.naa.gov.au/scripts/Imagine.asp?B=204341

[8] Archbishop Mannix's farewell address, *The Catholic bulletin and book review*, 11 (1921), 343-350.

[9] Gilchrist, *Mannix: Wit and Wisdom*, p. 101.

[10] Eamon de Valera letter to Archbishop Mannix, 6 November, 1922 (UCD Archives: Eamon de Valera Papers, P150-2909), reprinted in Patrick Mannix, *The Belligerent Prelate*, pp. 179-81.

[11] Papers of Fr James Murtagh, quoted in Griffin, *Daniel Mannix*, p. 73; further on Ellen Mannix, pp. 89-90.

[12] William T. Cosgrave letter to Archbishop Daniel Mannix, 17 December 1923, (National Archives of Ireland/NAI, D/Taoiseach, SI369-13), reprinted in Patrick Mannix, *Belligerent Prelate*, pp. 183-7.

[13] *Three Stepping Stones*, pamphlet, recording speeches made by His Grace, Archbishop Mannix made in the Rotunda, Dublin, 22 and 29 October 1925, pp. 1-12.

Chapter 5: The high tide of sectarianism in Australia

Australia in 1900 had a religious composition similar to Ulster. A dominant Protestant majority held most positions of influence, while a poorer Irish Catholic minority simmered with resentment over its exclusion. The potential for sectarian conflict was high, and up to the 1940s, tensions along sectarian lines were a significant theme in Australian social life.[1]

Those tensions never boiled over into serious violence, Ulster-style, because of the efforts of many on both sides of the divide to co-operate with or at least tolerate the other side. The comparatively relaxed and socially fluid atmosphere of the Australian colonies encouraged leaving behind the hatreds and bigotries of the old world. Australia did not have a fixed and ingrown ruling class in the same sense as Ireland and Britain, nor an established religion. In the late nineteenth century a great range of people, including Catholics, rose to the top of politics, business and medicine.

Certain issues, however, exacerbated sectarianism. The prime one was the education problem. In the 1880s the Australian states had withdrawn state aid to denominational schools and set up a free and secular state system. Catholics regarded state schools as "a system of practical paganism, which leads to corruption of morals and loss of faith,"[2] and felt obliged to set up their own complete system. For ninety years they sacrificed to pay for the Catholic school system, while being taxed to pay for the state system which they could not in conscience use.

Job discrimination was the other main issue, from the Catholic point of view. Banks, insurance companies, some government departments and the officer corps of the armed services had in many cases informal policies discriminating against Catholics. Many men in those institutions were Freemasons. Freemasonry, though not explicitly anti-Catholic, encouraged webs of influence and patronage which in effect favoured Protestants, as Catholics were forbidden by their Church to join.[3]

On the Protestant side, the Loyal Orange Lodge, imported from Ireland, and the Protestant Federation acted as pressure groups to "defend" Protestantism against alleged Catholic plots. Such bodies never had widespread strong support from the general Protestant population.

Certain Catholic policies acted to encourage Protestant suspicions. Until the 1960s, the Catholic Church did not admit the principle of religious freedom and supported the idea of confessional states, in which the true faith would be privileged by law. At a more personal level, anger was aroused by Catholic policies aimed at separating its members from personal connections that were thought to endanger faith. Forbidden were attendance at state schools (except where no Catholic school existed), attendance at Protestant religious services, and, most significantly, marriage in a Protestant Church. The papal decree *Ne Temere* of 1907 appeared to declare invalid marriages of Catholics outside the Church. Legislation making it illegal to promulgate the decree almost passed the New South Wales Parliament in 1924.[4]

And acting as a "lightning-rod" (his words) for these storms was His Grace, the Archbishop of Melbourne, Daniel Mannix. Though Mannix did not insult Protestants as such or attack their theology, his statements on the Empire and Ireland seemed to Protestants confirmation of their wildest claims about the disloyalty of Catholics, and the dangers posed by allowing them any leeway.

Mannix's aggressive strategy in the face of sectarianism certainly raised the self-esteem of a large part of the Catholic minority. It was very popular, especially among the poorer classes. Many more prosperous Catholics felt that by encouraging extreme Protestant reaction, it risked worsening the existing problems.

After World War II, sectarianism gradually waned. Intermarriage and other interactions, as well as higher standards of education, made it harder to take religious differences so seriously.

When Arthur Calwell and the Menzies government flooded Australia with a million Eastern and Southern European immigrants, the now "Anglo-Celtic" Australia had someone else to "construct as other".

Freemasonry, 'the great tumour'

Speaking to the annual meeting of the Catholic Federation in the Melbourne Town Hall on 14 February 1916, Archbishop Mannix covered the subjects of Freemasonry, social evils, educational injustice and the War. On the subject of Freemasonry, Mannix said he:[5]

> *". . . the Freemason brotherhood, which was the most insidious enemy of Australia. Freemasonry was a huge tumour growing upon the life blood of Australia"*

. . . would be glad if the Federation has been able to report that it had unmasked and overthrown the Freemason brotherhood, which was the most insidious enemy of Australia. Freemasonry was a huge tumour growing upon the life blood of Australia. Mr. Hughes had spoken of the parasites upon his party. It was to be wished that Mr. Hughes, a strong and courageous man, should feel himself strong enough to deal with those who were parasites not only upon one party, but were poisoning the life blood of both parties, were strangling the honesty of commerce, and, if allowed, would drag down Australia as they had dragged down some of the nations of Europe. (Cheers)

Continuing, Mannix said he:

. . . hoped that the federation would be able to supply a list of the brethren and to begin with a list of those Freemasons who sat in the Federal and State Houses. It would be of great interest in this democratic country at election times, and would be the key and the cue to many objectionable things that could not otherwise be explained, and things done behind the back of the people and against their will. (Cheers.)[*]

Protestant attacks

The heads of Protestant churches in Melbourne mostly had the good sense not to take the fight up to Mannix in his own terms. All-in brawling was left to certain ministers and propagandists, who would always rise to the Mannix bait. In the lead was the Rev J. Laurence ("Fighting Larry") Rentoul[†], always happy to write to *The Argus*.[6]

---

[*] On the causes and effects of the long struggle between Catholics and Freemasonry, see James Franklin, Catholics versus Masons, *Journal of the Australian Catholic Historical Society* 20 (1999), 1-15.

[†] Rev J. Laurence Rentoul, born in northern Ireland, was a Presbyterian minister and professor in the theological hall, Ormond College. He opposed the Boer War but was chaplain-general to the A.I.F. in WWI and supported conscription. His daughter was the celebrated illustrator of fairytales Ida Rentoul Outhwaite.

Dr. Rentoul on Catholic Ireland, 16/10/17

To the Editor of the "Argus."

Sir,

In his pronouncement on Catholic Ireland on Saturday, Dr. Mannix says, "He wished Catholics in Australia would get as much justice as the Catholics gave Protestants in Ireland." And his credulous audience gave "applause" to that! Now, those of your readers who have not seen with their own eyes, as I have seen, the sort of "justice" which Roman Catholics and their Hierarchy now "give to Protestants in Ireland," by capturing the national school system, had better study up the actual startling facts. If they cannot get at the official reports, they can get the story of the long struggle, set forth with statistical accuracy, in the writings, for example, of Mr Hugh O'Donnell, M.A. (formerly Home Rule M.P.), and of Mr. Michael J. F. McCarthy, B.A.[‡] "Roman Catholic graduate of Trinity College, Dublin: barrister-at-law," author of "Priests and People in Ireland," "Five Years in Ireland," "Irish Roman Catholic University and the Jesuits," etc. Mr. McCarthy's works have received the highest encomiums from the leading newspapers of Europe and America, and also from Dr. Mannix's friends, the Germans, for their "fearlessness, honesty, and impartial truth." Lord Rosebery terms them "broad, independent, and fearless." Now, what are the facts as to the "justice the 'Catholics' give Protestants in Ireland" in national education? [Here follow the "facts."]

J. LAURENCE RENTOUL.

Mannix was happy to take Rentoul's bait in return. At the end of a speech addressing a large audience on a range of topics, he wound down with a long attack on Rentoul. After some detail on how Rentoul had said the opposite in 1907 to what he had written in 1917, Mannix turned to more personal attack: [7]

I will not insult your intelligence by dwelling upon the contrast between the letter and the speech. The Rev. Professor, who can one day tell you that a certain writer has maligned his country in works which are a tissue of lies, and another day refer you to the same writer as a man of a world-wide reputation for 'honesty and impartial truth,' deserves to have a bust in his honour in the office of the "Argus." I do not want to brand the Rev. Professor Rentoul as he deserves. I leave that to you. (Applause.) If the press representatives are fortunate enough to get their reports inserted in the papers in the morning, I want the public to judge him and to brand him

> *"I do not want to brand the Rev. Professor Rentoul as he deserves. I leave that to you"*

[‡] Irish nationalist but anti-clerical author and former seminarian, who argued that the Catholic Church's influence and wealth in Ireland was hindering social progress.

as they think he deserves. I like a man of courage and a man of force of character, and I do not object if he speaks his mind forcibly at times. (Applause.) I can respect such a man, even when he differs from me, and attacks me if he thinks I merit his censure. (Applause.) But I cannot either respect or understand Rev. Professor Rentoul. I did not want to give you my estimate of Mr. McCarthy until I had first given you Rev. Professor Rentoul's estimate in 1907. I know Mr. McCarthy's history, and I know his works. After hearing the Rev. Professor Rentoul's 1907 opinion of him, you will be prepared for mine. He is on the level of a kindred character here; he is no higher, and he could not well be lower. He is the "Critchley" Parker[§] of Irish literature (Laughter and loud applause.). I part from Rev. Professor Rentoul with a question that I have put already: Was he honest in 1907? Is he honest in 1917? (Voices: "No, no!") Was he ever honest? Or has he been always honest, but irresponsible and negligible? (Loud applause.) He seems a fitting sponsor for the Protestant Federation, to which he has given his blessing. So I leave the Rev. Professor Rentoul. (Applause.)

Young Robert Menzies critical of Mannix

While the Rev Rentoul represented an extreme wing of Protestant opinion, more moderate Protestants were also offended by Mannix. Their views can be seen in a 1917 letter by the young Robert Menzies, addressed to a Catholic friend who had defended Mannix.[8]

Letter from Robert Gordon Menzies to Frank Corder, 18 September 1917

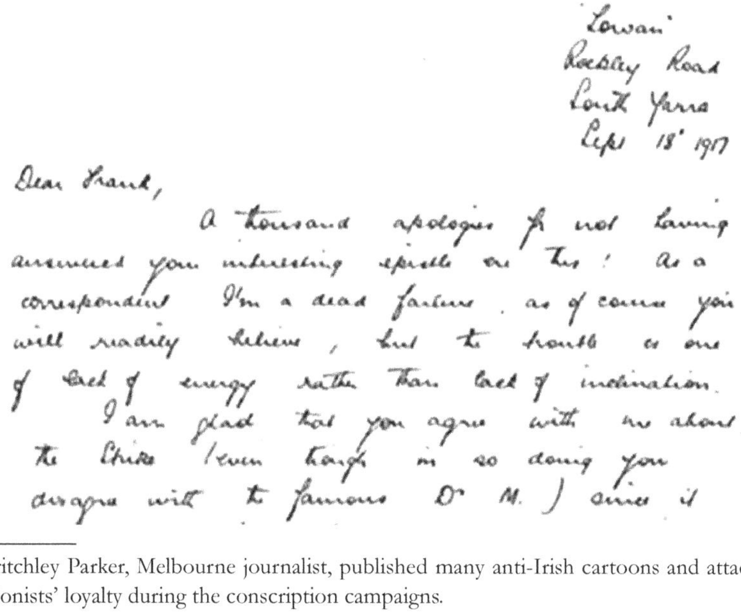

[Handwritten letter:]

"Lowan"
Rockley Road
South Yarra
Sept 18' 1917

Dear Frank,

A thousand apologies for not having answered your interesting epistle ere this! As a correspondent I'm a dead failure, as of course you will readily believe, but the trouble is one of lack of energy rather than lack of inclination.

I am glad that you agree with me about the Strike (even though in so doing you disagree with the famous Dr M.) since it

---

[§] Frank Critchley Parker, Melbourne journalist, published many anti-Irish cartoons and attacks on anti-conscriptionists' loyalty during the conscription campaigns.

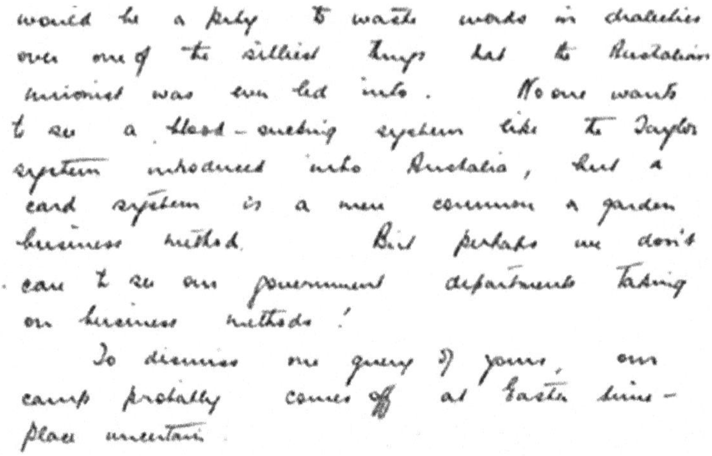

[handwritten letter excerpt]

In the second paragraph of this letter to his friend Frank Corder, a Catholic and Melbourne solicitor, Menzies refers to the General Strike of 1917. The strike began in New South Wales on 2 August 1917 and involved nearly 100,000 workers in all states, a large proportion of them Catholics. He agrees with Corder about the strike but says, "even though in doing so you disagree with the famous Dr M." On 2 September, just over two weeks before the date of the letter, at St John's Catholic Church in Clifton Hill, Archbishop Mannix strongly defended the strikers. In particular he attacked Taylorism or 'scientific management', which Menzies himself appears to disfavour.

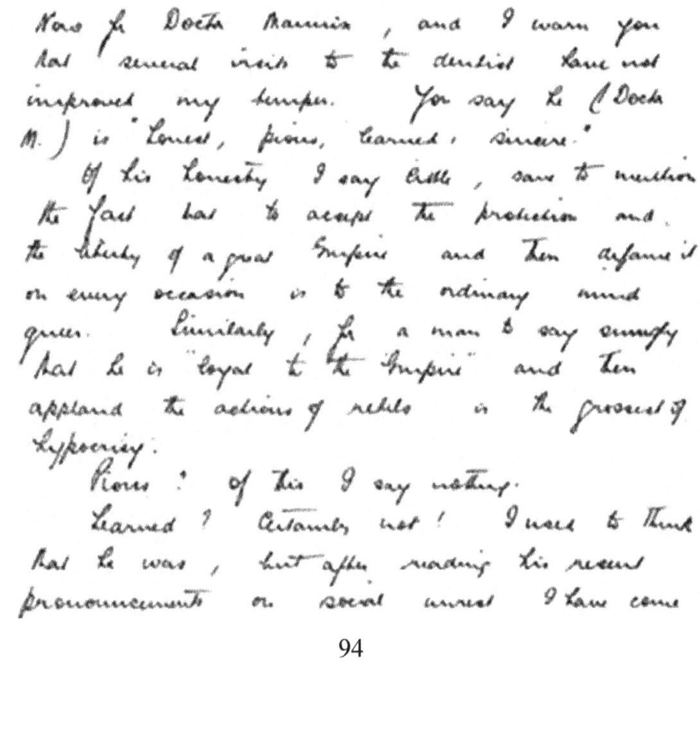

[handwritten letter excerpt]

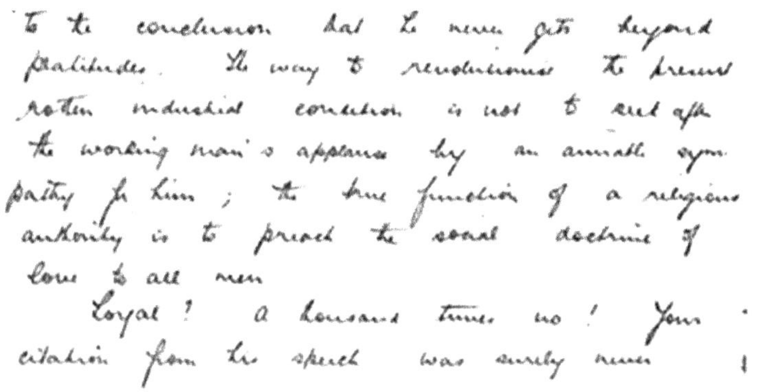

[handwritten text:]
'...to the conclusion that he never gets beyond platitudes. The way to revolutionise the present rotten industrial condition is not to suck after the working man's applause by an annual sympathy for him; the true function of a religious authority is to preach the social doctrine of love to all men.

Loyal? A thousand times no! Your citation from his speech was surely never...'

Menzies moves into a detailed analysis of 'Doctor Mannix'. Most of this page is his responses to Corder's claim that Mannix is "honest, pious, learned, sincere." In summary Menzies says:

'Of his honesty I say little, save to mention the fact that to accept the protection and the liberty of a great Empire and then defame it on every occasion is to the ordinary mind queer. Similarly, for a man to say smugly that he is "loyal to the Empire" then applaud the actions of rebels is the grossest of hypocrisy.

'Pious? of this I say nothing.

'Learned? Certainly not!

'Loyal? A thousand times no!' Your citation from his speech was surely never [to last page] calculated to impress anyone! It is easy to say, "I am loyal to the Empire." We would be ready to believe it if the reverend gentleman had ever wholeheartedly espoused the cause of the allies[1] and shown a little enthusiasm for their great ideals. But no. A cold word of praise, followed invariably by a wild Maynooth story about perfidious action and the fancied wrongs of Ireland. Has he ever encouraged recruiting by one word? Certainly not! By every power of suggestion and veiled speech he has sought to retard the Australian people in their progress towards a decently unselfish point of view.'

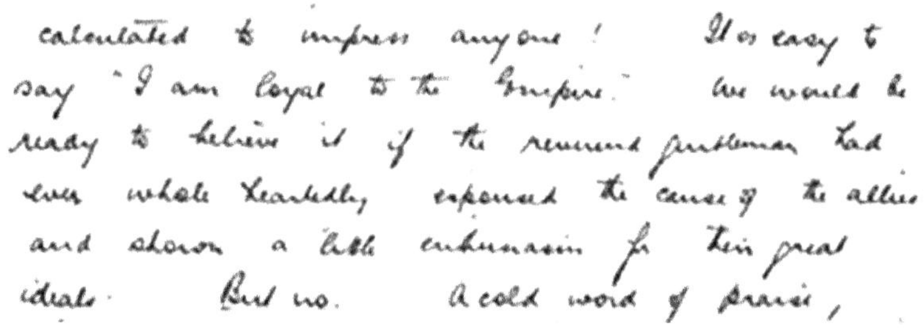

[handwritten text:]
'...calculated to impress anyone! It is easy to say "I am loyal to the Empire." We would be ready to believe it if the reverend gentleman had ever wholeheartedly espoused the cause of the allies and shown a little enthusiasm for their great ideals. But no. A cold word of praise,...'

---

[1] Menzies' own devotion to the allied cause did not extend to enlisting; he never explained why but it is generally believed that a family conference decided that with two brothers in the services the family had – as Mannix said of Australia – done enough.

In the next paragraph, Menzies writes,

'I don't think we'd better discuss Doctor Mannix. In my eyes he is a cunning, sinister, and a national menace! Selah!'[1]

---
[1] Selah: a Biblical word of obscure meaning usually taken to mark a break in a Psalm.

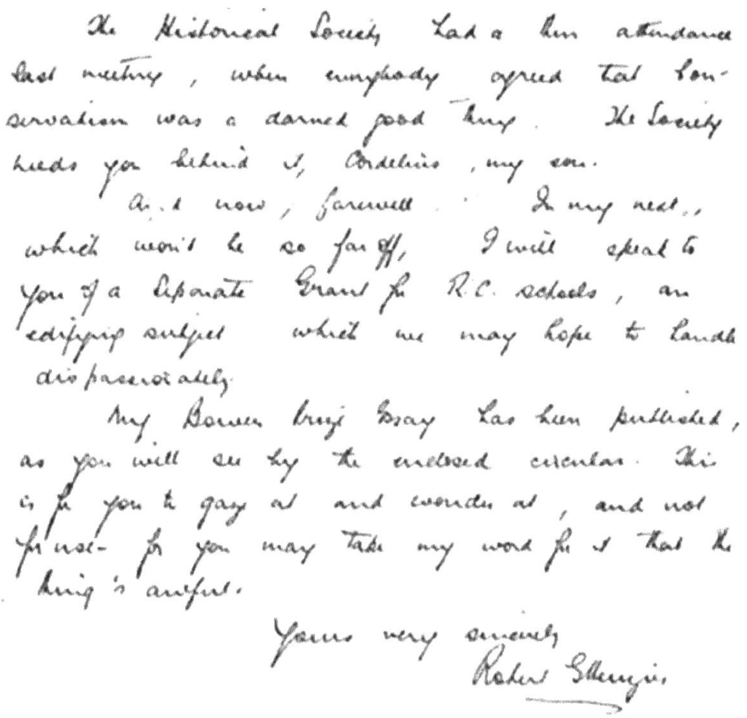

[Handwritten letter reproduced as image]

In the penultimate paragraph of the last page, Menzies writes,

I will speak to you of a Separate Grant for R.C. schools, an edifying subject which we may hope to handle dispassionately.

Dispassionate consideration of state aid was hardly on the agenda in 1917. But decades later, Menzies sometimes met Mannix on their daily walks to their respective work places. Someone who used to drive daily along the Mannix walking route remembered:[9]

Coming home, I'd just turned at the bridge over the Yarra at the bottom of Johnston Street and about 80 or 90 yards up, there was he and Bob Menzies walking. He [Mannix] was stepping it out and Bob was trying to step it out with him. I eased up and said 'Your Grace and Mr Menzies, would you care for a lift?' 'No', said His Grace, 'my friend might.' Well, Menzies got into the car and said goodbye to His Grace. Half way, Menzies said: 'He's fit enough to go to the Olympic Games and win a race there!'

It was to be Menzies who, in the last few days of Mannix's life, came through with the first offer of state aid for church schools. (Chapter 7 below) That was no more than fair recompense for Mannix's unwavering support for the Labor Split, which kept Menzies in power for a decade.

The Spanish influenza: No popery

By 1919 the influenza pandemic, the "Spanish flu", had reached Australia. As elsewhere throughout the world, the medical facilities were overwhelmed. The State Government proposed to create a temporary hospital in Melbourne's huge Exhibition Building. Archbishop Mannix offered to staff it by conscripting a small number of his army of religious sisters and brothers for the work. Only some had nursing experience, but the supply of trained people had simply run out. The Minister for Public Health, John Bowser, was initially enthusiastic:[10]

At first, I feared that the task might be too great for them, as it had proved for those whose place they proposed to take. But the more I saw of the volunteer Nuns who flocked in for service from city and country convents, the more confident I became of their ability to work the Exhibition Hospital. And then, when it was reported to me that patients were lying neglected and dying in their own homes – not for want of hospital space, because the Exhibition had room for an additional 1000 or 1500 patients, but for sheer want of nurses; when I learned that you were begging for nurses from other States, from New Zealand, and even from India; above all, when I was warned that a virulent epidemic later on might make the conditions infinitely worse – I hesitated no longer. I promised, first to Dr. Robertson [Chairman of the Board of Public Health], and then to you, that the Sisters would at once take over the Exhibition and, without fee or reward, would provide for a thousand influenza patients and as many more as the building would hold. You promptly accepted my offer, and the public, who had been hearing of the condition of things at the Exhibition, felt relieved that thence forward the Sisters would do for the sick at the Exhibition, as far as circumstances allowed, what they always do at St Vincent's for all creeds and classes.

The Archbishop's offer was made on Friday, 14 February, and on the same day the Government of the State of Victoria, in restrained official diction, 'welcomes the generous offer of the competent services of the Sisters,' and arranged that the Mother Rectress of St. Vincent's Hospital should take over the Exhibition Hospital at her convenience.

However, two days later, at Wesley Church, the excitable Methodist, the Rev. Henry Worrall,** denounced the deal:

The garb worn by the nuns and brothers, the ceremonies they observe, the customs they follow, are things that should not be introduced into a state hospital.

** See chapter 1 above.

Face masks worn by nurses during the Spanish influenza epidemic of 1919.[11]

The government backed down and Mannix felt he had to withdraw his offer. Nevertheless, to ensure that Catholics clearly understood the attack, Mannix later published his correspondence with the government in a pamphlet published by the Australian Catholic Truth Society. Even in a grave emergency, Catholics were not wanted. The pamphlet argues:

NO POPERY AND THE SPANISH INFLUENZA

At a time when, to use the words of the Chairman of the Board of Public Health, 'anything might happen,' at a time when the dearth of nurses was so great that we were calling for help from new Zealand and from India, the Ministry, abandoning every consideration for the welfare of the public menaced by an appalling calamity, actually begged the Archbishop to withdraw his offer of a host of devoted Nuns and Brothers who had volunteered to risk their own lives in the hour of peril.

The Archbishop's just refusal to adopt this proposal faced Ministers with the difficulty of finding some shadow of excuse for their action. They were too pusillanimous publicly to speak the truth, as the Minister of Public Health did privately, when he told the Archbishop that sectarianism, and nothing else, was the cause of the trouble.

On Tuesday 18 February, the chairman's explanation appears in *The Age*. This results in both the minister and the chairman being deputed to call on the Archbishop to ask him to withdraw the offer and the Cabinet proposes to offer another venue[††] for the Sisters. Mannix rejects the offer.

In the last act the Archbishop, while acknowledging the minister's letter, rebukes the government for conceding to anti-Catholic pressure and offers help in future if proper guarantees will be given by the government.

[††] The alternative venue offered was Melbourne High School which, in those days was close to St Vincent's Hospital. However, it would have to be fitted up to serve as a hospital, which would have taken extra time when the matter was urgent.

"Raheen," Kew, Victoria,
20th February, 1919.

Dear Mr. Bowser – I have received your letter of this date informing me that the present arrangements at the Exhibition cannot be altered. The decision of the Government is just what I expected. Their submission to sectarian dictation is abject and complete.

Now that the Government has set your agreement with me aside, I may say that it was with great reluctance that I consented to offer the services of the Sisters in the Exhibition.

[the first part of the next part of this letter is a word for word repeat of Mannix's offer letter]

> *"The decision of the Government is just what I expected. Their submission to sectarian dictation is abject and complete"*

I have purposely refrained from incumbering this correspondence with any reference to the statements of those who have since intervened to upset your arrangement with me. The whole community was shocked by their utterances, and no reputable person outside the Ministry has had a word to say in their defence. The only importance attaching to these people is that, at their dictation, the Government has now formally refused to ratify your agreement with the Sisters, the Christian Brothers, and the Jesuit Brothers. By an oversight I omitted to mention the Jesuit volunteers in my former letter. But I do not suppose that their inclusion would have been much of a recommendation in the eyes of the Government or of its sectarian masters.

However, I must not dwell upon matters now definitely settled. You are anxious to know whether the services of the Sisters and Brothers will be available in the event of a future outbreak. The answer is easy; my duty is plain and imperative. I should never have thought of making any offer to your Government, had I known that the acceptance of my offer by the Government would require ratification at open-air services now being held on Sundays at non-Catholic churches. President Wilson's proposals, we are told, will need ratification by the Parliaments of the countries affected. I do not know what are his chances of success in the ordeal, but I do know what chance any proposal of mine would have in certain quarters in Melbourne. Knowing, now, the Government with which I have to deal, I withdraw every offer which I have made to you.

The Sisters and the Brothers who generously came forward at the invitation which you have now withdrawn will return to their convent homes, and there, within their limited opportunities, will render such aid to the sick as they can. But, after what has occurred, the Sisters and the Brothers cannot be expected to offer their services to your Government.

The epidemic seems to have spent its force. I hope it has. But if, later, we have a virulent outbreak, and if the Government, in need of nurses, desires the services of the Sisters and the Brothers to fight the epidemic, I shall gladly consider on its merits any request or proposal that the Government may make to me; and the Sisters and the Brothers will forget the conduct of the Government in their desire to succour the suffering. I must add, however, that I will consider no application, unless it comes from the Premier and his Ministry, and with guarantees that will make a repetition of the present regrettable incident impossible. That much I owe to the Sisters and the Brothers. Perhaps I owe something also to the whole community, whose sense of decency has been shocked by the reception given by the Government to my over-trustful advances. I have learned a lesson, and will not sin again.

I dealt with the Melbourne High School proposal in my last letter. There is nothing to add.

I truly sympathise with you, Sir, in the treatment you have received from your colleagues. At the crack of the sectarian whip, they have over-ridden the wise agreement which you made with me at the end of last week, and which you defended in the Press on your return to town after the week-end. At any rate, *you were unsectarian from Saturday to Monday. That is a small thing; but it is the only redeeming feature in a transaction otherwise wholly discreditable.*

It is sad that the noble offer of the Sisters should have been the occasion of such an outrage on public decency and of such degradation on the part of the Government. I am handing this correspondence to the Press. – Faithfully yours,

† D. MANNIX

VCs ON WHITE CHARGERS

Although St Patrick's Day was an annual celebration for Melbourne's Catholics, because of the Spanish influenza epidemic in 1919, assemblies that attracted large crowds were restricted. So the St Patrick's Day parade, Saturday 20 March 1920, was the first since the end of World War I. It was an opportunity for a spectacular display in response to Protestant accusations of disloyalty. Fourteen[12] Victoria Cross recipients were rounded up and mounted on white chargers to head Mannix's progress through the throng – said to be 100,000, with 20,000 in the procession itself.[13] The civic authorities enforced display of the Union Jack and the Australian coat of arms.[14]

Archbishop Mannix in the St. Patrick's Day procession led by thirteen Victoria Cross recipients on white chargers, Melbourne, 1920.[15]

Archbishop Mannix with VC winners 1920[16]

Framed composite photograph[17] presented to Lieutenant John Hamilton VC by his Grace the Archbishop of Melbourne and the Irish citizens of Victoria on the occasion of the Saint Patrick's Day celebrations in Melbourne, 1920. Portraits of fourteen Victoria Cross winners (ten Catholics and four Protestants) with portraits of his Grace Dr Daniel Mannix and the entrepreneur John Wren, who helped with costs of the event.

The VC winners are Pte William Currey, Sgt George Howell, Cpl Walter Peeler, Pte John Jackson, Lt Joseph Maxwell, Lt John Dwyer, Sgt Maurice Buckley, Pte George Cartwright, Cpl Thomas Axford, Cpl John Carroll, Pte Edward Ryan, Sgt John Whittle, Lt John Hamilton, Lt Lawrence McCarthy.

At the time of St Patrick's Day, 1921, Mannix was still overseas, speaking in Britain and about to meet the Pope. But in Melbourne his spirit lived on. In response to the requirement that the Union Jack should be carried in front of the procession, an "elderly man whose appearance would not suggest him as a suitable leader of a procession" was hired to do the "dirty work". At Bourke and Collins Street he was assaulted by men from the crowd and had to be rescued by police.[18] "We paid an Englishman fifteen shillings to carry the Union Jack for we could not find an Irishman prepared to carry it," Mannix was reported as saying.[19]

Loyal Orange Lodge protests

Mannix's return to Australia after his speaking tour was greeted with protests by the usual suspects:[20]

The Grand Secretary of the Loyal Orange Lodge writes to the Acting Prime Minister, 13 August 1921, protesting against the government's action in allowing Dr Mannix to land in Australia without taking the Oath of Allegiance. If this is to be the government's attitude, they cannot rely on the support of the Protestant community.

Heydon's response to Mannix's 'Australia First' speech[21]

A part of Catholic opinion, especially the better off and more "assimilated" – less tribal – section, regarded Mannix's utterances as dangerous and counterproductive. The most direct attack from a Catholic came from Judge Heydon‡‡ during the second conscription campaign: [22]

THE CHURCH AND LOYALTY
MR. JUSTICE HEYDON'S VIEWS
TO THE EDITOR OF THE HERALD

Sir, – A wise rule prescribes that Judges shall take no public part in politics. But there is a distinction between politics and loyalty. Where the latter is concerned, and where the loyalty not of a man but of a body of men is brought under suspicion, the fact that one

---

‡‡ Charles Gilbert Heydon, judge of the Industrial Court.

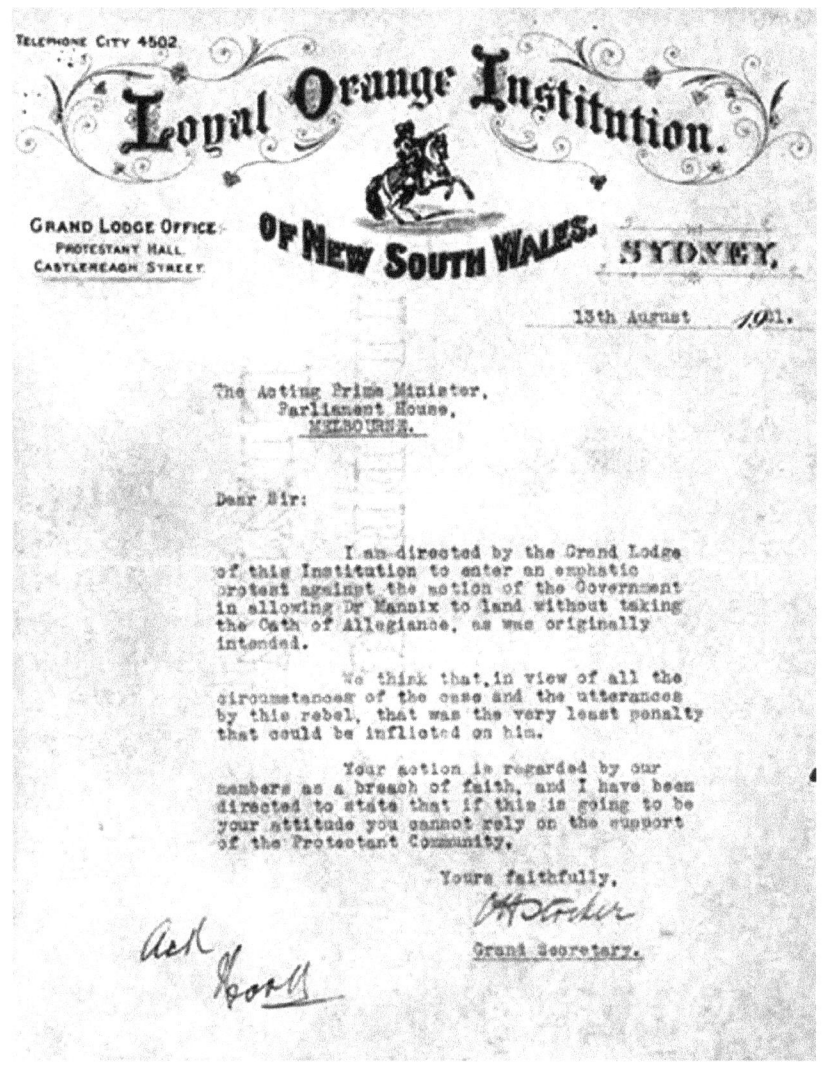

of the body holds, by the favour and confidence of his fellow citizens, the responsible and honourable position of a Judge may even make it his duly to speak, if possible with the tongue of a trumpet, in vindication of his fellows and of himself. Such a situation is created for me by the utterances of Archbishop Mannix, a prelate (I am ashamed to say) of the Church to which it is my highest and deepest blessing to belong. No man likes to appear in public opposition to a clergyman of his own denomination whose office he profoundly respects, but it may become a duty from which it would be cowardice to shrink. In proclaiming his sympathy with Sinn Fein, in urging us to put Australia first and the Empire second, the Catholic Archbishop of Melbourne has shown himself

> *"For a Catholic Archbishop to lead his flock along the paths of sedition is to disobey the clearest teachings of the Catholic Church"*

to be not only disloyal as a man but (I say it emphatically, Archbishop though he be, and simple layman though I be) untrue to the teachings of the Church of which by his office he should be a guardian.

Private assurances of this by Catholics to their fellow citizens have little weight; they say to each other naturally: "If Catholics do not agree with him, why do they not repudiate him?" And so infinite harm is done, and Catholics walk among their follow Australians whom they respect and by whom they desire to be respected, with a brand upon them. For a Catholic Archbishop to lead his flock along the paths of sedition is to disobey the clearest teachings of the Catholic Church. Obedience to and loyal co-operation with duly constituted authority and all its lawful commands (for there is, of course, a domain of conscience where no human laws can intrude) is by her most earnestly instilled. The political entity to which we belong is the Empire, of which we are a part as essentially as Victoria is a part of Australia, and as Melbourne is a part of Victoria, and as Archbishop Mannix is a part of Melbourne. The final issue of such teaching is that a man may put himself before his country, and such a man we call a traitor. He may do so if he chooses, but let there be no mistake about it, the Catholic of the British Empire who tramples the Empire underfoot tramples upon the teachings of his Church with it. The Catholic Church utterly reprobates treason, and strongly inculcates loyalty. The hierarchy of Ireland has recently reaffirmed, what all Catholics know, that the temporal authority of our rulers comes from the same Divine source as the spiritual authority of the Church itself. Cardinal Mercier,[§§] in maintaining the resistance of his Belgian people to the German invaders, has to take the ground – the demonstrably just ground – that the Germans are not, in Belgium, a lawful authority, but a set of bloody and cruel and tyrannical Invaders and treaty breakers. Will Archbishop Mannix dare to say that the Empire stands in that relation to Australia? Let us turn for a moment from the call of duty to that of gratitude; and from the call of gratitude to that of self interest; and what shall we find but the most overwhelming reasons why we should be faithful to our fellows who, all over the world, shelter with us under the glorious Union Jack? Of whom are we the child? Who gave us this great country of ours, as large as the United States? Who protected us, through war and peace, in the most profound calm, so that never once has an enemy fired a shot within our boundaries, or even against our shores, for now 129 years?

Who did this, during nearly the whole of the time, without charging us a single penny, and even while spending large sums amongst us? And it was done for us, even now a

---

[§§] Cardinal Désiré-Joseph Mercier, leader of the Thomist revival in Catholic philosophy, symbol of Belgian resistance to the German occupation in WWI.

mere handful, living in the great prize country of the world, the only great empty country remaining, which of ourselves we could never have held, and could not now hold. It was done for us all: Irish, Scotch, Welsh, or English – wherever our fathers came from. The arms of the Empire were round us all; and we were safe; and in that cradle grew up to be the Australian people; and now there is a man amongst us (but, thank God, not an Australian) who can tell us that in this war we should put Australia above the Empire. Or rather (let us be absolutely fair to him) above the British Empire,

"... overwhelming reasons why we should be faithful to our fellows who, all over the world, shelter with us under the glorious Union Jack? Of whom are we the child?"

our parent, our nurse, and our protector, the home of our fathers. As for that other Empire, the German, which would tread out in blood our language and. our nationality, we are to come under that; and indeed, if we listen to him, most richly shall we deserve it. Truly there are hatreds which ask for very costly food to glut them.

I say in protection of my fellow Catholics who already suffer, and will suffer more, through the indignation which is rightly felt at such teaching, this: That such hatreds and such treasons, though they may be cherished by individuals, are no part and no fruit of Catholic teaching, but have their root quite elsewhere. In America we have seen Monsignor Cassidy, the son of a Fenian, addressing Catholic soldiers of Irish descent, telling them that their cause was "freedom, liberty, and righteousness." If that is true in America, outside the Empire, is it less true in Australia, within the Empire? Can Archbishop Mannix alter a single one of those words? And if not, will he still tell us that Australia should put herself above freedom, liberty, and righteousness? Perhaps he will. It is only in a country as free as Australia that freedom can be abused and such things can be said. What would be done in Italy at this moment were some Sicilian Bishop to have the audacity to rear his head and tell his flock before all the world that they ought to put Sicily above Italy and Italy beneath the Austrian? Would his life be safe? Yet what would be the difference between his teaching and that of Archbishop Mannix?

"... this stab in the back of the Empire ..."

I might say something of the time chosen to inflict this stab in the back of the Empire; this time of strain and difficulty, with heavy clouds of disaster louring around, and a special call for unity of counsel and effort; but, perhaps, it would be better not to enlarge on that. If I said what suggests itself I do not think that Daniel Mannix the man could complain, but I cannot forget, however he may seem to do so, that Daniel Mannix is also an Archbishop in my Church. I will only say (speaking generally and without any reference to current controversies) that if Australia accepts his doctrines, and holds herself free to give anything less than the fullest fidelity to the Empire, she will indeed have made the great refusal. History will be unable to point to any example of more faithless disloyalty, or blacker ingratitude, or more enormous folly. And nothing in the teaching of the Church, I will not say prescribes it, but even permits it.

I am. etc.,

CHAS. G. HEYDON.

Booreen, Darling Point. Nov. 17.

An attack from within the Church, especially one as well-reasoned as that, hit Mannix where it hurt. His reply descends to a level of personal abuse rare for him:[23]

Dr Mannix replies to Justice Heydon
Melbourne, Nov. 20.

Archbishop Mannix, speaking at Croxton Park to-night, referred to the criticism levelled against him recently by Sir (sic) Justice Heydon of Sydney. "People," said Dr. Mannix, "are under the impression that this person is an Irishman. He is not an Irishman. His father was an Englishman, and I believe that he was born in Australia. People are also under the impression that he is a Judge of the High Court. He is not.

> *"He is a Judge of the second or third class of some kind or other"*

He is a Judge of the second or third class of some kind or other. He went to the Bar; but I know nothing remarkable about him there. Later he got on to the Bench, and he became quite a famous person for a day or two. The whole thing is amusing. You can imagine the Judge putting on his wig, and ordering the court officer to call "Silence in the Court" while he delivered judgment, as if the whole of Australia were listening. I do not want to reply to him. I do not think myself that the whole letter is worth any reply. If he were to go to address Catholics in Sydney he would not get as many to listen to him as would fit in a lolly shop.

"No Irish need apply": Did Mannix increase employment discrimination against Catholics?

The increase in sectarian feeling, they said, increased employment discrimination against Catholics. Herbert Moran,¶ a prominent Sydney Catholic doctor, attempted a pen-portrait that highlighted the potentially toxic aspects of the Mannix phenomenon:[24]

¶ Herbert "Paddy" Moran, Wallabies captain on their first overseas tour 1908-9, served on Gallipoli with the Royal Army Medical Corps, later a pioneer in the use of radium to treat cancer.

Doctor Mannix was a dignified and commanding figure with two small eyes set deeply in the large sockets of a long and heavily lined face. His nose was straight and fine, his mouth like a fissure in granite, his complexion muddy and unhealthy. There was about him something of the air of a mediæval recluse suddenly projected into the lists of a political contest. If Hughes was the leader of a new jingoism, Doctor Mannix was the self-appointed head of a movement of what might be called little Australians. His case was that the war was a sordid commercial affair, that in any case Australia had done enough and more than enough. Doctor Mannix at that time had been in Australia some three years. It was as an Australian citizen, not as a priest, that he claimed he always spoke.

The main antagonists descended to bitter personalities at times but no lower. The partisans outside the ring, however, were guilty of using every conceivable weapon. For example, there were sown broadcast and anonymously the most vile and filthy attacks on Catholic institutions. They could only have been produced by men with the minds of low perverts. All this was done in the name of patriotism.

The whole country was split on the question. It divided the people in the presence of a great war. If Hughes had made, as many thought, a grave error in asking the people to decide such an issue, the decision of a religious leader, and above all, an Irishman, to lead the opposition was incredibly foolish. The Catholics among the population had volunteered as well as any others; there was no actively disloyal element at any time in the country. By his attitude Doctor Mannix attracted to him a most fervidly enthusiastic crowd of supporters by no means exclusively Catholic, but drawn chiefly from the labouring classes. The extreme Irish section, lay and clerical, formed a very prominent part of those who noisily cheered his every appearance. It is necessary, however, to stress this point: when the vote was taken, on each occasion, more non-Catholics than Catholics voted against the proposal.

". . . the decision of a religious leader, and above all, an Irishman, to lead the opposition was incredibly foolish"

In two different referenda, the first in October 1916 and the second in December 1917, the answer was given in the negative. The social unrest caused by them was very great. The Archbishop's temerity split the Catholic body into two hostile layers. The upper social classes, strongly loyal, bitterly opposed their own ecclesiastic. A Catholic judge [Sir Charles Heydon] in a letter to the public press, in caustic terms disowned him. His example was followed by others of the same religion. These in turn were denounced from some pulpits where, under the guise of sermons, anti-English propaganda had been more or less openly practised. Such disloyal clergymen were few in number; the Easter executions in Ireland had excited them. But it was the Archbishop of Melbourne who had given the lead in defeatism. He had assumed the mantle of the Saviour of Australia.

In one speech before a great assembly of people he pointed out that he had become the lightning conductor for all the abuse in Victoria, but he added, humorously, that in a thunderstorm the lightning rod usually escaped damage. Nothing was ever truer in his own case. Every time the clerical orator went forth to speak a frenzied mob of admiring partisans followed him. The speech over, the Archbishop returned to the serenity and the simple amenities of "Raheen" and retired to sleep with the applause of thousands still ringing in his ears.

". . . after every such display of eloquence in every State humble Catholics were discharged from their jobs"

He himself suffered no personal injury or discomfort. But after every such display of eloquence in every State humble Catholics were discharged from their jobs. Thanks to the Archbishop a system of boycott against Catholic workmen and tradesmen was set up throughout the whole Commonwealth. In calling for applications to fill a position nearly every large firm adopted, though they did not publish it, the old formula, "No Catholics need apply." But the lightning rod stood untouched amid the ruin. William Hughes, himself, created a secret police force.[25]

Obviously, Doctor Mannix should have been the last person in the world to set himself up as leader in such circumstances. There was no spiritual question at stake. Although in Ireland Doctor Mannix had been himself suspected by the extreme Nationalists – he had opposed the introduction of Gaelic and had warmly entertained King Edward VII at Maynooth – his utterances in Australia confirmed the suspicion that he was implacably hostile to British rule. It was surely not a statesmanlike thing, still less a charitable thing, to declare publicly, during 1920, while he was passing through the United States: "England was your enemy, is your enemy, will be your enemy for all time." He could not then have been speaking in the assumed role of an Australian citizen.

It was a painful epoch for Catholic citizens; they became now the scapegoats for every social evil. In both the laity and the clergy a great gulf divided two sections.

Lukewarm Catholics publicly denied their faith. Many who didn't, became bitterly anti-clerical, speaking of some of their own priests with crude offensiveness. Doctor Mannix achieved nothing more than a notoriety which seemed strangely gratifying to his austere mind.

"Doctor Mannix achieved nothing more than a notoriety which seemed strangely gratifying to his austere mind"

An instance of Catholics losing a job occurred in 1918 at Royal Women's Hospital, Melbourne, an overwhelmingly Protestant establishment. The Committee of Management proposed to appoint a Catholic as Medical Superintendent. The appointment was objected to and did not go through, mention being made that "everybody has been stirred up by Dr Mannix".[26]

Mannix did have a reply to these charges:[27]

Some good people say that I have made a great many enemies; that I have stirred up a wave of sectarianism that will sweep the Catholic people into the sea. [Laughter] But bigotry did not begin with my arrival, nor is it confined to Victoria or to Australia. I was never in New Zealand, and probably my name, so familiar here, is not even known in that country. Still, there is a wave of sectarianism and stupid bigotry passing over New Zealand that is quite as high and mighty as the wave which threatens to engulf us here. [Laughter][***]

A MAD DOG FROM MAYNOOTH

More colourful and less well argued was an article by an anonymous 'Australian Catholic', entitled 'A mad dog from Maynooth' and helpfully reprinted as a pamphlet by the Protestant Federation in 1921. One paragraph gives the flavour.[28]

For a time the bigots outside raised secretly the tocsins of *revanche*. "No Irish need apply." He was warned that it would be raised and worked. He would not heed. He had his palace, but there were those of his own flock who, if they had "where to lay their heads," did not know where the next day's food was to come from, by reason and effect of what he had done. He seemed to care no more what might happen to them than the Hohenzollern and Hapsburg Caesars when they flung their people to the Moloch of war in gratification of their own dynastic ambitions and personal egoisms and arrogances. The civil authority in Australia cannot save us from this awful infliction. The Vatican can and should.

MANNIX, ECUMENIST?

From the early 1920s the tide of sectarianism gradually went out. Mannix made fewer inflammatory speeches; extreme Protestantism lost support.

Suggestive of a friendlier communal atmosphere was the Archbishop's presence at an inter-faith gathering arranged by the Mayor of South Melbourne in late 1926. There he rubbed shoulders with Methodist and Anglican churchmen, perhaps for the first time since arriving in Australia, and offered some unwontedly tactful and conciliatory words:[29]

[***] Although New Zealand did not have a Mannix, it did not lack similar figures. The pro-Irish coadjutor Bishop of Auckland, James Liston, was prosecuted for sedition in 1922.

A bishop usually takes a motto on the day of his episcopal consecration. The motto which I selected was: 'All things to all men'. When I selected that motto, I wished to convey that as far as was consistent with my conscience, I would make no distinction between man and man, creed and creed, nationality and nationality. It is not easy to live up to that motto. I know well that a great many people would not give me credit for having tried to live up to it and to do everyone justice. My intentions, however, have been good, and if I have fallen short of that ideal, I hope to do better in the future. It has always been my earnest desire to do or say nothing that would cause ill-feeling between religious bodies and to bring their members together and to enable them to be friends without bartering their religious convictions.

By the 1950s, sectarianism was on the wane. Mannix was involved in an event sometimes thought of as the last gasp of sectarianism in Australia, the 1954 dispute over whether Catholic soldiers should have to attend a service at Duntroon that included an element of Anglican rites. By the standards of 1920, it was a storm in a teacup.[30]

MINE ENEMY GROWS OLDER: MANNIX AND HUGHES RECONCILED

As a result of Archbishop Mannix's campaigning against conscription during World War 1, Mannix and Billy Hughes, then prime minister of Australia, became bitter enemies and, as we saw, freely gave their views on each other in their speeches. In 1920, Hughes was reported to have said:[31]

When he arrived in Australia seven years ago Australia was freer from sectarian bitterness than any country in the world. Spurred by boundless personal ambition and hatred of Great Britain, Archbishop Mannix has fanned the dying embers of religious bigotry into a fierce blaze, gathering around him every fanatic alien and Sinn Feiner in the country. He worked incessantly during the war to prevent recruiting and to help the enemy defeat the allies, working great harm to Australia.

The breach between the two was overcome many years later. In 1937, Hughes' daughter died suddenly. Mannix sent a letter of condolence, which was well received. Hughes made a special trip to 'Raheen' in Melbourne to meet and thank the Archbishop personally, and they spent a day together. On subsequent visits to Melbourne Mr. Hughes always called on the Archbishop.

'Did you ever discuss the conscription campaign with him?', Mannix was once asked. 'Oh, yes,' said the Archbishop, 'I asked him why he didn't do what the New Zealand Government did – simply pass a Conscription Bill instead of holding a referendum. Mr. Hughes replied, 'Because I am a democrat.'[32]

Hughes was a good friend to have, when it came to matters of mutual interest. In 1941 Hughes, despite his great age, was federal Attorney-General and thus in charge of the secret doings of the Commonwealth Investigation Service. A concern of the Government was the efforts of Communist unionists to sabotage the war effort.[33]

The CIS distributed money to anti-Communist groups in the unions, a fact revealed by a disaffected public servant to the Labor opposition. Hughes was reported to have said, then denied having said, that one of the recipients of these sums was Catholic Action. The truth remains unclear.[34]

Action was certainly forthcoming in the matter of the Jehovah's Witnesses in the same year. Mannix asked the Administrator of St Patrick's Cathedral to complain to the Commonwealth Investigation Branch (CIB) in April 1940, enclosing a copy of a Jehovah's Witness publication distributed during Anzac Day. The publication savaged Roman Catholics and linked Mannix to major figures in organised crime such as Al Capone, 'Legs' Diamond and others. Mannix requested an investigation. This request was forwarded to Hughes, who promptly approved it and referred the matter back to the CIB.[35] The Jehovah's Witnesses were banned in 1941, the only Christian sect to be banned in Australia in the twentieth century. (The ban was overturned by the High Court.)

By the late 1940s Mannix and Hughes – the elder by a year and a half – had outlived most of their contemporaries. They continued to communicate:

From Archbishop Mannix to William Hughes 9 November 1949

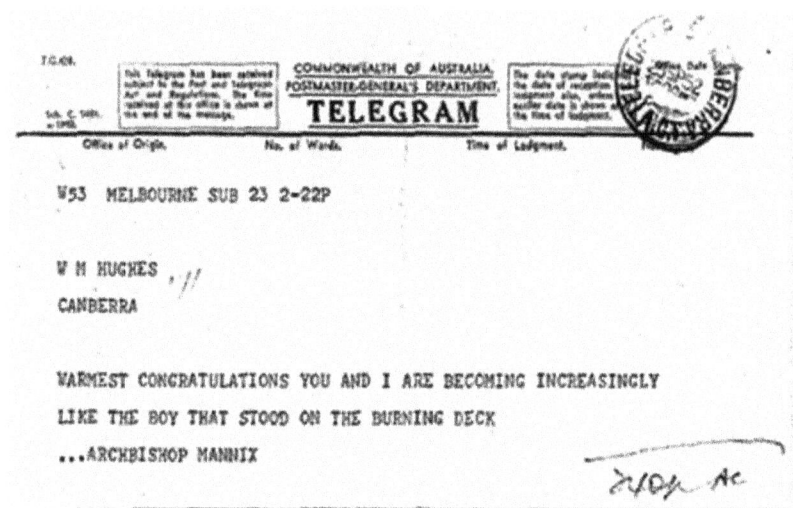

From Archbishop Mannix to William Hughes on 25 September 1952, the occasion of Hughes' 90th birthday[2]

Hughes died a month later. Mannix said: 'I have reason to think that the last letter Hughes wrote was written to me.' It was to say that he would be making a business trip to Melbourne and would be calling. 'He never arrived,' said the Archbishop, 'he was dead in twenty-four hours.'[36]

---

[2] The boy stood on the burning deck/Whence all but he had fled;/The flame that lit the battle's wreck/Shone round him o'er the dead. (Felicia Dorothea Hemans, Casabianca)

1. Overviews in Michael Hogan, *The Sectarian Strand: Religion in Australian History* (Penguin Books, Melbourne, 1987); Patrick O'Farrell, Imagination's Stain: Historical Reflections on Sectarian Australia (2009): http://www.patrickofarrell.com/pdf_download.php.
2. Archbishop and Bishops of N.S.W. Pastoral, Catholic Education Sydney, 1879, repr. in P. O'Farrell (ed.), *Documents in Australian Catholic History*, vol. 1, London, 1969, pp. 386-99.
3. James Franklin, Catholics versus Masons, *Journal of the Australian Catholic Historical Society* 20 (1999), 1-15.
4. Brigid Moore, Sectarianism in NSW: the *Ne Temere* legislation 1924-1925, *Journal of the Australian Catholic Historical Society* 9 (1987), 3-15.
5. Reported in *The Age*, 15 February, 1916, p. 8, repr. in O'Farrell, *Documents in Australian Catholic History*, vol. 2, p. 265.
6. *Argus*, 29 October 1917, p. 5.
7. Cyril Bryan, *Archbishop Mannix: Champion of Australian Democracy*, Chapter XXI, The Town Hall Lecture, pp. 132-9.
8. Copy obtained by Michael Gilchrist from John Corder, 1970s.
9. Michael Gilchrist, *Daniel Mannix: Wit and Wisdom*, Freedom Publishing, 2nd edition, 2004, p. 187, n. 80, quoted from an interview with Mr P. Tobin, Malvern, June 1981.
10. John Bowser, Minister for Public Health, to Mannix, in Brendan Hayes, Archbishop Mannix and the Spanish influenza: a week in 1919, *Footprints* 22 (2), 2005, 17-44.
11. Image AWM P1102/40/21 from Australian War memorial, Forging The Nation–Towards the Future: http://www.awm.gov.au/exhibitions/forging/future/changing_nation.asp
12. *The Advocate* reported 14 VC winners, which is also the number pictured with Archbishop Mannix in a photographic tribute to Victoria Cross winners from Archbishop Mannix on St Patrick's Day 1920: http://www.awm.gov.au/collection/P01383.018; 13 riding in the procession according to http://nla.gov.au/nla.pic-vn4507207. The chargers are variously reported as white or grey.
13. *Advocate*, 25 March 1920, cover and inside.
14. *Barrier Miner* (Broken Hill), 9 March 1920, p.1.
15. Image from: http://nla.gov.au/nla.pic-vn4507207
16. Scanned from Niall Brennan, *Dr Mannix*, Rigby Limited, Adelaide, 1964, facing p. 49. Also photo by News Ltd: *NPX91575*.
17. Image: AWM P1383/17, from Australian War Memorial site: http://www.awm.gov.au/exhibitions/forging/future/changing_nation.asp
18. *Argus*, 21 March 1921, p. 7.
19. Bertha Walker, *Solidarity Forever! . . . a part story of the life and times of Percy Laidler, the first quarter of a century . . .* National Press, Melbourne, 1972, p. 221: http://www.cpa.org.au/resources/classics/solidarityforever.pdf
20. NAA, A1606, F42/1 ATTACHMENT 3: Disloyal utterances – Dr Mannix - Oath of allegiance.
21. See text of "Australia First" speech, this book, ch. 1.
22. *Argus*, 19 Nov 1917, 'Archbishop Mannix'. p. 6, http://nla.gov.au/nla.news-article1664211.
23. *The West Australian* (Perth), 21 November, 1917, 'DR. MANNIX.', p. 8, viewed 18 July, 2013: http://nla.gov.au/nla.news-article27461117

24 H.M. Moran, *Viewless Winds: Being the Recollections and Digressions of an Australian Surgeon*, Peter Davies, 1939, pp. 156-9r.

25 Moran, *Viewless Winds*, p. 158, also C. Cunneen, Steward, Sir George Charles Thomas (1865–1920), *Australian Dictionary of Biography* 12 (1990), http://adb.anu.edu.au/biography/steward-sir-george-charles-thomas-8657, and Glenn Calderwood, A question of loyalty: Archbishop Daniel Mannix, the Australian Government and the Papacy, 1914-18, *Footprints* 22 (1), 2005, p. 27, n. 78.

26 Janet McCalman, *Sex and Suffering: Women's Health and a Women's Hospital: The Royal Women's Hospital, Melbourne 1856-1996*, Melbourne University Press, Carlton, 1999, pp. 149-50.

27 Catholic principles speech, *Advocate*, 3 November 1917, pp. 4-7, at p. 7.

28 A mad dog from Maynooth, by 'An Australian Roman Catholic', Australian Protestant Federation, Melbourne, 1921, reprinted from the *National Review*, January, 1921, p. 657.

29 Michael Gilchrist, *Daniel Mannix: Wit and Wisdom*, Freedom Publishing, 2nd edition, 2004, pp. 126-7, n. 74, quoted from *Tribune*, 23 September 1926; expressions were less polite in the controversy of 1934 with the Anglican archbishop, see David Schütz, "May I write to you…?": The correspondence between Catholic Archbishop of Melbourne Daniel Mannix (1864-1963) and Anglican Archbishop of Melbourne F.W. (Frederick Waldegrave) Head (1974-1941) concerning the Eucharistic Procession Controversy, *Footprints* 28 (2) (2013), 8-48 and 29 (1) (2014), 3-44.

30 John Steinback, Sectarianism's last stand?: Mannix, Menzies and the 1954 Duntroon colours controversy, *Australian Defence Force Journal* 146 (2001), 19-26.

31 Walter A. Ebsworth, *Archbishop Mannix*, H. H. Stephenson, Armadale, 1977, p. 125.

32 *Advocate*, 14 November, 1963.

33 Hal Colebatch, *Australia's Secret War: How Unions Sabotaged Our Troops in World War II*, Quadrant Books, Sydney, 2013.

34 Patrick Morgan, ed, *B.A. Santamaria: Running the Show: Selected Documents 1939-1996*, Miegunyah Press, Carlton, 2008, pp. 110-11; 'Mr Hughes denies money paid to Catholic Action', *Newcastle Morning Herald and Miners' Advocate* 3/10/1941: http://trove.nla.gov.au/ndp/del/article/134072906; Sydney parallels in J. Franklin, Catholic thought and Catholic Action: Dr Paddy Ryan MSC and the Red Peril, *Journal of the Australian Catholic Historical Society* 17 (1996), 44-55.

35 Jayne Persian, "A national nuisance": the banning of Jehovah's Witnesses in Australia in 1941, *Flinders Journal of History and Politics* 25 (2008); Mannix-Hughes telegrams in the National Library of Australia collection: 'Letters' from Papers of William Morris Hughes, Circa 1865-1958 (Bulk 1930-1949).

36 *Advocate*, 14 November, 1963.

Chapter 6: Loyal son of the Church?

Cardinal Pell rightly says that Mannix was "the most influential churchman in Australian history".[1] One expects from a great churchman a number of qualities which Mannix possessed – personal piety, an ability to think and speak well on religious matters, energy to advance appropriate agendas, skills in inspiring associates and the public. One also expects prudence in keeping clear of non-religious controversies, and obedience and loyalty to the head of the church. Those virtues Mannix did not have.

The prime duty of an Archbishop is the care of souls. That is incompatible with a career as a rabble-rousing nationalist icon. The Apostolic Delegate told him that. His brother Australian bishops told him the same and eventually forced him to draft a resolution promising restraint on his part. The Australian and British Governments urged the Vatican to remind him. The Vatican did so, time and again. Mannix resisted every such effort to the last, and eventually made the efforts public. Yet he escaped any public censure. If there is one thing the Church abhors more than disobedience, it is admitting it has made a mistake.

At one crucial point, however, Mannix unexpectedly received support from the highest level. As he approached Rome in 1921 after being refused entry to Ireland and creating political disturbances throughout Britain, the British Government had high hopes that he would be well and truly carpeted and that the Pope would condemn Irish Republican terror. Instead, the meeting between Mannix and His Holiness was cordial and the resulting statement by the Pope condemned the violence of both sides in Ireland in an even-handed way.

The British were livid.

Mannix on his right to speak

Before we start, let us consider Mannix's own view on why a Catholic bishop should talk politics. In 1917, he laid down a view from which he was never to deviate:[2]

There are people who say that freedom of speech is a valuable thing, but that it should be denied to Catholic Bishops and Archbishops. They should confine themselves to the sacristy, and have no opinions on public questions, or, if they have any, they should not be allowed to speak them above a whisper. Now I may claim to know something about the Catholic Church, and I know that the countries in which the Church has failed most disastrously are those countries in which ecclesiastics kept within the sacristies and took no interest in the temporal concerns of their people or in public affairs. I do not accept the theory that the Catholic Church in Australia will best be safeguarded when Bishops retire within the sacristy, keep their opinions to themselves, and so lose touch with the people to whom they should belong.

"the countries in which the Church has failed most disastrously are those countries in which ecclesiastics kept within the sacristies and took no interest in the temporal concerns of their people"

Two years before his death the Archbishop indicated that he had remained faithful to that view:[3]

When a man becomes a bishop he doesn't cease to be a citizen, and as a citizen and as a responsible man he has the right to make up his own mind and his own conscience and to follow it.

Vatican, Foreign Office and Bishops fail to restrain Mannix

As the second conscription referendum approached in 1917 and Mannix made his "ordinary trade war" speech, the Australian and British governments tried some lobbying with the Vatican and its representatives. In early 1917, the Governor-General met the Apostolic Delegate and reported to London:[4]

He [Cerretti] said that for a Catholic Archbishop to express himself as Dr Mannix had done was to do his church much harm, that he greatly disapproved of his action and that on his arrival in Rome he intended to have a letter of reproof sent to him which the Archbishop will not dare to disregard.

"... the Government of the Commonwealth may find it necessary to take action against him under the Defence of the Realm regulations..."

The Foreign Office sent a veiled threat of action against Mannix to their representative in the Vatican, Count de Salis:[*]

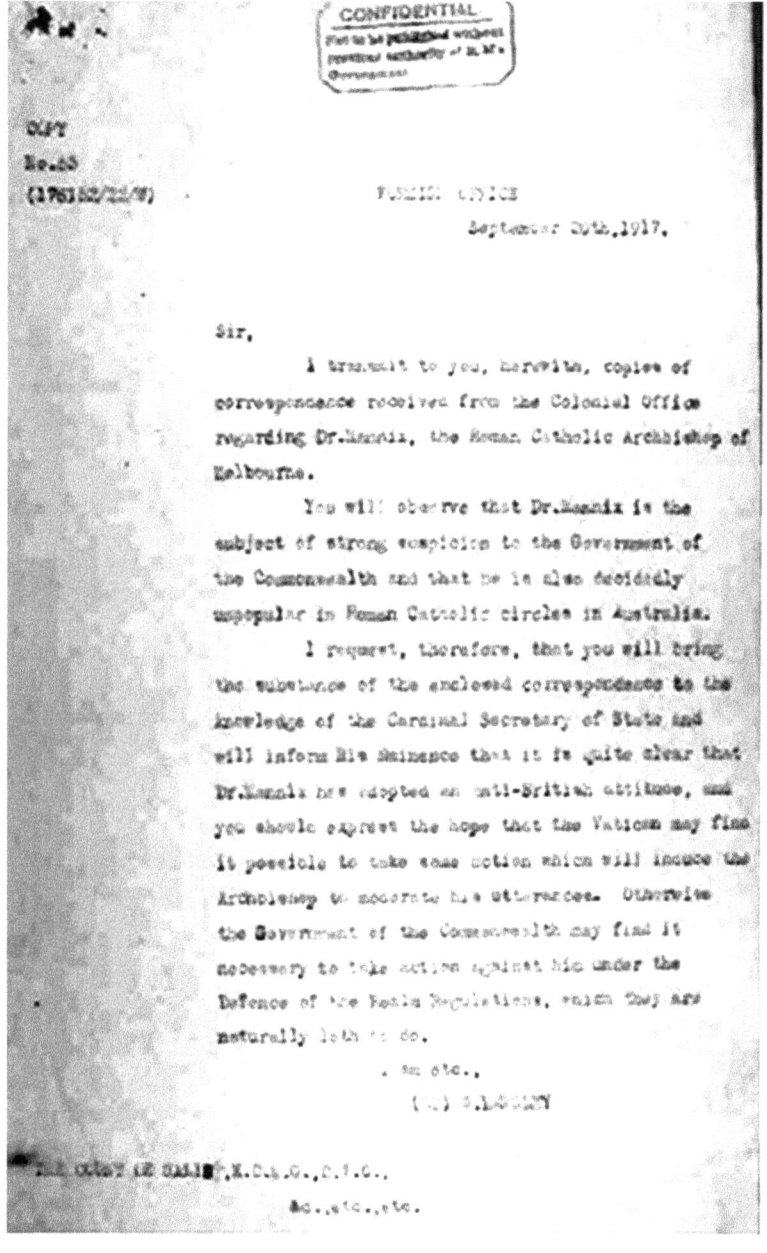

---

[*] Sir John Francis Charles de Salis, 7th Count de Salis, KCMG, CVO, envoy extraordinary and minister plenipotentiary on a special mission to the Holy See, 1916–1923; arrested by the Serbians in connection with his secret report detailing their atrocities in Montenegro.

The Vatican was sensitive to these representations, and also of a report presented by Archbishop Cattaneo, the new Apostolic Delegate, following the representations made to him by leading Catholic layman Sir Thomas Hughes and by Judge Heydon.

On 3 April 1918 Cardinal Van Rossum, Prefect of the Congregation of Propaganda Fide, addressed a letter to Mannix (This and other letters from Rome criticising Mannix appear in B.A. Santamaria's *Daniel Mannix*, presumably after Mannix provided them to Santamaria.):[5]

From various sources the Holy See has received information of grave and profound divisions which have unfortunately occurred among the Catholics of your Archdiocese on the occasion of the referendum relating to compulsory military service. Although the Holy See has no intention whatsoever of entering into any discussion on the issue or of expressing any viewpoint on the merits of the question, nevertheless it must remind Your Grace that the office of pastor is primarily to restore harmony among souls, to reduce discord, and to prevent [its] initiation or renewal.

". . . [the Holy See] must remind Your Grace that the office of pastor is primarily to restore harmony among souls, to reduce discord . . ."

On the basis of that principle I make a warm appeal to the zeal and the prudence of Your Excellency, hoping that in the future, while retaining your own freedom of private judgement and action, you will take care, for the good of souls, for the interest of Holy Church, and for the preservation of your own episcopal dignity, to avoid hostile discussions on questions which are purely civic and political, which could be the cause of disharmony and of unfortunate and dangerous antagonisms.

Archbishop Cattaneo convened a meeting in Sydney of the Australian hierarchy to discuss "the best means of re-establishing calm and avoiding further causes of trouble". Mannix was allowed to draft the motion (of course not made public) urging restraint on himself, which was carried unanimously:[6]

In view of the present difficulties it is necessary that the bishops and clergy should use prudence and caution in dealing with public questions. Public declarations must be well-weighed, especially when relating to conscription, recruiting, the Irish question and other matters concerning the participation in the war of this country: care must be taken to avoid saying or doing anything which in present circumstances might estrange anyone, and everything must be avoided which can give cause for the accusation against Catholics of disloyalty to the Empire and the legitimate aspirations of the country.

Cerretti, now in Rome, added his friendly advice, urging Mannix to keep to the spirit of the motion:

> To His Grace, Most Rev. D.Mannix, D.V. Archbishop of Melbourne
>
> SEGRETERIA DI STATO
>
> August 24th, 1918.
>
> DI SUA SANTITA
>
> Your Grace, I hope you have received a cable from which I sent you to-day informing you of the approval of Constitutions of the Sisters of Mercy. Finally we have the approval after many years and troubles notwithstanding all my insistences I could not hasten the work of the Congregation. The principal reason of the delay has been due to the Codex which has introduced many changes for the religious life.
>
> The expenses incurred are as indicated in the note enclosed with the constitutions, lire Italiani 475.50. You will explain to the Sisters that the money is Italian and Pounds sterling!!!
>
> I take this opportunity to inform Your Grace that I have followed with great interest the agitation and public discussion that have taken place in Australia. It is most fortunate that I am so familiar with conditions there, and know so well the purpose of certain people. Owing to this fact the Holy See has defended Your Grace very strongly. You will understand however the necessity of avoiding in the future any occasion or pretext for complaint. This recommendation which I make to you in the most friendly way is the same which your Grace suggested at the last meeting of the Archbishops in Sydney.
>
> I cannot say to you now in a letter all that I would wish but as soon as the War is over I hope you will come to Rome when I can inform you of all the details of the case.
>
> I recall with the greatest pleasure all your kindnesses to me and I assure you I shall never forget my relations with Melbourne.
>
> Whatever I can do for you I hope you will let me know.
>
> I hope you have received the Cappa Magna and that you are pleased with it. In these times it is very difficult to procure material which is very expensive as you know through the good ladies who presented you with the Cappa Magna.
>
> With every best wish and sentiment of highest esteem.
>
> I remain,
> Yours very sincerely in J.C.
> (s) B.Cerretti
> Arch. of Corinth.
>
> Postmark:- Rome xx Italy

There was hope all round that the Mannix problem was now solved. Cardinal Gasparri, Secretary of State, wrote to the British that Mannix should now be quiet, but at the same time warning of the obstacles to taking action against him:[7]

... Finally, it must not be forgotten that Monsignor Mannix, wrongly or rightly, enjoys a great influence upon the working classes – proofs of this are the imposing and clamorous demonstrations of Melbourne and Sydney – therefore, severe measures taken against him by the Holy See, would undoubtedly aggravate the situation and create grave difficulties for the Government itself.

The Holy See is confident that His Majesty's Government will find the foregoing explanations satisfactory and with the fervent wish besides that Monsignor Mannix's line of con-

"Mannix ... enjoys a great influence upon the working classes ... severe measures taken against him by the Holy See would undoubtedly aggravate the situation ..."

duct will henceforth conform to the rules laid down by the Episcopate and approved by the Holy See.

British Foreign Secretary Balfour seeks to reassure Hughes

In a personal note to Billy Hughes on 26 June 1918 Balfour, the British Foreign Secretary,[†] sought to reassure Hughes that the Vatican disapproved of Mannix but feared there was little they could do:[8]

My dear Hughes,

I understand the position of affairs with regard to Archbishop Mannix is somewhat as follows.

"His revolutionary, or semi-revolutionary, attitude in Australia meets, I gather, with no approval at the Vatican"

His revolutionary, or semi-revolutionary, attitude in Australia meets, I gather, with no approval at the Vatican. On the contrary, remonstrances have been twice addressed to him from Rome, although apparently with little or no effect. Of course these remonstrances were private, and we know of them only through private, but authentic, sources of information. The secret of their existence should be carefully kept.

As, however, they have been, to all appearance, quite ineffective, the question still remains: can anything more be done?

Evidently, the position of the Vatican is a difficult one. Archbishops are not in any case to be turned off at a week's notice; and it seems that, from the ecclesiastical point of view, Archbishop Mannix, however indiscreet in his behaviour, has not so far violated the letter of the ecclesiastical law.

I am myself but imperfectly acquainted with the overt proceedings of the Archbishop. That his policy, judged by its objects, is treasonable, I have no doubt; but I am not sure that in his acts he has ever sailed close to the wind. Nor, if he has, do I know whether the Australian Government would care to take proceedings against him. Of this, however, I am fairly confident that the Vatican would view with the most extreme disfavour any action on the part of the Archbishop which brought him within reach of the law, and, rather than that this would happen, they will probably take the very strongest steps in their power to prevent it. Perhaps you could give me some further information about the Archbishop's methods.

"... these remonstrances were private ... The secret of their existence should be carefully kept"

[†] Arthur Balfour, 1st Earl of Balfour, philosopher, British Prime Minister 1902-05, Foreign Secretary 1916-19 and responsible for the Balfour Declaration promising the Jews a national home in Palestine.

Hughes asks for Mannix's recall

When Hughes held out for recalling Mannix, Balfour wrote to de Salis, requesting him to take the matter up with Gasparri:[9]

> Mr Hughes, Prime Minister of Australia, has talked to me very earnestly about the case of Archbishop Mannix. He is most anxious that the Vatican shall recall him – nothing less, in his opinion, is sufficient, and he tells me privately that, if the Archbishop remains, a rebellion may result from his activities. The matter is so serious that nothing short of recall will meet the case.

"Mr Hughes, Prime Minister of Australia ... is most anxious that the Vatican shall recall him ..."

Lord Robert Cecil, Under-Secretary of State for Foreign Affairs,[‡] urged a higher level of threat in a letter to Hughes:[10]

> Matters might of course be brought to a head by telling the Vatican that unless the Archbishop is recalled within – say – a month, he would be arrested and tried, but you will probably agree that it is wiser not to force matters so greatly at present. If we do make the threat and the Vatican refuse to yield it will of course be necessary for the Government of Australia to carry it into execution.

"Matters might of course be brought to a head by telling the Vatican that unless the Archbishop is recalled ... he would be arrested and tried ..."

Writing on 5 November 1918, the Apostolic Delegate, Dr Cattaneo, sent a personal note of warning to Archbishop Mannix:[11]

> From all this, and the other things that Your Grace knows, you will easily understand that very strong representations must have been made to the Holy See from high quarters.
>
> I have no doubt that Your Grace will fully realise the delicacy of the position of the Holy See, and act accordingly.

[‡] Edgar Algernon Robert Gascoyne-Cecil, 1st Viscount Cecil of Chelwood, CH, PC, QC, Under-Secretary of State for Foreign Affairs 1915-19, awarded the Nobel Peace Prize in 1937 for his role in the foundation of the League of Nations.

Mannix unrepentant again

What Mannix himself thought about these attempts to restrain him can be gathered from the way he incorporated them into his personal myth, as told to his confidants years later. B. A. Santamaria recorded later retellings:[12]

"Couldn't you bring him back to Rome and put him in charge of a college?" "God forbid! At least in Australia he's that far away."

The story which he most enjoyed was one to which in later years he kept referring. In the middle of the First World War, "Billy" Hughes had made urgent representations to the British Government to induce the Vatican to get this troublesome prelate finally recalled from Australia. Balfour or Asquith – I forget which of the two British statesmen – met Cardinal Gasquet[§] at a garden party at Buckingham Palace.

The request was put to the Cardinal in a private conversation to be passed on to Pope Benedict XV. Cardinal Gasquet, perhaps startled by the request, perhaps playing for time, said: "But what could we do with him? Where would we put him?" "Well" said the English leader, "couldn't you bring him back to Rome and put him in charge of a college?" "God forbid!" replied the Cardinal. "At least in Australia he's that far away." The Archbishop never ceased to chuckle when he told that story at his own expense.

The total result of these herculean efforts of diplomacy behind the scenes was of course zero. That was 1918. In 1920 Mannix set off on his world tour to the US, Ireland (almost) and Britain, on his way to Rome.

The diplomatic system went into high gear again.

Archbishop of Dublin?

As Mannix progressed across America attacking Britain, a truly alarming rumour reached the British Cabinet. If Mannix arrived in Ireland, he might stay there – as Archbishop of Dublin. The aged Archbishop Walsh[¶] was ill and Mannix might succeed.[13] Cabinet determined to make urgent representations to the Vatican to prevent this worst-case scenario:

CABINET 37 (20).

CONCLUSIONS of Meeting of the Cabinet, held at 10, Downing Street, S.W., on Thursday, June 24th, 1920 at 12 Noon.

[§] Cardinal Francis Aidan Gasquet, English Benedictine and historian.
[¶] William Walsh, Archbishop of Dublin, who had ordained Mannix to the priesthood at Maynooth in 1890, died on 9 April, 1921.

> BISHOP
> MIX.
>
> (2) The Cabinet had under consideration what action, if any should be taken in regard to Archbishop Mannix, the Roman Catholic Archbishop of Melbourne, who has left Australia and, it is reported, will not return there. In Australia he has been delivering speeches of a violently anti-British character, and there is every reason to suppose that, if permitted to land in Ireland, he will resume this practice. There is also some reason to believe that he may be made Archbishop of Dublin.
>
> In view of the serious effect which they were informed would be produced on public opinion in Ireland by prohibiting the Archbishop from landing in Ireland, the Cabinet could not sanction this procedure.
>
> It was agreed —
>
>> That the Secretary of State for Foreign Affairs should follow up the representations he had already made to the Vatican on this question, and indicate the undesirability, in the present acute state of Irish affairs, of appointing as Archbishop of Dublin a person of pronounced and publicly-proclaimed anti-British sentiments. He should also suggest to the Vatican the desirability, if possible, of finding some employment for Archbishop Mannix outside the United Kingdom.

This Cabinet decision resulted in the following telegram being sent to Count de Salis, still the British representative in the Vatican. It contained a veiled threat to "alter our feelings" for the Holy See.

De Salis, faced with the unenviable task of delivering a threat, found himself under intense pressure from London to get results, as Mannix's speeches in the US continued. A Foreign office official, Alexander Cadogan,** minuted on 22 July:[14]

". . . in the event of our complaints with regard to Archbishop Mannix being disregarded ... it is more than likely we should alter our feelings for and dealings with the Holy See

---

** (Sir) Alexander George Montagu Cadogan, OM, GCMG, KCB, PC, career diplomat and diarist, influential in British foreign policy in World War II.

Paraphrase of telegram No. 16. to Count de Salis Vatican, Rome.

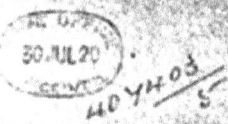

----------oOo----------

We have heard that Archbisop Mannix is to be appointed to the Archbisopric of Dublin if a vacancy occurs there. We have had reason to complain to the Vatican on several occasions about this man, who made an extraordinarily bad name for himself in Australia by his Sinn Fein behaviour and speeches.

The Vatican should be informed by you that not only would His Majesty's Government view such an appointment with the highest disfavour but that in the event of our complaints with regard to Archbisop Mannix being disregarded and the appointment made, it is more than likely we should alter our feelings for and dealings with the Holy See. As the presence of Archbisop Mannix in Ireland at present is highly undesirable, we are anxious for you to exert your power to prevent this contingency from arising.

Both the British and American Governments have been grossly insulted by his views and conduct while in the latters Country.

The Vatican ought to be in a position to prevent him from openly preaching sedition and conducting a campaign with the avowed object of promoting ill feelings between England and America. Count de Salis should call serious attention to the utterances and performance of the Archbishop and express the very definite hope that the Pope will signify his disapproval of his political activities. I hope we shall not allow the Archbishop to land in Ireland.

"The Vatican ought to be in a position to prevent him from openly preaching sedition ..."

> "... *Vatican will communicate with Archbishop Mannix ... on the subject of the Lack of Restraint in his utterances. Vatican will also support any decision of the British Government not to allow him to set foot in Ireland.*"

There was talk in the Foreign Office of de Salis's "weakness", and Curzon, the Foreign Secretary,[††] found de Salis's replies "profoundly unsatisfactory" and as "reflecting neither credit on Count de Salis nor on the Vatican". De Salis advised that the Vatican was sympathetic and that is was not advisable to play the strongest diplomatic card – breaking off relations – "to prevent what is not going to happen. It is not a card you can play very often."[15]

The anxiety was unnecessary. No-one agreed more with the British position than the Vatican. When de Salis met him, Gasparri assured him there was "no semblance of likelihood" about the Dublin rumour. Furthermore, the Vatican supported the British decision to prevent Mannix landing in Ireland, and promised to communicate with him on "the lack of restraint in his utterances", when he arrived in Rome.

```
Paraphrase of telegram:    From Vatican No. 35.

Your cable No. 26 July 25th.

    Yesterday I interviewed Cardinal Secretary of State,
and made a communication to him on the exact lines of your
instructions.  He wishes me to let you know immediately that
the Vatican will communicate with Archbishop Mannix as soon
as he reaches Rome on the subject of the Lack of Restraint in
his utterances, Vatican will also support any decision of the
British Government not to allow him to set foot in Ireland:
they are not sure if they can get into touch with him before
his arrival in Rome.  Cardinal reiterated, however, that he
was unable to promise to prevent Mannix going to Ireland if
England did not prohibit it.
```

[††] George Nathaniel Curzon, 1st Marquess Curzon of Kedleston, Viceroy of India 1899-1905, Foreign Secretary 1919-24.

> As instructed in your telegram I also touched on probable uselessness to British Government of continuance of relations if Mannix was allowed to continue doing what you had indicated.
>
> I have made every effort to make the Cardinal see the seriousness of what is happening and the danger of the irritation which it is causing. You said formerly I might indicate the possibility of a severance of relations in the event of Mannix becoming Archbishop of Dublin.
>
> As I have said before, there is no chance of this happening just now and Cardinal asked me to say that there was no semblance of likelihood about this rumour.
>
> Consequently I am glad you modified my orders so as to enable me more usefully to employ this argument in the present case.

MANNIX MEETS THE POPE

After a leisurely time in Britain giving Irish nationalist speeches, Mannix finally arrived in Rome and met the Pope in April 1921. The British, Mannix and presumably Gasparri expected that he would be chastised severely. We have only Mannix's word for what happened, but on the evidence of the Pope's subsequent statement, his account appears to be true. Santamaria recalled Mannix's telling of the story years later. Australia was apparently not mentioned;[16] it was Ireland on the agenda:[17]

He told me once that when he visited Rome in 1921, in the middle of the Irish troubles, he more than half expected to be recalled from Melbourne because of the embarrassment which some said he caused the Church. He made three calls on Pope Benedict XV and nothing was said. He was still uneasy.

"The Pope laughed at my impudence"

Finally, in the last audience, the Pope said to the Archbishop: "What do they think of me in Ireland?" The Archbishop thought that this was the opening remark in a conversation which would end in his recall. He admitted that he was tempted to go quiet, for he was in deep water as it was. But he could not have lived with himself if he had not told the truth.

"Holy Father" he said, "The Irish people find it very strange that you seem to be against them, when for so many centuries they have been so faithful to Rome."

"But I am not against them" said the Pope. "I am for them."

"Then, Holy Father" said the Archbishop, "you should write to let them know."

"The Pope laughed at my impudence" said the Archbishop, "and then surprised me."

"You draft me a letter and if I agree with it I will sign it."

The Archbishop drafted it.

The Pope agreed with the suggested text, and when his pronouncement on Ireland appeared on 22 May 1921 it clearly bore a Mannix imprint:[18]

We are most especially concerned about the condition of Ireland. Unflinching even to the shedding of blood in her devotion to the ancient faith and in her reverence for the Holy See she is subject today to the indignity of devastation and slaughter . . . neutrality . . . by no means prevents us from wishing . . . that a lasting peace . . . may take the place of this terrible enmity . . . we do not perceive how this bitter strife can profit either of the parties, when property and homes are being ruthlessly and disgracefully laid waste, when villages and farmsteads are being set aflame, when neither sacred places nor sacred persons are spared, when on both sides war resulting in the deaths of unarmed people, even of women and children is carried on. We exhort English as well as Irish to calmly consider . . . some means of mutual agreement.

The British were outraged that their violence was condemned in the same terms as Irish republican violence (despite this being not long after the depredations of the Black and Tans). "Just the kind of casuistic performance that might have been expected from the Vatican," said Curzon.[19]

Mannix did give at the time an account of one aspect of the meeting with the Pope. In London on his way home to Australia, he gave an Irish nationalist speech which played up the Pope's support for Ireland.[20]

> "The Pope has his sympathies, the natural sympathies of an honest man . . . will not be denied by the Pope to his suffering Irish children"

When I went to Rome recently many people thought *I was going to face my Waterloo*. Now I am not going to say much nor indeed anything at all about the Pope. I deprecate a good deal of what we hear about the Pope and about the Vatican in regard to Irish affairs. These references to the Pope and to the Vatican and their intervention in Irish affairs helps to keep up the idea that Ireland has been governed, is governed, and can be governed by the Vatican.

The Vatican never claimed to govern Ireland and does not claim at the present moment to rule Ireland. The Pope has his sympathies, the natural sympathies of an honest man, and the sympathy that went out to the Armenians, to the Poles, to the Belgians and even to the Jews, will not be denied by the Pope to his suffering Irish children.

When I went to Rome, however, and met the Pope for the first time, the very first thing that he said to me was, not what some of our friends the enemy would expect – he asked me if I wished him to use the ordinary diplomatic channels in order to have the ban upon my movements removed, and I did not require any time in which to frame my reply. "Holy Father," I said, "I have not condescended to ask from the British Government anything that they might regard as a favour or as a concession, and what I would not condescend, myself, I should not like your Holiness, to ask in my name." If the Pope had asked a removal of that ban, I think it is extremely likely that it would have been removed.

The British did have a small win. Mannix went quiet for a while. Winston Churchill sent to the Australian Governor General in 1922 a report from de Salis of his meeting with Cattaneo, recently back from Australia. De Salis congratulated Cattaneo on the lack of news from Australia, and conveyed to the British the difficulties of being Apostolic Delegate in Australia:[21]

For instance, he would be invited as representative of the Pope to be present at the opening of a church or convent or some other function of the most praiseworthy character; before the proceedings were over one of the local clergy, even a bishop, would get up and without warning deliver a speech devoted largely to current politics. The practice is anything but desirable; it was the more difficult to put it down as the people seemed to expect it.

POLITICAL ACTION DEFENDED

Both in Ireland and in Australia, Archbishop Mannix was continually at pains to assert his right to hold opinions and speak "as a normal citizen", not an Archbishop. His 1925 speech in Dublin explains:[22]

When a man becomes a priest he does not cease to be a citizen, he has a right to his own opinions like other citizens. (Applause)

If I might say just one personal word. I know right well there are people, and a great many people, who think it is an extraordinary thing that I should do the things I have done, and say the things I have said. 'After all,' they say, 'what is one amongst so many?' People who say: 'Would it not be wiser if the Archbishop of Melbourne would let others do the thinking and talking for Ireland – those who are nearer the centre of things in Ireland, and who may be presumed to know more about the things regarding which he talks.' I know right well that a priest has quite enough to do, and a bishop has quite enough to do also, without, as a rule, mixing himself up in political affairs, and it is only on compulsion that I ever entered on political affairs. I can say with truth that when *"it is only on compulsion that I ever entered on political affairs"* I left Ireland twelve years ago, I had never spoken from a political platform. But I found when I went to Australia that it was necessary that someone should defend Ireland in Australia, and as nobody stepped into the breach, I thought my place was there. (Applause). And when Ireland here raised her Flag of Freedom, the Flag of the Republic, I realised that it was the Flag of Justice and of Right, and I thought if I could do nothing else, I could, at all events, give it the sympathy of my tongue, and there, as well as here, when you were making the fight against England, I was recognised to be on your side. (Applause).

Rebuke from the Apostolic delegate

Mannix's criticism of General O'Duffy, who had recently organized the Irish Blueshirt Movement following the model of the Fascist Movement in Italy, became the occasion of the most serious criticism Mannix ever received from Rome. The Apostolic Delegate to Australia, Archbishop Philip Bernardini, addressed the following letter, dated 11 January 1934, to the Archbishop. Its meaning it clear. It is a direct order from Rome to shut up:[23]

Your Grace,

In accordance with instructions received from the Holy See, permit me to bring under your notice the following:

1. It is known with what paternal solicitude the Holy Father follows the vicissitudes of the Catholic religion in Ireland. This predilection, repeatedly manifested by the Supreme Pontiff has its reason

> a) in a sense of profound gratitude for the Irish people, who with serenity and firmness faced centuries of persecution in order to preserve intact that Faith, which, according to the mysterious designs of Divine Providence, it would one day have to implant in countries apparently destined for Protestant propaganda; [. . .]

5. [. . .] The situation is, in fact, so acute that any statement whatsoever of a political character, even apparently innocent, if it comes from an ecclesiastic who rightly enjoys national esteem, is given the greater publicity; the which, even unintentionally, aggravates a situation already serious.

6. An example of all this is had in the 'remarks', jokingly directed at General O'Duffy, and pronounced by Your Grace on the occasion of a conference given by the Reverend Doctor English in Melbourne before his departure for Ireland. The words of Your Grace were repeated and diffused, provoking lively replies and passionate comments,

> "... *you would do an act most pleasing to the Holy Father, and a precious work for the welfare of the Irish nation, if in the future you would cautiously avoid public discussions* ..."

hindering, certainly contrary to the intention of Your Grace, the patient and laborious work of pacification, that the Holy Father has so much at heart.

7. For these reasons, I am directed to let Your Grace know that you would do an act most pleasing to the Holy Father, and a precious work for the welfare of the Irish nation, if in the future you would cautiously avoid public discussions or statements which could be evilly interpreted and used by those who, from a division of minds, or from a religious disturbance of the noble Irish nation, have everything to gain.

I would be very thankful to receive a line of acknowledgement of this letter.

I take the opportunity of renewing my sentiments of profound esteem towards Your Grace, and remain,

Yours sincerely in Christ,
† Philip Bernardini
Apostolic Delegate.

Mannix sent his reply on 21 January 1934. He was, as always, unrepentant:[24]

Excellency

[. . .] The political condition in Ireland being as I have described, and the peril to religion being in my judgement so grave, my occasional intrusion into Irish affairs from a distance of 13 000 miles is not surprising as it might seem to one unacquainted with the facts. At all events I had nothing to gain personally by such intervention.

On the contrary, I was made to feel – and with much distress – that I was exposing myself to criticism and even to estrangement from some of my oldest and best friends among the Bishops and clergy of Ireland, as well as to possible misunderstandings at Rome, of which Your Excellency's present letter is the latest evidence. I do not complain, nor ask for exemption from criticism for my mistakes. But, as an Irishman, I am proud that my countrymen in most difficult times have not faltered in their traditional allegiance to their faith and to the Roman See. I should be also proud if I could think that by any act or word of mine I helped others in some

> "*I should be also proud if I could think that by any act or word of mine I helped others in some small measure to dispel from the minds of the Irish people the hateful idea that their Church was hostile to their legitimate political aspirations*"

small measure to dispel from the minds of the Irish people the hateful idea that their Church was hostile to their legitimate political aspirations.

[. . .] I must apologise for the undue length of this letter. But, your kind letter has given me the opportunity of saying many things which I have long wanted to say and which I cannot say in public, nor indeed in private, unless in such a letter as this.

With great esteem and all good wishes,

I am,

Sincerely yours,

† D. Mannix

---

1. George Pell, preface to Michael Gilchrist, *Daniel Mannix: Wit and Wisdom*, Freedom Publishing, North Melbourne, 2nd edition, 2004.
2. Frank Murphy, *Daniel Mannix: Archbishop of Melbourne*, The Polding Press, Melbourne, 1948, epigraph.
3. Gerard Henderson, *Mr Santamaria and the Bishops*, 1982, pp. 158-9. Also, *Sydney Morning Herald*, 7 November 1963, p. 2: http://news.google.com/newspapers?nid=1301&dat=19631107&id=h8pQAAAAIBAJ&sjid=sOUDAAAAIBAJ&pg=4162,1955912
4. Glenn Calderwood, A question of loyalty: Archbishop Daniel Mannix, the Australian Government and the Papacy, 1914-18, *Footprints* 22 (1) (2005), p. 21, n. 44: Extract from Memorandum (Confidential) from the Governor-General of Australia, 8 May 1917.
5. Cardinal Van Rossum to Mannix, 3 April 1918, quoted in B. A. Santamaria *Daniel Mannix: The Quality of Leadership*, Melbourne University Press, Melbourne, 1985, p. 97.
6. Quoted in Michael McKernan, Catholics, conscription and Archbishop Mannix, *Historical Studies* 17 (68), (1977), 299-314, at p. 311: Cardinal Gasparri to Count de Salis, 24 June 1918, http://recordsearch.naa.gov.au/scripts/Imagine.asp?B=1653030; McKernan writes that the language is stilted and quite unlike Mannix's masterly control of English. The explanation is that Cattaneo translated Mannix's motion into Latin for Gasparri, who translated it into French for de Salis, who translated it into English for Hughes.
7. NAA, A1606, F42/1 ATTACHMENT 1, 1917-1922, Cardinal Gasparri to Count de Salis, 22 August 1918, translation, pp. 82-5: http://recordsearch.naa.gov.au/scripts/Imagine.asp?B=1653030.
8. Foreign Secretary Balfour to Prime Minister Hughes, 26 June 1918, quoted in *Santamaria, Daniel Mannix: The Quality of Leadership*, p. 100.
9. Colm Kiernan, *Daniel Mannix and Ireland*, Alella Books, Morwell, Victoria, 1984, pp. 123-124: Chapter Seven: Archbishop of Melbourne, 1971-1919, n. 31: AJ Balfour to Count J de Salis, 26 July 1918, Calwell papers.
10. Lord Robert Cecil (Assistant Secretary of State for Foreign Affairs) to Prime Minister Hughes, 27 August 1918, quoted in *Daniel Mannix and Ireland*, p. 101.
11. The Apostolic Delegate (Dr Cattaneo) to Archbishop Mannix 5 November 1918, quoted in Kiernan, *Daniel Mannix and Ireland*, pp. 100-1.

12 Morgan, *BA Santamaria: Running the Show,* pp: 327–328; also mentioned in *Cardinal Gasquet: a memoir,* by Shane Leslie, Burns Oates, 1953, p. 16, as well AA Calwell, *Be Just and Fear Not,* Lloyd O'Neil in association with Rigby Ltd, 1972, p. 149.

13 Dermot Keogh, *The Vatican, the Bishops and Irish Politics 1919-39,* Cambridge University Press, 2005, pp. 47-8.

14 Keogh, *The Vatican, the Bishops and Irish Politics 1919-39,* p. 48.

15 Keogh, p. 48.

16 Mgr. Patrick Lennon, President of St. Patrick's College, Carlow, Ireland, reported in *The Carlovian* – the Carlow College magazine, 1965 – on his 'Australasian Journey,' June to September, 1962, that on 2 July he visited Archbishop Mannix at 'Raheen', and Mannix told him that Australia was not mentioned in his talks with the Pope.

17 *Running the Show,* p. 328; originally from Santamaria's TV broadcast of 10 Nov 1963; a similar recollection by Arthur Calwell in *Be Just and Fear Not,* Lloyd O'Neil Pty Ltd, in association with Rigby Ltd, 1972, p. 150; overview in Keogh, *The Vatican, the Bishops and Irish Politics,* pp. 69-70.

18 Tim Pat Coogan, *Ireland in the Twentieth Century,* Palgrave Macmillan, New York, 2004, p. 89; Keogh, p. 70.

19 Keogh, p. 70.

20 Archbishop Mannix's farewell address, *The Catholic Bulletin,* Vol. XI, June, 1921, pp. 344-8 (speech at the Cannon Street Hotel, 21 May 1921).

21 NAA, A1606, F42/1 ATTACHMENT 1, 1917-1922, De Salis, 24 Mar 1922, http://recordsearch.naa.gov.au/scripts/Imagine.asp?B=1653030

22 Dr. Daniel Mannix, *Speeches of His Grace most rev. Dr. Mannix, Archbishop of Melbourne in the Rotunda Dublin, 22 and 29 October, 1925* [Mellifont Press, Dublin, 1925], p. 16.

23 Santamaria, *Daniel Mannix: The Quality of Leadership,* pp. 142-4 and n. 19.

24 Santamaria, *Daniel Mannix,* pp. 144-5 and n. 20.

Chapter 7: Mannix as Church leader

Besides his low regard for obedience to Vatican directives, Mannix the churchman displayed several other divergences in emphasis from the typical prelate of his day.

First, in an age of clericalism where bishops and priests distrusted the laity and believed their purpose was, in the classic phrase, to "pay, pray and obey", Mannix genuinely encouraged lay initiative. And the style of lay initiative that he particularly favoured was in the intellectual realm – and in the realm of political action formed by ideas. The need for university education for Catholics had been an unexpected theme of his first speech in Australia. It was soon followed up by the foundation of Newman College at Melbourne University and of St Kevin's College, a secondary school to provide the highest academic standards for boys. In 1923 came the foundation, with his friend Fr Hackett, of the Catholic Central Library to provide a wide range of solid Catholic reading for church members generally. The 1930s saw the flourishing of the Campion Society of university-trained intellectuals and the publication of the associated journal the *Catholic Worker*. These developments were largely unique to Melbourne. As emphasised by B. A. Santamaria – St Kevin's graduate, prominent Campion member, editor of the *Catholic Worker* – Mannix really was normally content to leave direction to the lay organisers and to resist requests for direction by himself.

Secondly, his personal intellectual preoccupations showed little interest in theology, canon law or the ethics of personal morality. His conflicts with Protestantism were vigorous, but rarely concerned with any but the broadest questions of theological differences. When he discussed sex education in schools, his views were comparatively relaxed. But he did have a well-developed passion for the ethics of social and political questions. As we will see in chapter 9, Mannix and politically active Catholics associated with him were excited by the thinking on labour and capital of Popes Leo XIII and Pius XI, an area of Catholic ethical thought that has been very much a minority interest in the Church. Mannix spoke regularly on the sins of capitalism and Communism; it is hard to imagine him matching Archbishop Kelly of Sydney in condemning the evils of mixed bathing.[1]

Thirdly, Mannix's conception of Catholicism has the Irish sense of tribalism. As in Ireland, the priest embodies leadership of a tribe. He works to advance its interests and embody its prestige, while maintaining its uniqueness of thought and practice against a competing culture.

THE INTRICACIES OF CANON LAW

We begin with some brief extracts from Mannix's first surviving writings – sadly, his earlier dissertation on 'The salvation of the heathen' is lost, as well as the 'Manual of etiquette and good manners' that he issued for Maynooth students.[2] These publications are replies to questions from priests on detailed issues of canon law, written for the *Irish Ecclesiastical Record* in his capacity as Professor of Moral Theology at Maynooth. These very elaborate conundrums, generated by the Church's very detailed mass of canon law accumulated over centuries, are perhaps best seen as relics of the obsession with rule-based trivialities from which Mannix, and indeed the whole Church, needed to extricate itself.[3] It is unclear quite how seriously Mannix took these exercises. When Archbishop in Melbourne later, he showed no interest in such matters. Indeed, the "animadversions" sent to the preliminary deliberations for the Second Vatican Council, under his name and approved by him, show an impatience with legalistic understandings of the Church. He was said to have believed "you can't make people good by punishment."[4]

The following excerpts are from *The Irish Ecclesiastical Record*. Vol. III (Jan. to Jun. 1898).

NOTES AND QUERIES
THEOLOGY
PROTESTANT WITNESSES AT THE MARRIAGE OF CATHOLICS
CAN CATHOLICS VALIDLY MARRIED AT A REGISTRY OFFICE, OR IN A PROTESTANT CHURCH, AFTERWARDS RECEIVE THE NUPTIAL BLESSING?

REV. DEAR SIR, – 1. Can a priest on the English mission permit Protestant witnesses to a marriage in his church on his own responsibility? They are valid witnesses I know – are they licit?

2. Can he (a priest on the English mission) give the nuptial blessing – privately of course – to a Catholic couple who were married in the Registrar's office, or in a Protestant Church?

Yours, &c.,

SACERDOS [PRIEST]

1. A priest should not, on his own responsibility, admit non-Catholics to assist as witnesses to a marriage. An answer to this effect was given by the Holy Office, 19th August, 1891:

Se sia lecito assumere gli eterodossi a testimoni nel matrimonio dei Catholici. [If it be licit to accept the unorthodox as witnesses to the marriage of Catholics]

And the reply was:

Non esse adhibendos; posse tamen ab Ordinario tolerari ex gravi causa, dummodo non adsit scandalum. [It is not done; it may however be tolerated by the Ordinary (local bishop) for grave cause, provided no scandal arises.]

According to this reply, therefore, non-Catholics should not *per se* be admitted as formal witnesses of a marriage. They may, however, for a grave cause be admitted where no scandal will be given. The bishop – not the officiating priest – is the judge of the sufficiency of the reason for their admission. If there be anywhere a recognised custom of admitting non-Catholic witnesses, we may assume that the bishop regards their admission in that place justified by the circumstances, and we require no express authorisation to follow the usual practice.

2. In England – for it is to that country only our correspondent refers – even Catholics may, of course, marry validly before a registrar or a Protestant clergyman. We assume that they are not perigrini [visitors from elsewhere] contracting in *fraudem legis* [to get around the law]. But such a marriage is gravely sinful; and if the parties contract before a heretical minister (as such), and with a heretical rite[*], they incur excommunication, specially reserved to the Holy See in the Bull *Apostolicae Sedis*.[5]

Manifestly a priest's first duty, in regard to such persons, is to bring them to repent of their sin, make reparation for the scandal given, and seek absolution from censure, if a censure has been incurred. In some dioceses special legislation defines the manner in which public reparation of the scandal given is to be made. Having succeeded in getting

---

[*] A practice naturally common in British countries with majority-heretical populations. Ben Chifley incurred excommunication by marrying in a Presbyterian church in 1914.

the parties to repent of and repair the evil done, our correspondent asks whether he should give them the nuptial blessing.

By the nuptial blessing, we may understand either the simple blessing of the Ritual or the solemn blessing of the Missal. Many theologians hold (and rightly, we think) that *per se* there is, in ordinary cases, an obligation sub veniali [under pain of venial sin], to seek the solemn blessing.[6] All must admit that there is *per se* a[n] obligation to give the solemn blessing to those who ask it. Others think it is not strictly obligatory to receive the solemn nuptial blessing, though the Church strongly exhorts the faithful to receive it.[7] But, outside a case of necessity, Catholics contracting marriage are bound, under pain of mortal sin, to receive the blessing of the Ritual, and that even where the law of Trent has not been promulgated.[8] Nor does this obligation cease when a marriage has been, lawfully (in case of necessity) or unlawfully, though validly, contracted without the presence and blessing of a priest.

Clarum est [says Gasparri[†]] *inito valide matrimonio praeceptum grave manere sponsos petendi hanc Ritualis benedictionem . . . Haec vera sunt non modo de matrimonio defectu parochi coram testibus contracto, sed in genere de matrimoniis validis clandestinis.* [It is clear, says Gasparri, that in a marriage entered into validly, there remains a grave obligation on the couple to seek the blessing of this ritual . . . this is true not only when the marriage lacks pastor and witnesses, but in general for all marriages valid but clandestine.]

Catholics, then, who have contracted validly, in the office of a registrar or in a Protestant church, are still bound to present themselves to receive, and the priest should impart – if the parties have satisfied the requirements above mentioned – the simple blessing of the Ritual. The matrimonial consent is not to be renewed, for the marriage is already, we assume, certainly valid. The priest does not recite the words of the Ritual: *Ego vos conjungo* [I join you together] &c.; but everything else is done as the Ritual prescribes in the ordinary marriage rite. So much for the blessing of the Ritual.

May the solemn blessing of the Missal be also given to such persons at a nuptial Mass? …

D. MANNIX.

Mass on board ship

REV. DEAR SIR, – I will ask you to reply to the following questions:

1st. Is a priest on a voyage from Ireland to America or Australia justified in saying Mass on board without special permission, in order to give himself and the other Catholic passengers an opportunity of hearing Mass?

[†] Pietro Gasparri, later cardinal, responsible for the 1917 revised Code of Canon Law, Secretary of State who concluded the Lateran Treaty that brought to an end hostilities between the Vatican and Italy; the same Gasparri troubled by the Foreign Office in the previous chapter.

2nd. In case special permission is required, from whom should it be obtained?

SACERDOS [PRIEST]

The priest in question would not be justified in celebrating Mass without special permission. He would require a special indult, which, at the present day, at all events, is granted only by the Pope, or, in virtue of special facilities, by the bishop of the place from which the ship sails.[9] The indult is granted subject to the condition that there be no danger of irreverence. It is usually required, moreover, that there be a second priest or a deacon to hold the chalice.

D. MANNIX.

CATHOLICS IN AUSTRALIA: PANEGYRIC ON ARCHBISHOP CARR

By the time Archbishop Carr died in 1917 and Mannix became Archbishop of Melbourne in his own right, he had developed a view of Australian Catholics as a persecuted minority, now coming into its own. His panegyric for Carr develops the ideas seen in their initial stages in his Easter speech of 1913. Australian Catholics have a hard past and a bright future.[10]

Truly, the hand of God is visible in the history of the Church here. It is His Providence that often the weak things should confound the strong. A century ago, and for long after, the outlook of the Church in Australia was unpromising indeed, Catholics were few and far between; a rejected, despised people, without cohesion, without anyone to defend them, without anyone to give them hope or ambition or leading. "Upon the rivers of Babylon, there we sat and wept when we remembered Sion. . . . For there they that led us into captivity, required of us the words of songs" (Ps. 136). The ruling caste among the early settlers had brought with them the bad traditions of dark and evil days in Ireland and in Great Britain. Those who were set to shape the policy and the destiny of Australia in those early days were probably no better and no worse than most men of their time and of their class. But, at all events, the mind and purpose of some of them was that the Catholic Faith should get no footing in Australia. We who live in better days, and in comparative freedom, find it hard to realize how much our fathers in the Faith suffered, in order to hand on the heritage to us. We are even told that we should forget those far-off, evil days. But, David, in his prophetic vision, did not forget that his people sat and wept by the rivers of Babylon; and to ask us to forget the beginnings or our history in Australia is to invite us to ignore the dealings of God with a chosen people. We may explain, extenuate, forgive; but we do not, and we ought not, to forget. Australian Catholics owe too much to God to forget that, in their fathers and in themselves, He made the weak things confound the strong; that He Himself led them out of the house of bondage.

> *"Those who thought to give the Catholic Church no foothold in this fair land did not reckon with the invincible, unconquerable faith of the Irish exiles..."*

But it is not my purpose to make more than a passing reference to these things today. I mention them merely for the purpose of setting the present position of Catholics in its true light and perspective.

Those who thought to give the Catholic Church no foothold in this fair land did not reckon with the invincible, unconquerable faith of the Irish exiles; they dropped out of their calculations the Providence of God, which, all the world over, has shielded and strengthened the faith of the Irish exiles wherever they have made a home. Often, and in many places, they have met with opposition, even with repression and persecution. But God, in His own patient, wise, leisurely way, if I may say so, has worked out His own designs. The Irish exiles came here one hundred years ago, broken in spirit, without education, without wealth, without the instincts, the habits, the traditions that make for success in this world. In the century that has passed they and their children have suffered from the poverty and the limitations of the early days in Australia. Catholics are, of course, but a minority of the people, and they must be content with the modicum of justice that a minority can win. In business and trade they have been outdistanced; in education they have not yet fully reached their own ideals; in public affairs and in political life they have not yet secured their due place or their proper influence. Indeed, so hard does ascendancy die that any effort on their part to secure equality is even still enough to awaken resentment and to stir up angry passions. But, whatever may be true of worldly success and progress, in all that belongs to God Catholics have no rivals in Australia. They have done more – I say it in no spirit of boasting, but in a spirit of gratitude – out of their poverty than others, with the best intentions, have been able to do out of their wealth. They alone, or almost alone, have resisted the temptation to accept from the State godless schools, which have banished God Himself from every land into which they have been admitted. Their Christian schools, maintained by the heroic sacrifices of the teaching Orders and by the marvellous generosity of their people, are studded over the land; and, as a consequence, and as a reward, while others, I grieve to say, have to complain of dwindling congregations and empty churches, the Catholic churches are multiplied beyond numbering, and their churches are filled with worshippers.

> *"... while others ... have to complain of dwindling congregations and empty churches, the Catholic churches are multiplied beyond numbering..."*

Here as elsewhere, it is proved by experience that the Christian school is the ante-chamber of the church. To the schools, undoubtedly, we owe our strength; to the schools we owe that progress of which there is abundant evidence around us. It is but a hundred years since an Irish priest, who had crossed the seas to minister to his fellow countrymen, was haughtily told that no Popish priest would be tolerated under the Southern Cross.‡ But, thank God, no puny Governor, with his fleeting authority, could permanently bar the working out of God's design; and the Catholic Church in Australia today is almost perfect in its organisation, with its Apostolic Delegate, the direct representative in this southern land of the Father of all the faithful, with its Archbishops and Bishops, and clergy, secular and regular; with its marvellous organizations of Brotherhoods and Sisterhoods working in schools, orphanages, hospitals, and other institutions designed to draw out every latent capacity and meet every need. The progress of a hundred years could scarcely be brought home to us more pointedly in any way than by recalling the fact that Australia, even non-Catholic Australia, which one time refused to admit even one Irish priest to minister to his brethren, has in our day given a welcome, which was frank and warm and gracious, to another ecclesiastic, who came straight from the See of Peter with the Pope's commission for his passport and the Apostolic Blessing for his recommendation. It is, indeed, a change – a change of which Catholics are all the more sensible, and for which they are all the more grateful, not because they forget, but just because they remember the change from the old days.

Now, how has this marvellous success of the Church in Australia been achieved? God, of course, it was Who gave the increase. But God works out His plans through human agents. And, under God, the growth of the Church in Australia has been due to the strong, living, generous faith of the Irish people who have made this fair land their home. Other nationalities, no doubt, have contributed. There have been in Australia great prelates and priests and laymen who did not come from Ireland. But the sum of their contributions, great though it was in itself, is by comparison negligible. It is not, therefore, surprising that in common speech, the words Catholic and Irish have come to be synonymous in Australia. It is a rough generalisation of the facts. And it is our joy and glory that Catholic Australia has borrowed from Ireland its temper and its spirit; its depth and its solidity; its generosity, and grace, and charm.

The Church's Mission

This is not the time or place to discuss at length the attitude of the Catholic Church towards error in religion. But, for my purpose, the case of the Church may be very briefly stated. The Church has no doubt about her Divine commission. She claims that she alone has been sent to teach the nations. She is to gather them into her fold, not by force or violence, however, but by persuasion. She vindicates for herself the right

---

‡ Fr Jeremiah O'Flynn was deported by Governor Macquarie in 1818 as he had been refused permission to come by the Colonial Office on the grounds of his unsuitability.

> "... *physical repression of heresy had lost it power, and therefore its justification* ..."

to teach and appeal to outsiders without hindrance. She further claims the right to protect her own subjects from the corruption of error, and in the exercise of that right and duty, she further claims the right to use, at every period, and amid the changing conditions of the world, the means which she deems necessary and expedient for her purpose. For many ages after the triumph of Christianity, while there was still but one fold, and while there still seemed to be a hope of maintaining religious unity, the Church inflicted upon former heretics – i.e. those of her subjects who rebelled against authority – *not* merely spiritual chastisements, but also physical punishments of various kinds. Later on, a time came when the union of Christendom was hopelessly broken, when changing civilisation had bred new ideas, and then it became more and more evident that physical repression of heresy had lost it power, and therefore its justification, until, in our own day, no Catholic, from the Pope down to the humblest layman, dreams of suggesting oppressive measures against heretics.

That is the whole case in a few words. The Church will not admit that she exceeded her right in having recourse to physical punishment as long as it was effective and suitable for the attainment of her ends.

Neither will she admit that, in the present condition of the world, she is bound, in consistency or in any other principle, to use a weapon of defence which has become useless, or worse, in her hands.

The world changes and the Church adapts herself to new conditions. She is now as sincere and as single-minded in her tolerance as she was earlier in her efforts at the repression of religious error [. . .]

> "*[the Church] is now as sincere and as single-minded in her tolerance as she was earlier in her efforts at the repression of religious error* ..."

CATHOLIC TOLERANCE

[. . .] I omit to explain that the Catholic church recognises that at the present day heretics may be, and that they are, in good faith in their errors and if they are in good faith, they have the right and the duty, unmolested, to follow their conscientious religious convictions [. . .]

You were told that you were bound, if possible, to persecute even unto death your non-Catholic neighbours. You may have wondered in what great storehouse of theological learning this confident assertion was uncovered. If you did consider the matter, it was, no doubt, a relief to find, as the controversy went on, that, after all, this unfamiliar and intolerant doctrine was attributed to the Catholic Church on the authority of a shilling pamphlet written by a Protestant Bishop.

The panegyric on Carr was something Mannix was proud of. Calwell recalled:[11]

I said: 'You must have written some things that have survived, your Grace.' He said: 'Since coming to Australia I have led a lazy life. I have written very little.' I said: 'The splendid panegyrics that you have delivered over the coffins of departed priests were all expressed in classical English. Fortunately, they have survived.' I added: 'You wrote a magnificent panegyric in St Patrick's Cathedral at the funeral of your illustrious predecessor, Archbishop Carr.' He said: 'Well, that is possibly the only thing I did write. I haven't done much else.'

CATHOLIC PRINCIPLES

In 1917 Mannix gave a long speech – two and a half hours – on 'Catholic principles'. It might have given him an opportunity to say what religious principles inspired him, but there is little about that in the content of the speech. Jesus and anything said by Jesus are almost absent, except for his setting up the Church. Mannix took his Melbourne audience to be Christians of either Protestant or Catholic persuasion, and hence meant by 'Catholic principles' those principles which distinguish Catholics from Protestants. He had what came be called after Vatican II a "triumphalist" view of the Church, proud of its unity and uniformity in distinction from warring Protestant sects. We include some brief extracts on the strictly religious questions – the later sections of the speech on the rights of workers and other social questions are quoted later in the chapters on social justice and population:[12]

Dr Mannix meets Lady Godiva, Bega Budget, 4 February 1920.

I do not mean tonight, so far as it can be avoided, to say anything that might be considered unreasonably polemic or unreasonably controversial. (Applause.) I know that people attribute to me a rather warm Celtic temperament. (Laughter.) Somebody wrote to me about it this very morning. (Laughter.) But I do not intend on this occasion, and

Melbourne Town Hall, 23 October 1917, for lecture by Archbishop Mannix on "Catholic Principles" to which 20,000 people were unable to gain admission. (His Grace may be seen with Fr. Lockington near the centre of the picture)[13]

I never intended on any occasion, to let my Celtic temperament run away with me, and make me say anything that could give reasonable offence to any human being. (Applause.) …

I assume that I am addressing believers in Christ; those who know that, while here on earth, He prayed for His followers with a prayer that cannot have been in vain, "that they may all be one, as Thou, Father, in Me, and I in Thee, that they may also be one in Us: that the world may believe that Thou has sent Me." To the unbeliever, of course, these words have no special importance. But to the believer in Christ they are full of meaning

… the Catholic Church claims within her own sphere absolute independence from secular control of any kind whatever. (Applause.) She has her charter from Christ, and she has to obey God rather than man. (Applause.) The Catholic Church, too, claims that she has from Christ Himself the right to teach with authority – that is, the right to teach and bind her members to accept her teaching. She claims, moreover – I am not saying just now whether the claim is well-founded or not – that in exercising that teaching power she has the infallible authority of God upon which to rely. (Loud applause.) It is a big claim to make, but still she is not afraid to make it. (Applause.) You will find it characteristic of the Catholic Church

> *"The Catholic Church claims within her own sphere absolute independence from secular control of any kind whatsoever"*

> *"The Bible was written and collected by the Church..."*

that she knows her own mind, so to say, and that she is not afraid to speak it. (Applause.) The body of doctrine which the Church is to teach, she finds in the Bible and in the traditions handed down from Apostolic times. She admits, of course, that the Bible is the work of God, divinely inspired, but, besides the Bible, she relies upon tradition. Christ did not commit His teaching to writing, and the Church had to get on for many years without the New Testament writings. (Applause.) The Bible was written and collected by the Church, and it is only by tradition, by the authority of the Church, that we can know that we have any divinely inspired Book at all. I have been merely running over the heads of Catholic doctrine. That was the kind of Church the world knew when there was only one Church. (Applause.) The people did not have to choose between 200 or 300 different sects, all claiming to follow Christ, and all warring with each other. (Applause.) There was only one Church then, and the people received the Word of God through the priests and Bishops, with the infallible Roman Pontiff at their head. (Applause.) The church was human, and, like all things human, she had her defects, and they were not few or small ...

The Catholic Church today stands where she stood 1800 or 1900 years ago. (Applause.) Her unity is intact today, as it was on the day on which the Apostles came out from the chamber on Pentecost Sunday with the Holy Ghost newly come into their souls. (Applause.) Today, 300,000,000 people are said to be in the fold of the Catholic Church. All of that vast host – men and women, priests and Bishops, from the Pope down to the youngest child confirmed in Melbourne – believe exactly the same doctrines, and all are prepared to submit to the same infallible teaching authority. (Applause.) These 300,000,000 people belong to all nations, and they are of all ages: they differ in culture, in civilisation; they differ in their economic, social, political principles; they are often poles apart. Some belong to kingdoms, others to empires, and others to democracies; sometimes they are at peace, and sometimes, unfortunately, at war. But, whether in peace or in war; whether at one end of the earth or the other; whether advanced or backward in civilisation, all are in one faith and belief – a solid body behind the Pope of Rome. (Loud applause.) ...

> *"All that vast host ... believe exactly the same doctrines..."*

Mannix's piety

One would like to know more of Mannix's personal piety and pastoral work – sermons, visitations, confessions. There are fragments remembered. He was certainly seen to pray a lot. Santamaria wrote:[14]

He had a deeply Christian fear – more properly described, respect for God. There was

> "... how often, when you went in to see him at "Raheen" you would find him saying the Rosary"

nothing else in his life to which he had any real attachment. Today all the talk is of a man's "image", whatever that may mean. His "image" was that of a national or ecclesiastical leader. I wonder whether those who "fitted" that image on to him knew about the five hours a day which he would spend before the Blessed Sacrament in the chapel at "Mandalay" at Portsea. I wonder if they knew how often, when you went in to see him at "Raheen" you would find him saying the Rosary.

But, of course, apart from God, he was afraid of no one. King or Prime Minister, Pope or Cardinal, he paid them all the highest respect of never being afraid to speak what was in his mind.

He spent long hours in the confessional.[15]

The Archbishop occupied his confessional every Saturday night from 7 o'clock till well towards 11, his box still surrounded long after the others had been deserted. One Saturday night, the Administrator, Fr. Lonergan, remonstrated with the numbers still waiting their turn.

An hour later, he received a mild rebuke, "Never do that again. If people want to come to me, let them come."

What was it like to go to confession to Mannix? The young found the Archbishop an approachable confessor – and what could be discussed ranged more widely than one might imagine:[16]

He had the habit of putting his hand through [the grille] and patting your hand as you told him your confession. He'd have a little talk: 'Play football? Where do you live?' And so on ...

I found it easy to discuss things with him in confession. There was no feeling of trepidation. I was 19 before I knew anything about sex. I found a book by Marie Stopes which mentioned French letters and *coitus interruptus* – things I didn't understand. He gently explained so that I got a faint idea. He was somewhere between being frank and modest, but very kind.

A priest who knew Mannix well recalled:[17]

My maternal grandmother had a dreadful experience in her life and he helped her. Her husband took off to Adelaide, and had left her in Mt Gambier with seven children, the youngest just a baby ... My poor old grandmother, after a few years there, left Mt Gambier with the seven children and came to Melbourne, and raised the children there. Then, the husband decided, after some years, he wanted to come back. When she refused to take him back, she was told by a priest that she was a wicked woman, and she could never go to Communion. She went on for years, and never received Communion until she plucked up courage to go to Archbishop Mannix for confession one Saturday night. He was kindness itself. This is what I heard from my mother. He told her that the priest was wrong, and he was sorry, and that she could go to Holy Communion. So he helped her. She just worshipped the ground he walked on.

The Archbishop regularly celebrated the 8am Mass each Sunday in the Cathedral and preached homilies that were recalled as "gems, quietly and beautifully spoken, and extremely practical".[18]

He was also involved in major liturgical ceremonies such as Tenebrae, during Holy Week. A part of this involved the extinguishing of candles, one by one, until the Cathedral was plunged into darkness. The liturgy could be long and tedious for young altar boys – as one from this period remembers – and some of them fell asleep. When the lights came on again, the Archbishop would notice:[19]

There were sure to be within his reach, sitting on the steps of the Bishop's Throne,

Young Paradian Bill Korf accepting the sprinter's trophy from Archbishop Mannix, late 1920s.[20]

three or four boys, sound asleep. He would remove one of his sandals and gently tap each one of the boys on the head. I am sure he derived considerable amusement, as the rest of us did, from this manoeuvre, although his face showed no sign of it.

Yet in some important ways, his pastoral experience was surprisingly limited. As rector of a seminary and then archbishop, he had served only briefly as a parish priest. In an interview late in life, he was asked about his achievements:[21]

Achievements? There are so many things I have not achieved. I have not baptised a person, I have never married anyone.[§] I have never given the Last Rites or administered Extreme Unction.

Santamaria broke in,

Your grace has baptised at least one person. My second child.

The Archbishop looked up sharply and sighed.

That is so. I had forgotten that.

Mannix's attention to the rubrical accuracy and appearance of the liturgy went with a sense of how the Church could give a poor impression. He "constantly referred to clerics in France and Italy as not being fully masculine: they wore soutanes in public and rode girls' bicycles…"[22]

Newman College

From his very first speech after his arrival in Australia from Ireland in 1913,[23] Daniel Mannix made it clear that quality education for all Catholics, including university education, was one of his major preoccupations. The foundation of Newman College at Melbourne University was one of his earliest initiatives. Protestant denominations had colleges, so must Catholics.

Cardinal Newman provided a suitable role model:[24]

Cardinal Newman assured the scientist that he need not fear that the Church or the theologian would always be at his elbow to raise a warning finger at every new step that for the moment may seem to diverge from received Catholic opinion.

A passenger on board a sailing ship did not run to remonstrate with the captain every time the vessel, to suit the tides, the currents, the winds, tacked about from one side to the other. He did not expect that the prow would always point to the port of destination.

---

§ Untrue: Mannix had conducted a few weddings in West Melbourne, 1913-17: Val Noone, Archbishop Daniel Mannix in West Melbourne 1913-1917, *Footprints* 27 (2) (2012), 6-18.

An individual theologian might be nervous without cause, and remonstrate without authority. But Cardinal Newman rightly held that the Catholic Church was too old and too wise to fear the results of true science, or the investigation of true scientists.

> "Cardinal Newman rightly held that the Catholic Church was too old and too wise to fear the results of true science..."

Mannix remained realistic about what could be achieved with the resources available. A Catholic university might be the ideal, but was not on the cards at present:

Of course, Cardinal Newman's ideal was a Catholic University, in which, side by side with the other sciences, theology would take its place, and an honoured place. Unfortunately, we were not within sight of that ideal in Australia, and, therefore, I think I might venture to say, that if Cardinal Newman were today in Melbourne, he would urge Catholics to make the best of their opportunities, and to avail themselves of the University which was in their midst.

A smiling Mannix with Cardinal MacRory, Papal Legate to the National Eucharistic Congress, 1934[25]

THE LAITY

Mannix was unusual in his time for his promotion of lay Catholic intellectual life and action. His founding of the Catholic Central Library, support for the Catholic Evidence Guild, and, as will be seen later, support for the *Catholic Worker* and its associated political activities, placed him outside the mainstream of the Australian (and world) Catholic hierarchy, who generally insisted on clerical control of all possible church-related activities. Mannix used the occasion of the December 1934 Melbourne Eucharistic Congress to advance the cause of lay Catholic Action. At a convention of Catholic university societies, he expressed his willingness to listen to ideas from the laity (in their proper sphere, of course):[26]

His Holiness the Pope himself has been sending a clarion call to the whole world, not directed to the Bishops and priests, but to the laity, who, for the greater part, are inclined and satisfied to leave the major portion of the work to the Bishops and priests, and to be spectators of the work that is being undertaken. The Pope is very anxious at the present time that Catholic men and women should, as it were, pull their full force and strength as Catholics . . .

You are the leaders of the people . . . Your body represents the universities of Australia, and any ideas that you may initiate to make things better than they are at present will receive a cordial welcome, and will be assured of the utmost consideration. And I can assure you that I shall leave nothing undone to give effect to any feasible proposal that may emanate from this important convention of yours.

B.A. Santamaria, with long experience of Mannix, found that he meant what he said:[27]

It was one of Mannix's deepest convictions that the laity had functions to perform and responsibilities to fulfil which were not open to bishops or priests . . .

"allocation to the laity of a role in which they would be permitted to operate with genuine independence"

This conviction led him to describe himself, with somewhat impish humour, on more than one occasion as 'anti-clerical'.

It was, of course, intended jokingly, but merely emphasised his belief not only in the necessity for lay commitment, but in the allocation to the laity of a role in which they would be permitted to operate with genuine independence. In this he differed greatly from almost all other bishops of earlier and later epochs.

And Catholic Action, in Mannix's terms, was not to mean just praying and marching in sodalities. It meant political action:[28]

I am sometimes uneasy that Catholic Actionists should be so engrossed with their own special work that they take no interest, or little interest, in public affairs. Some would ask them to believe, for example, that politics is just a sordid game that decent people and Catholic Actionists especially should shun. To my mind that policy leads to disaster . . . Catholic Actionists are constantly reminded that they should try to change their environment. Without tying themselves to party politics they might well spend some of their energy in changing their environment for the better. If they were to stand aside from public affairs, their political adversaries might easily destroy in one day of revolution the work of years spent in building up the Mystical Body and Christian civilisation.

Regular visit to the Little Sisters of the Poor hostel for the aged, 1940s[29]

SEX EDUCATION

In the early 1940s Mannix took up an issue that would not normally be expected from a Catholic archbishop aged almost 80 – sex and moral education.[30] He gave the main address at a meeting of boys' secondary school principals to discuss "the difficult subject of sex education and training in chastity". A memorandum was published embodying "the wishes of His Grace in regard to the improvement of moral training in schools" which was sent to boys' secondary school principals, religious training colleges and the heads of teaching Orders.

The memorandum had wide-ranging criticisms of how things were done. There were references to smaller classes for religious instruction, the encouragement of discussion, the discouragement of corporal punishment and harassment for examination success, and the removal of any stigma attached to "impurity" as "the greatest of sins". The memorandum suggested that the training colleges for teaching brothers were excessively rigid and caused "the suppression of personality and frankness for the sake of external obedience and conformity to rule".

During 1943, the Archbishop turned to Catholic girls' schools and delivered several forthright addresses to the principals. The audiences were no doubt startled to hear criticism of the "regimentation" of the "First Friday", the "false conscience" and exaggerated "gravity" regarding sins of impurity. Sexual curiosity, he declared, was "good and natural" and school discipline should be based on pupil loyalty to teachers "who deserve loyalty by their upright character". Turning to the characteristics of Catholic religious teachers, he confessed that "all of us are too puritanical in matters of sex", a phenomenon which he attributed to Irish heritage.

Despite Mannix's best efforts, there was little uptake of these ideas.

VATICAN II SUBMISSION 1962

After Pope John XXIII announced the Second Vatican Council, preparations included the drawing up of a number of draft documents which the Council was expected to approve, possibly with amendments. In 1962 they were sent to Church leaders for comment. The documents were very conservative in nature, and in the event were thrown out by a Council possessed by a reforming spirit. Mannix sent comments on the first document, *De Ecclesia* (On the Church), which show him very critical of its conservative line. The comments were drafted by Eric

D'Arcy,[31] ¶ but the covering letter makes it clear that they represent Mannix's views. The comments are highly critical of the reactionary nature of the documents, and show Mannix on the side of the mood for change. The comments on the laity and on obedience summarise something of Mannix's long-standing non-standard views on those topics:[32]

OF THE SECOND VATICAN COUNCIL: NOTES ON THE SCHEMA ON THE CHURCH FROM THE ARCHBISHOP OF MELBOURNE
22 FEBRUARY 1963

GENERAL NOTES

Overall decision on the Schema On the Church: <u>I VOTE AGAINST</u> *for the following reasons.*

1. The Schema smacks more of a legal document than a spiritual proclamation of religious faith, and least like an evangelical one; for it treats too much of the juridical aspects of the Church, which is almost exclusively represented as a juridical society rather than a participation in the sacrament hidden from the world in God. Even baptism itself seems to be considered more as establishing a juridical relationship with the Church than as a New Creation.

> *"The Schema is too preoccupied with the rule and rights of a Church desiring power and authority, like 'Kings of the Nations'..."*

2. The Schema is too preoccupied with the rule and rights of a Church desiring power and authority, like 'Kings of the Nations' who 'rule their own' and always 'ask what is theirs.'

The tone of the schema suggests a certain hardness, and perhaps even pride, sometimes more redolent of 'To you I give the power of this world and the glory of it' than of 'Learn from me, because I am gentle and meek of heart.' ...

Chapter VI: On the Laity

It is asked** that the Council affirm the following:

II

1. The field of apostolic work proper to the laity is therefore found in the temporal order in political, social and economic life. The laity ought to work so as to transform the earthly city, in accordance with the intention of the Gospel and with the norms of the social doctrine of the popes, into the kingdom of justice, love and peace.

¶ Eric D'Arcy, Movement chaplain, author of *Conscience and its Right to Freedom* (1961), later head of the University of Melbourne Philosophy Department and Archbishop of Hobart.
** Murphy's translation has "demanded".

2. In our days especially the duty lies with the laity of allotting Christian form and structure to the world of industry and labour; for this end religious motives and moral strengths are not enough, but practical experience and the ingenuity derived from experience in political and social practice are also required, both in its strategy and tactical methods.

3. The laity who, whether as individuals or in the collective action of organizations, exercise such apostolic activity in the temporal order – social, political or economic are by no means to be exempted from the authority of the Roman Pope and Bishops in matters of faith and morals.

". . . the laity acts on its own responsibility, and rejoices in full freedom, both of obedience and action"

4. But in all other aspects of their temporal activity, whether concerning the practical policies to be chosen or the strategic and tactical methods to be preferred, the laity acts on its own responsibility, and rejoices in full freedom, both of obedience and action.

Chapter VIII:

On Authority and Obedience within the Church

1. It is asked that the Council affirm more clearly that authority in the Church is humble service and ministry to all, according to the spirit and example of the Lord, who became a servant for our sake; who came not to be ministered to but to minister, and washed the feet of the Apostles as an example to their successors.

2. By no means are the apostolic helpers of the Hierarchy, whether clerical or lay, to be conceived of or represented in the manner of an instrument, 'which is not moved except insofar as it is moved by the principal agent'; for all adult Christians are required to show initiative and exercise due prudence and responsibility.

Chapter IX:

On the Relationship between Church and State (I)

It is asked that the Council affirm the following:

1. Although Christ the Lord embraced all, without exception, in his redemptive love, he always exhibited special predilection for the poor and afflicted, and those 'labouring and oppressed'; this example of its Founder the Church always holds as a norm, as much of its doctrine as of its practice.

2. Let the Church therefore commend and bless all those societies, whether clerical or lay, which provide visitation, solace and assistance to the poor, the sick, the captive and others in any way afflicted; not only when individuals are helped, but also nations still less developed in the state of industrial progress.

3. Let the social doctrine proposed by the Roman Popes and national Hierarchies be commended to all. For although this doctrine is connected with natural law and strictly human rights, yet it proclaims that which strict justice requires, in asserting which the Popes were inspired by the spirit of the Gospel, and constrained by the love of Christ for the poor and labouring.

> *"Let the Church approve no social order ... in which there is a great discrepancy between the luxury and wealth of a privileged few, and the wretchedness and material indigence of the many"*

4. Let the Church approve no social order, even if it claims to be 'constituted by legitimate authority', in which there is a great discrepancy between the luxury and wealth of a privileged few, and the wretchedness and material indigence of the many. It has been falsely asserted, since it was propagated by enemies of religion, that the Catholic Church has always been identified with the 'status quo' or existing order, or that it has always supported the rich and privileged classes (even those generous to the Church), or that it holds in suspicion those political parties which emphasize social reform.

On the Relationship between Church and State (2)

It is asked and sought that the Council by no means disturb the good relationship which exists between the Church and the Civil Authorities in many regions, or even put them in danger, by passing a definition concerning the necessity of any formal union between Church and State. For in many places – in Australia indeed and New Zealand, as in North America, in Ireland, and in many regions of Northern Europe – although a theoretical separation exists, there is in practice harmony and equilibrium between the spiritual and temporal powers. The Church, full of freedom and independence, rejoices, and indeed in many things rejoices in the privilege of law and governing bodies.

On the Relationship between Church and State (3)

It is asked that the Council clearly affirm the duty and obligations by which the State is held to be responsible for and provide religious liberty to all its citizens, both to Catholics and to those who are not members of the true Church but follow their own conscience in good faith.

Let it be affirmed, moreover, that this freedom must be extended, not only to choosing the lesser evil – e.g. for avoiding civil strife, or for avoiding the persecution of Catholics in various regions – but to a strict right; which right indeed is most closely connected with the obligation of each and every one of us to follow faithfully the

> *"... the obligation of each and every one of us to follow faithfully the dictates of our own conscience, formed in good faith ..."*

dictates of our own conscience, formed in good faith; but it is more deeply founded on respect for the human person, created in the image of God, which God Himself holds in respect and embraces in love, even if the gift of true faith is no longer evident in it.

STATE AID: THE FINAL VICTORY

In the last weeks of his life, Mannix finally received the good news that the tide had turned on state aid for church schools. Santamaria was able to inform him that a breakthrough would be announced in the Prime Minister's policy speech on 12 November. Santamaria recalled:[33]

"... that I could tell Archbishop Mannix that something would be done to acknowledge the principle of state aid in the Liberals' policy speech"

... on the eve of the 1963 election – and that took place, I think it was on the 22 November, give or take a day[††] – he [Harold Holt, the Treasurer] got in touch with me and asked me to see him. And he said that he'd discussed the matter again with Menzies, and Menzies intended to make some gesture – that's all that he said – and that I could tell Archbishop Mannix that something would be done to acknowledge the principle of state aid in the Liberals' policy speech. But it was very interesting. I spoke to Archbishop Mannix about it, before the end of October as far as I remember, and it was lucky that I did. I could see that he was naturally delighted, because he had campaigned for state aid ever since he came to Australia in 1913, and he said, 'I have worked all my life in Australia for this. But in the end it's not due to my efforts, it's due to the efforts of the men', – was the phrase he used – by which he meant the DLP and so on. What was lucky about it was that I told him this before the end of October and he died on November 6, before Menzies had given his policy speech. So if I had not mentioned it he wouldn't have ever known. So he was quite happy about it. He died.

Menzies announced help for science blocks in all schools. It was the thin end of the wedge. Fifty years later, Australia has one of the most generous systems of public funding of church schools in the world.

[††] Menzies easily won the federal election on 30 November 1963.

[1] Archbishop Kelly in *The Sun*, 15/8/1911, repr. in P. O'Farrell, *Documents in Australian Catholic History*, Geoffrey Chapman, London, 1969, vol. II pp. 258-61.

[2] Griffin, *Daniel Mannix*, pp. 97, 101.

[3] Australian examples of this genre collected in Pat Mullins, Looking back on the way we were, *Australasian Catholic Record* 75 (1998), 323-5, repr. in *Journal of the Australian Catholic Historical Society* 33 (2012), 163-6; Mannix's position discussed in John Murphy, Dr Mannix and the integrity of confession, *Australasian Catholic Record* (Jan 1902), on which see Griffin, Daniel Mannix, p. 100.

[4] James Griffin, 'Mannix, Daniel (1864-1963)', *Australian Dictionary of Biography*, National Centre of Biography, Australian National University: http://adb.anu.edu.au/biography/mannix-daniel-7478/text13033.

[5] [Footnotes in original] Cf. Collect: Prop. Fid., n. 2,202: Bucceroni, Comment De Constit. Apos. Sedis p. 7, n 9.

[6] Sanchez, St Alphonsus, Becker, De Spons. et Mat., p. 358; Gasparri, De Mat., n. 1,021; Rosset, De Sac. Mat., v., n. 2.868.

[7] Lehmkuhl, ii., n. 693; Feije, n. 554.

[8] Cf. Lehmkuhl, ii., n. 693.

[9] See Putzer, 161, iii. c., 4th ed.

[10] Walter A. Ebsworth, *Archbishop Mannix*, H. H. Stephenson, Armadale, 1977, pp. 163-5.

[11] Calwell, *Be Just and Fear Not*, p. 157.

[12] *Advocate*, 3 November 1917, p. 4-7, 24.

[13] *Advocate*, 3 November 1917.

[14] Patrick Morgan, ed, *Running the Show, B. A. Santamaria, selected documents: 1939–1996*, Miegunyah Press, Carlton, 2008, p. 328.

[15] Ebsworth, *Archbishop Mannix*, p. 431.

[16] Gilchrist, *Daniel Mannix: Wit and Wisdom*, p. 131, n. 89, quoted interview with Mr N. Tobin, Ballarat, March 1981.

[17] Leo M. Clarke, Archbishop Mannix: what was he like? *Footprints* 20 (1) (2003), 28-48.

[18] Gilchrist, *Daniel Mannix*, p. 131, n. 90, quoted recollection by Mr D. Dillon, Surrey Hills, Vic, 9 March 1981.

[19] Gilchrist, *Daniel Mannix*, p. 131, n. 91, quoted recollection by Mr D. Dillon, Surrey Hills, Vic, 9 March 1981.

[20] Courtesy of Old Paradians' Association, http://www.oldparadians.com.au/FullArticle.aspx?Article=Korf

[21] Peter Hastings interview in *The Bulletin*, quoted in Vincent Buckley, *Cutting Green Hay*, Penguin Books, Ringwood, 1983, p. 143; an almost identical recollection on a different occasion in Leo M. Clarke, Archbishop Mannix: what was he like? *Footprints* 20 (1) (2003), 28-48, at p. 45.

[22] Interview with Eric D'Arcy, 15/11/1976, quoted in Anthony S. Cappello, To be or not to be an Italian: BA Santamaria, culture, descent and the social exclusion of Italian-Australians, PhD thesis, Victoria University, 2009, ch. 7.

[23] See 'First impressions', this book p. 2.

[24] 'Daniel Mannix, John Henry Newman, Catholic higher education and the idea of a residential college', Simon Caterson, Mannix College Occasional Papers, published by Mannix College,

Wellington Road, Monash University, Victoria, 2011, in the series Gabrielle McMullen FRACI, Reflections on Catholic Identity and Mission, pp: 1 and 4.

[25] Image from Ebsworth, *Archbishop Mannix, p.321.*

[26] Gerard Henderson, *Mr Santamaria and the Bishops*, Sydney, 1982, p. 12.

[27] Gilchrist, *Daniel Mannix*, p 152, n. 64, quoted from B.A. Santamaria, Mannix and the laity: after 25 years, *AD2000*, November 1988, p. 4.

[28] Address to 1948 YCW conference, in Henderson, *Mr Santamaria and the Bishops*, p. 34.

[29] Original image supplied by Michael Gilchrist.

[30] The story is taken from Gilchrist, *Daniel Mannix*, ch. 7. The original documents cannot be found.

[31] Michael Costigan, Vatican II as I experienced it, *Journal of the Australian Catholic Historical Society* 33 (2012), 83-104, at p. 100.

[32] Jeffrey J. Murphy, The lost (and last) animadversions of Daniel Mannix, *Australasian Catholic Record* 76 (1999), 54-73.

[33] Santamaria interviews conducted for the Australian Biography project, interviewer: Robin Hughes, recorded April 23, 24 and 25, 1997, interview 9: http://www.australianbiography.gov.au/subjects/santamaria/interview9.html

Chapter 8: Mannix and Labor:
The First Round

As we leave religion for politics, we need to go back in time. Mannix twice sought political power through Catholic control of the Labor Party – once during World War I and again during the 1950s. Both attempts ended in complete failure, though the first was more quickly repaired than the second. The first attempt was directly focussed on the education grievance, but the result was no progress on that and a near-split in the Labor movement. Grave suspicion of Catholic designs was left among both Labor supporters and Protestants.

As foreshadowed in his first speech in Australia, Mannix aimed to achieve political results, in particular state aid for church schools, by organising the Catholic vote. The Catholic Federation – a non-party political organisation formed before Mannix's time but given increased impetus by him – during 1914 demanded to know which Labor candidates supported state aid and then attempted to gain control of the Labor party organisation. The Party reacted by refusing to give pledges to outside bodies and then by expelling Catholic Federation members.[1]

The crisis was defused through the efforts of men like James Scullin, the future Prime Minister, who, like Arthur Calwell decades later, were dedicated both to the Catholic faith and to Labor principles. They believed that the inclusion of State aid in the Labor platform would be electoral poison and so would prevent the achievement of Labour aims that were the surest way to benefit both Catholic and non-Catholic workers.

Catholic Federation members were soon readmitted to the Party, on the implied condition that there were no more organised attempts at Catholic infiltration.

Catholic education

In July 1913, only a few months after arriving in Melbourne, Mannix said:[2]

It is necessary in Australia for Catholics to stand together. Minorities have only to bide their time, and use their power, and the opportunity will come to them. The contending parties are more evenly balanced than in Britain; consequently it is easier for Catholics in Australia to hold the balance of power.

Victory did not then seem to be fifty years off.

At a very well attended meeting held in the Melbourne Town Hall on the evening of 26 October 1914, under the auspices of the Australian Catholic Federation, Mannix gave his major speech on Catholic educational justice and how to achieve it politically:[3]

CATHOLIC CLAIMS
GRANT FOR INSTRUCTION
SPEECH BY DR. MANNIX
ANSWER TO CRITICS

We have met to vindicate a great cause. The Catholic Federation has been exposed many a time to criticism from various quarters but by our presence in such huge numbers tonight the meeting is passing a vote of confidence in the federation and endorsing fully its methods and its action (Applause). We have been told many a time that the education question is closed for all time in Victoria, that the Education Act is the last word that can be said in this State. We have met under the presidency of the Lord Mayor to say that the last word has not been spoken in Victoria (applause) and that the last word will never be spoken in Victoria until the educational grievances of the Catholic people and others similarly circumstanced are redressed.

We have a noble cause to fight for and whatever other mine goes undeveloped this one must be worked, and the ore that is taken from it must ring true and pass current in this world, not in another. We have been told that the present is no time to ventilate our grievances and that Australia has plenty to do to face the dreadful war and the ravages of the drought. With these menaces opposing us, so we are told, there should be a truce in the campaign. That is a very paltry answer to a very pressing question. One would think that the Catholics of Victoria are able in some way like the Jews of old in the land of Pharaoh to sprinkle their door posts so that the angels of famine and of war shall pass us by. The Catholics of Victoria have to face the burden of war and drought as well as the other citizens. While we are bearing these burdens and bearing all the other common burdens of the State are we to be told – we who are less than one fourth of the State in the matter of population and not the richest fourth – are we to go on through the war bearing that burden?

Questioning Candidates

We are told that the methods of the federation are at all events very exasperating – (laughter) – that we talk too loud and talk too much. We are interfering at election times and we actually have the audacity to put questions to candidates who are looking for our votes. That interference is intolerable (Laughter). That is a dreadful menace to the democracy of Australia. Now, whatever may be said of the federation, I think we should agree in this – that the federation is the best judge of its own methods and its own business (Applause). I think that the federation can justly claim that by its methods at the present moment the educational claims occupy a place in the public mind that they have not occupied for many a day. Our politicians, and I have the greatest respect for them, have come to a course just like you see posted up at your level railway crossings – they have come to "Stop, look, listen" (Laughter). They are having a look-out for the federation express – (applause) – and possibly, too, for they are able to look both ways, some of them are keeping a look out as well for a freight train that is coming in an opposite direction from the Scripture Campaign Council (Laughter). So much has been said and so much has been written about this educational question that one would imagine in this late day that our claims should be a little understood. It may be that people are not prepared to grant our demands but this at all events, we may expect that they should know what we are looking for. Yet within the last few days in the daily papers of Melbourne we have been reading a letter from a gentleman about whom I wish to speak with respect – the president of the Methodist Conference. The president of that conference states that if the Catholics succeed in getting their claims met by the State of Victoria then the Methodists would be looking for a grant for the upkeep of their Sunday schools. One would think that there would be nobody in the State and perhaps least of all the president of the Methodist Conference, who would be found to think that we are looking for a grant for religion, either for our churches or our Sunday-schools. We have never looked for anything of that kind, and we are not going to look for anything of that kind. I can't understand why, if we get what the Methodists and other bodies like the Methodists have had for 40 years, why Methodists should be entitled to get something for which we never asked (Applause). We are asking payment simply for secular work done in our schools provided that teaching is up to the standard decided by the State examiners. That is what the Methodists and other bodies like the Methodists have had for 40 years. It is not too much for us to ask now for what they have been enjoying for 40 years and if we get it I for one cannot recognise that the granting of our claims is any claim for Sunday schools for Methodists.

A Professor of Logic

"It must be said for the president of the Methodist Conference and I am glad to say it in his defence – (laughter) – that he is not the only one that does not understand our claims. The British Association visited this country recently and the Federal Government very properly presented it with what is called a handbook in which Australia was dealt with by various writers. The Professor of logic in the University of Sydney makes, in a paper written by him, the statement to the members of the British Association, that the claims of the Catholic body were more specious than real. He was speaking to the learned members of the British Association, and the learned members of the British Association came from countries where these claims are acknowledged and granted. (Cheers) It certainly must have been very flattering to the learned members of the British Association and they must have received the news with great gratitude from the professor of logic in the Sydney University* when they learned that, owing to the fact of the want of logical acumen in the old countries they themselves in England and elsewhere have been spending enormous sums of public money in order to satisfy claims which are more specious than real.

> *"Catholics, like their neighbours, are paying education taxes and all that we are looking for is that, not that we get other people's money but that we should get the whole or even a portion of our own"*

That professor goes on to make the following astounding statement and it is for the sake of this statement I have introduced his name. If the Catholic claims were granted the State, and mark the words the State of Victoria or New South Wales as the case might be, would be subsidising a religious body and paying their clerics and their teachers at the expense of the majority. This gentleman, who is teaching logic in the Sydney University makes himself responsible for that statement. Imagine a statement of that kind coming from a chair of logic established at the public expense and submitted to the learned members of the British Association.

This gentleman does not seem to know that the Catholics, like their neighbours, are paying education taxes and all that we are looking for is that, not that we get other people's money but that we should get the whole or even a portion of our own. I might give many of the statements given by many other distinguished gentlemen which would go to show that in other quarters our demands are not understood. However the purpose I

---

* (Sir) Francis Anderson, Professor of Logic and Mental Philosophy, educational reformer and opponent of state aid to church schools.

wish to serve is simply this, to remind you, as I have so often reminded myself that we must go on repeating the exposition of our claims, and that we must be patient, because there are those who, in a hazy and reluctant way, are waking up after a sleep of 40 years.

Rights of parents

While education is made compulsory the State allows the parents to comply with the law by sending their children to either State schools or schools of their own choice, thereby acknowledging the basis of their claim. Catholics have no intention of admitting the claim that it is only by privilege that Catholics are allowed to maintain their own schools and send their children into them. That idea was working in the minds of a large number of those who are the bitterest opponents of the Catholic faith. The school chosen by the parent is largely to take the place of the home and the teacher is to some extent to take the place of the parent. Therefore the schools into which Catholic children were put should be Catholic schools. Curiously enough this principle is recognised in the laws of Victoria. When the State takes over the care of neglected children care is taken to send the waif into homes where the foster parents are of the same religion as the parents of the child (Applause). All that Catholics are asking is that they should not be penalised for endeavouring to do what the State does for the waif which falls into its hands. It will be seen how it was that 40 years ago, when Catholics were offered secular schools they told the Government that they were unsuitable for them. In spite of being as they are now, in a minority and comparatively poor, Catholics undertook to keep and maintain their own schools. They have never regretted that decision and have never given up any school for any bribe that the State was empowered to offer (Applause). When the State set up the secular schools it might justly have said, "If you are not going to use our State schools, taxation for their upkeep will not be imposed on you." If exemption from the tax was inconvenient the State might have said, "We will tax you for education in common with all the people, but as you are not going to use the schools, you will be allowed to take your proportion out of the public taxes." The State had no more right to set up these schools than it would have to appoint State Ministers of religion. If it had done so it would have been called gross religious persecution. In many parts it is heard that it costs practically nothing to educate our 40,000 children as they were educated by nuns and Christian Brothers. There is an indirect way, however of arriving at the saving to the State. The cost to the State per child for education is £6/10/-. The 40,000 children educated by the Catholics therefore save the State something like £250,000. I demand not merely that the Catholics should be relieved of this unjust burden but I also ask that the nuns and the Christian Brothers and the self sacrificing lay teachers shall at this late hour be paid a living wage … [section on Anglican policy deleted]

Labor Party's attitude

The Labor Party has also considered its attitude, and for my part I sincerely regret that the attitude taken up by it is not the same as that taken up by their Liberal opponents. The Labor Party has considered the question, but has shown no indecent haste in giving us the benefit of its decision.

> *". . . every candidate who gets up for election with the endorsement of the Labor Party will be bound to oppose a grant or aid of any kind to the Catholic schools"*

It has leaked out in well informed quarters, that the decision come to by the Labor Party is that every candidate who gets up for election with the endorsement of the Labor Party will be bound to oppose a grant or aid of any kind to the Catholic schools. Labor candidates are totally bound to refuse even a Royal commission to inquire into the defects of the Education Act. I do not come here to gloss over anything on one side or the other, and I say, speaking on behalf of the Catholic body, that the treatment received from the Labor Party is shameful. When I speak of the Labor Party I do not lay this outrageous treatment at the door of the Labor Party as a whole. I have too much respect for many of the Labor Party, whom I know too well to believe that they would be capable of endorsing such a suicidal policy. I know that this action has been taken, not by the Labor Party, but by a very small knot of extremists, who for the present moment have it in their power to say what shall be the platform of the Labor Party, and who are to be the candidates at the coming elections. I know that the decision of this small extreme body has been received by many Catholic men in the country districts with the greatest possible regret. Catholic men who belong to the Labor Party are preparing a drastic lesson for the Labor Party. There is time yet to set these things right and personally I should be sorry if it were necessary for the Catholic body to teach a lesson to the Labor Party which it should not learn at the polls.

The cause of the Catholic Church is the cause of God and justice, and it cannot be swept aside by any caucus or any party. Any political party which faces a quarrel with the Catholic body is facing a big and difficult battle and when the issue of that battle is declared I believe that you will be able to say that it is perfectly safe in the hands of the Catholic people (loud and continued applause).

> *"The cause of the Catholic Church is the cause of God and justice, and it cannot be swept aside by any caucus or any party"*

Catholic interests and the Labor Party

Attempts to extract promises from by-election candidates in January 1914 had little positive outcome, but Mannix reassured members of the Catholic Federation as to the future:[4]

At the recent contest the Catholic Federation was only taking its preliminary canter, and he thought its enemies began to feel uneasy when it was seen to be getting into its stride. He hoped that the Federation would before the next election embrace within its ample orbit every Catholic in the State, and that every Catholic would have his or her name on the rolls, in order to give their enemies in that educational struggle the answer they deserved. The Federation had behind it the Archbishop, the Bishops and priests, and Catholic people of Victoria, and he took no risk when he promised their opponents a very uneasy time in every constituency of Victoria at the coming general election.

The next plan, announced with an openness that would have been inconceivable in the 1950s, was:[5]

"The work before the Catholic Laborites is to capture the Labor machine"

The work before the Catholic Laborites is to capture the Labor machine.

Enemies of those manoeuvrings naturally began to feel very uneasy indeed. They organized in response, and Labor's Central Executive determined to expel from the Political Labor Council (the official name of the Party organization) all pressure groups attempting to seize control of it from the inside:

. . . that the Australian Catholic Federation, Licensed Victuallers' Association, Loyal Orange Lodge, and Women's Political Association are Political Associations within the meaning of Rule 38 (g) and members of such Organizations cannot continue membership of the P.L.C.[6]

The Labor conference of 1915 backed the executive and the Catholic Federation subgroup was roundly defeated. Archbishops Carr and Mannix addressed a large meeting at Melbourne Town Hall on 28 April, to express anger at this rebuff by their natural political allies. Mannix threatened Labor with the turning of the Catholic vote against them:[7]

Catholics had not met that night to widen the breach between those who ought to be their friends and allies . . . Catholics did not want war either in State politics or in Federal politics, but they had met that night to tell all whom it might concern that if any State party made war upon them they would leave no stone unturned to defeat that party everywhere it showed itself. If Federal politicians thought that they stood upon neutral ground, he thought that Catholics would teach them that they were very much mistaken . . .

If the next Labor Conference left Catholics where they were today, he would not be one to hold back those who wanted an open and straight fight with the Labor Party.

This attack of the Labor Conference was not upon the Catholic Federation, but upon the Catholic Church, and upon every loyal Catholic in Victoria. The Catholic Church was an organization which in the past whenever religion was threatened or conscience violated had supported, and, if need be, had selected, candidates for Parliament, and he could tell the Political Labor Conference that in similar circumstances in the future it would do the same thing again.

Fighting words, but passions soon cooled. Catholics needed Labor and Labor needed its Catholic members. A relatively innocuous Catholic Workers' Association within the Labor Party was formed to "educate" party members in the justice of Catholic claims concerning education. The C.W.A. was accepted by the next Labor conference as an allowed organization. But the aggressive campaign for state aid had completely failed.

Scullin: state aid as electoral poison

Many Catholics in the Labor movement feared that aggressive single-issue politics in the style of Mannix would split Labor and place in jeopardy all the broader gains that Labor had made and might make in the future. Their reasoning is explained by James Scullin, who was fifteen years later to be Australia's first Catholic Prime Minister. Scullin, editor of the *Evening Echo* in Ballarat, had joined a study group on the Catholic social justice thought of the papal encyclical *Rerum Novarum*,[8] and remained enthusiastic about those ideas, but opposed the separatism of the Catholic Federation:[9]

> . . . At no time have I disguised my opposition to making questions of religious controversy party political matters. The Labour movement has been developed by men and women who, having a common economic faith in general principles, have agreed to a platform designed to give legislative expression to those principles. The Labour conference represents the Labour organizations, and delegates have the responsibility of seeing that a majority does not impose on the minority measures which they are fundamentally opposed to.
>
> For nearly twenty years I have assisted to strengthen the growth of the Labour movement, and the members have at all times, whilst not denying religion, steadfastly refused to allow subjects of religious controversy to become part of the platform. When the Orange lodges sought to have convents inspected and brought under factory

laws,† they were repulsed by the Labour party. When the Scripture Campaign Council endeavoured to graft religious instruction on the State system of education, the Labour party answered by upholding secular education as a plank of the platform. That attitude was approved then by all Catholics, clerical and lay, and the non-Catholic Labourites who comprise the majority of our movement were taunted with being "dragged at the heels of Rome."

It is true that the Catholic educational claims are financial, but unfortunately, they were so urged as to make it impossible to separate them from religious controversy, and would undoubtedly divide men and women who are otherwise agreed on economic principles which have been a greater gain to Catholic workers than twenty grants such as are being asked for would be.

". . . I could not . . . vote for the inclusion of a plank in the platform which would entirely disrupt the Labour movement . . ."

I am a strong believer in religious education, and will continue to support our Catholic schools, but I could not, having in mind my responsibility as a delegate of Catholic and non-Catholic workers, vote for the inclusion of a plank in the platform which would entirely disrupt the Labour movement, while the Catholic claims would be no nearer realization, but would be further off than ever. Those who seek, by jaundiced sneers, to question my sincerity as a Catholic, I think I can afford to treat with silent contempt. My life and actions are the test of that. – Yours, etc,

J H SCULLIN

Ballarat, May 8

Decades later, Mannix was to preside at Scullin's funeral. The panegyric did not neglect to mention the foundation of Scullin's thought in *Rerum Novarum*.[10]

---

† Reference is to the "Magdalen laundries" in convents which competed with commercial laundries using unpaid labour; see James Franklin, Convent slave laundries? Magdalen asylums in Australia, *Journal of the Australian Catholic Historical Society* 34 (2013), 70-90.

1. Celia Hamilton, Catholic interests and the Labor Party: Organized catholic action in Victoria and New South Wales, 1910-1916, *Historical Studies* 9 (1959), 62-73; Patrick Morgan, Santamaria and the organised Catholic vote, *Quadrant* 56 (10) (Oct 2012), 47-49.
2. Quoted in Hamilton, p. 66.
3. *Argus*, 27 October 1914, p. 8.
4. *Advocate*, 14 Feb 1914; Hamilton, p. 67.
5. *Advocate*, 5 Dec 1914; Hamilton, p. 68.
6. Hamilton, p. 68.
7. *Catholic Press*, 6 May 1915; Hamilton, p. 69.
8. Colin H. Jory, *The Campion Society and Catholic Militancy in Australia 1929-1939*, pp. 13-14 and n. 22; *Tribune*, 8 May 1941, p. 1
9. *Advocate*, 13 May 1915, p. 23. An editorial in the same issue vigorously attacks Scullin.
10. Scullin's Funeral – Thousands Watch, *Sunday Herald*, 1/2/1953, http://trove.nla.gov.au/ndp/del/article/18516210

Chapter 9: Social justice and political action

There is probably no aspect of Catholic theory as poorly understood by Protestants and other outsiders as its teaching on "social justice". Most Catholics too have either ignored it or, like Tony Abbott, dismissed talk of social justice as mostly just "socialism masquerading as justice".[1] Yet it is one of the most significant and unique contributions of Catholicism to modern thought. Mannix showed an enthusiasm for it, an enthusiasm not always evident in his views on some other Catholic doctrines. He shared that commitment with some of his closest and most influential political associates, Scullin, Calwell and Santamaria.

The social justice tradition is an aspect of the Catholic natural law tradition of ethics, itself poorly understood in general. On that view, ethics is not fundamentally about rules, or divine commands, or the greatest happiness of the greatest number, or habits ingrained by evolution and custom. It is about the irreducible worth of persons – the irreducible equal worth of persons – and what follows from that. Because a human being is of immense value, a human death is a tragedy. That is in contrast to the explosion of a lifeless galaxy, which is just a firework. So humans have a right to life and (to put the same thing from the point of view of others) murder is prohibited. Because humans have a particular nature, their rights and duties are of particular kinds. For example, because they are intellectual beings, knowledge is central to a full human life, which is to say they have a right to education.

This objective view of ethics applies not just to personal morality, the actions of individual persons. It extends to social, economic and political systems, which are human creations for the purpose of serving the common human good. Humans are essentially social beings in a certain way, and it follows that certain ways of organising society are ethical and others not. So at least the most general features of economic and political organisation are conceived to be, not matters of "policy" to be decided by democratic political processes, but absolutely right and wrong as much as murder is wrong and charity right.

As industrialisation pushed generations of men into poorly-paid, dirty and dangerous assembly line work, conflict arose between capitalism and revolutionary socialism. Marxism advocated violent overthrow of the system, while *laissez faire* capitalism argued that any interference with economic forces would make things worse. In contrast to both sides of the conflict, Leo XIII's 1891 encyclical *Rerum Novarum* laid out a cooperative vision of society that respected the rights of workers but also the right to private property. A society should consist of many organizations of different sizes and purposes cooperating in the context of an acceptance of moral rules. Families, trade unions, guilds, businesses, clubs and the state should pursue their own aims, respecting each other's spheres of action and cooperating to build a just society.[2]

In Australia, one thesis of *Rerum Novarum* in particular struck a chord – its teaching on the right to a minimum wage, enough to support a "frugal and well-behaved wage-earner". The phrase was taken over in the 1907 Harvester judgement, which laid down a basic wage "enough to support the wage earner in reasonable and frugal comfort".[3] Debate continues on the economic effects of the basic wage, but it became an essential part of the "Australian settlement", ensuring that workers gained a share of increased productivity.[4]

The ideology of the Australian Labor Party had certain synergies with the ideas of *Rerum Novarum*. It was against revolution in the cause of socialism – drawing Lenin's ire, as he understood the competition for the workers' allegiance that would arise if workers began to achieve gains by working within the system.[5] Initially, Labor's support for nationalisation of industries posed a problem of incompatibility with the popes' defence of the right to private property.[6] That problem was solved with the party's 1921 adoption of the "Blackburn interpretation" of the socialist objective, which stated that instruments of production would not be socialised if they were used "in a socially useful manner and without exploitation". Mannix stated that the Blackburn interpretation was "exactly what the bishops in their pamphlet [*Socialisation*] have set out."[7] The way was free for Catholic men of the working class to join – sometimes dominate – the Labor Party.[8]

"Hard-headed" ideologues of both Left and Right regarded it as ludicrously naïve to address the urgent problems of capitalism, labour and depression by forming study groups to discuss a papal encyclical. Nevertheless, Catholics interested in political and economic questions who took their faith seriously maintained interest in Church social teaching.[9] A few took it very seriously indeed, and, as we will see, Scullin, Calwell and Santamaria, in different ways, saw their work as advancing the Catholic understanding of social justice.

Political developments in the later twentieth century, from the social engineering of Chifley's government to the Hawke Government's Accord and present-day "regulated capitalism" or "market socialism"[10] are closer to Leo XIII's vision of a cooperative society than they are to either of the extreme nineteenth-century options of revolutionary socialism and *laissez faire* capitalism.[11]

The close fellowship between the Church and the workers' cause had important consequence for both Australian Catholicism and for politics. The situation was entirely different from countries like France, where the Church became identified with monarchism and reaction and lost the support of the working class.[12] That was not going to happen in Australia, where the Church *was* the working class, or a significant part of it. There was an element of self-interest in the Vatican's comment in 1918, mentioned in chapter 6 above, that Mannix's great influence with the working classes stood in the way of action against him. There were not many Catholic archbishops in the early twentieth century who could draw tens of thousands of cheering workers.

THE CHURCH AND THE WORKERS

Mannix's 'Catholic principles' speech of November 1917, after dealing with strictly religious issues, went on to address social issues:[13]

... The Church which protects the woman is also, and for a like reason, the Church of the toilers and of the poor. (Applause.)

"The Church stands, first of all, for the worker's right to a living wage"

The Church stands, first of all, for the worker's right to a living wage. (Applause.) Leo XIII seems to have opened the eyes of the world when he boldly proclaimed, not so many years ago, that the workman had a right to a living wage – a first claim on the wealth that he produced. (Applause.) And, of course, his right to a living wage gives him a right to such a share of the wealth he produces as will enable him to bring up his family in decent surroundings and in reasonable comfort. All this the Pope said, was due, not merely by reason of the wealth produced, but also by reason of what is due to man's nature. Man has a right to live upon the earth, and it is by his labour that this right is exercised. Now, though I feel that I am treading on ground which many call dangerous, I am convinced that the principle on which Pope Leo XIII relied has a wider application than it sometimes receives. It seems evident to me that, on the Pope's principles, the Government is strictly bound to see that industry is organised so that those who are willing to work will find work, or, failing to find it, will have a right to decent sustenance. (Applause.)

To my mind, Governments are bound to provide against unemployment so far as may be, and then to provide for the unemployed. (Applause.) It is very poor consolation to tell a man that when employed he has a right to a living wage, if at the same time he is starving for want of work. (Applause.)

> *". . . Governments are bound to provide against unemployment . . ."*

If as Pope Leo says, the inherent dignity of man's nature entitles him to a living wage when he is at work, the same requirement of his nature should imperatively demand for him a decent sustenance when he is willing to undertake, but, through no fault of his own, is unable to find work. (Applause.) If the right to work and the right to support during unemployment were recognised, as I think they ought to be recognised, I promise you that Governments and capitalists would try to find work for all. (Laughter and applause.) I know that people will say that I am playing fast and loose with the rights of property. Of course, I am putting upon the State, and upon society, duties which they are naturally reluctant to undertake. But the problem of unemployment has never been frankly faced, and it once and for all must be faced, and with the conviction that a man's life is more sacred than the rights of property. (Loud applause.) Of course, we shall be told – it is the old story – economic society would go to pieces. (Laughter and applause.) Yet those who stand aghast at the demands of the worker – we know it is now to our cost – those same people are able to find untold millions in order to wage war in Europe. (Applause.) Heaven and earth would have been moved and all the devices of Parliament exhausted before an hundredth part of that expenditure would have gone to improve the lot of the poor man who labours for a living. (Loud applause.) When the war is over, will the workman, who has had his eyes opened, and has seen what has happened, be satisfied with the excuse that money cannot be found – that the old system must go on?

Voices: No! (Applause.)

The Archbishop: I do not think he will. (Applause.) I believe that great changes will come as a result of the war, and as a result of the awakening that has come to a great many of us – myself amongst that number. (Applause.) It is true that the condition of the workers has been improved in some respects – old age pensions are provided and the doles are given in times of accidents and sickness. But all these benefits come from the fund – from the wealth – which the worker has himself produced. It only shows how distorted is our view of economic relations, if we claim credit for giving the worker what is really his due. (Applause.) These things are his right, and it is really no credit to the State to have provided them. (Applause.) Even now the worker is getting less than he is entitled to, and much less, probably, than he will insist on having himself before many years are over. (Loud applause.) Doubtless, even in the very best form of society, there will be inequalities, hardships, suffering. But that is no reason for leaving things as they are, for saying that the workers have no grievance; that they have nothing to complain of; that they ought to be patient; and that their religious guides should keep them quiet in this world, and offer them a great reward in the other. (Laughter and applause.) When I read what is sometimes written by the capitalist press, and when I read between the lines, as I always try to do, I seem to discover that we have many who value religion mainly – perhaps solely – for keeping the proletariat quiet. (Applause.) That is the religion they believe in (Applause.) They believe that religion is a good thing for the poor man because it will help to keep him quiet. Even if he were quiet, we would not be absolved for giving him what is justly his due.

> *". . . we have many who value religion mainly . . . for keeping the proletariat quiet"*

Mannix recognised that if the existing system did not protect the workers, they would be tempted to try another:[14]

It was a fundamental principle, recognised in Australia, at all events, that men had a right to a living wage. The Government accepted and enforced that principle. But it was a barren principle if the Government did not see men had a chance of working for their living . . .

> *"What wonder if idle, starving men find themselves driven into socialism?"*

It was small consolation to 800 unemployed carpenters to tell them we must economise and that we must win the war . . . But why were all the economies to be at the expense of the poor and the working man? The man who had five thousand a year was never displaced . . . No; if one thousand pounds or one million pounds had to be saved, it was always done by throwing the poor men, in tens, and in thousands, out of employment. Within the past twelve months, well-paid officials had their salaries increased, while poor working men had been turned out idle in hundreds. What wonder if idle, starving men find themselves driven into socialism?

Mannix wrote in his foreword to the first issue of a new Catholic monthly *Australia* in 1917, approving workers' control of industry:[15]

'The War had made men and women think much and think hard: They would not cease thinking when the war was over. They would not be satisfied to be cogs in a wheel. More and more they would try to control the industries in which they were engaged. It would be hard to convince them or convince anyone that they were not entitled to industrial control as they were to political power. The people were just now in the temper to assert themselves – politically, socially and industrially. And if they were to move along safe lines it was never more necessary than it was now that the public mind should be leavened by Catholic principles.

Responding to the Seamen's Strike in 1919, he queried whether:[16]

. . . any of the sneering critics would undertake to balance the family budget on the strikers' wages and at the present cost of living: Would they live in the conditions, in the holds, or in the slums, on sea or land, in which the strikers had been living? If they themselves were the workers, would they patiently bear their lot in the face of all that was said about the profiteers, and especially about the shipping interests? People's sympathy was asked for the man who, owing to the strike, had to change his hour of rising or be content with a cold breakfast! What about the women and children who had to be thankful if they had any kind of breakfast, hot or cold? The sooner people understood that the worker must get, not just a living wage, but a fair share of the wealth he produced, the better.

Mannix (centre), with some workers, Broken Hill, 1922[17]

Capitalism and Depression

Less was heard from Mannix on the workers during the 1920s, as he spent more effort on Irish affairs. But with the onset of the Depression, the issues resurfaced. He told the Annual Conference of the Hibernian Society in October 1931:[18]

All over the world, people were experiencing a very anxious time: They were only now beginning to realise how wise Pope Leo XIII was when he told the world, about forty years ago, that if radical change were not made in society, much trouble, and even revolution, might have to be faced. There was more unemployment in the world than had ever existed before, and people were worse off than when slavery existed. Slave owners had to feed, clothe and look after those subject to them, but many who called themselves free men today had scarcely anybody to look after them. Until the unemployment problem was solved, the world would never be at rest.

By 1933, the danger of the workers turning to Communism was more acute. The failure of capitalism made that inevitable:[19]

One could well understand how people were driven to extremes in times like the present. Millions of men and women in all lands were actually starving while the world was full of wealth.

> *"The first line of defence against Communism and Socialism was to acknowledge humbly and sorrowfully that the system under which they were living had been a complete failure . . ."*

The first line of defence against Communism and Socialism was to acknowledge humbly and sorrowfully that the system under which they were living had been a complete failure . . . People who were genuinely alarmed about Communism and Socialism should first put their own house in order . . .

Countries that prided themselves on being most progressive, such as Germany, England and the United states had been badly affected by the depression... This was due to the capitalistic system, which concentrated the wealth in the hands of the few. His Holiness Pope Leo XIII and his successors had pointed out that concentration of wealth in the hands of the few left the multitude without the wherewithal to pay for the things that could be produced . . .

Speaking in Newcastle in 1938 – now accompanied by Santamaria – he again condemned the failure of unrestricted capitalism, even though by this time the problem of Communism was moving to centre stage:[20]

Catholic Attitude to Social Justice
ARCHBISHOP MANNIX SPEAKS
NEWCASTLE, Thursday.

Archbishop Mannix said that it was not a question of production in the world, but of distribution of the wealth. America, of all places in the world, where unrestricted capitalism could be expected to succeed, had been dragged down by unrestricted capitalism. 'The most wealthy States and the States of great industrial development are the places that have suffered most,' he continued, 'If it fails there, where can it succeed? Nowhere.'

No logic in basic wage

Archbishop Mannix added that one of the national necessities was child endowment. Australia claimed to be advanced in regard to social legislation, yet it deliberately laid down a basic wage which was intended only for a man and his wife and two children. There was no logic in it. Or rather, there was logic – abominable logic.

'You get the benefits of the State legislation if you have two children, but if you have more we will not help you. God help you. That is the attitude,' he added.

'I am old enough to remember when Pope Leo XIII was regarded by many people as a socialist or Communist of the time because he told us that human labour was not merely a commodity to be bargained for, but that human dignity had to be considered, and that a man was entitled to a living wage for himself and his family.

'It is the big financial experts of the world who control the money. These are the people to whom the Pope has addressed his most caustic remarks, and these are the people who will have to release their grip of the world.'

Mr. B. A. Santamaria, M.A., LL.D., proposing a vote of thanks, said that the three requirements for social justice in Australia were redistribution of income, redistribution of property, and the installation of vocational groups as the controlling force in industry.

The problem of credit would not be solved in Australia inside 10 years, and reform could not wait so long. An increase in the basic wage and the institution by the Commonwealth of a national system of child endowment was necessary. The motive force of Catholic action was not primarily against Communism, but against social injustice. The position of Communism was incidental and secondary. There was only a thin line between Capitalism and Communism.

"The motive force of Catholic action was not primarily against Communism, but against social injustice"

Women

At the conclusion of one of a series of adult education lectures in 1917, Archbishop Mannix spoke after a lecture titled "Woman and the state", which was presented by a woman guest lecturer:[21]

Mannix indicated his agreement with the view that women should play more active political roles in the life of the country:

> "... *women have a very great work to do, not merely in the home, but also, in the conduct of public affairs* ..."

... women have a very great work to do, not merely in the home, but also, in the conduct of public affairs ... It is only by taking her proper place in every public movement that she can make her own home – and the homes of other women – what these homes ought to be.

In his 'Catholic principles' speech, Mannix connected the Church's support for women with its protection of the weak and its opposition to divorce:[22]

... circumstances make her always and everywhere the Church of the weak against the strong. (Applause.) Therefore, it is as we learned during the course of the lectures, that the church has always been the guardian and the champion of the rights of women. (Applause.)

Man has been inclined to make woman his slave, or his plaything and his toy, but the Church extends her protecting hand over women. (Applause.) She has always endeavoured to uphold the dignity of women, of the wife and the mother, and she has always stood for the sanctity and purity of the home. (Applause.) To the world the Church may seem to have been too rigid and unbending in her view of marriages and divorce, or the breaking of the marriage bond. (Applause.) But she has her commission from Christ, and it is written – "What God has joined, let no man put asunder." (Applause.) The Church takes her stand on that and she is true to principle. It might sometimes have seemed worldly wisdom if she could change her principles, as some persons change their minds. (Laughter.) Take the classic case of Henry VIII. If the Catholic Church has been an opportunist Church; if she had done what other religious bodies have sometimes done, and bowed her head to the storm, she might have managed in some way to give a bill of divorce to that much-married individual. (Laughter and applause.) If she had done so, England might never have been separated from the Holy See. (Applause.) But the Catholic Church did not swerve from her duty, though she knew full well that resistance to Henry probably meant a break with the English nation. (Applause.) The years have gone by, but the Church does not repent; rather we glory in her unflinching fidelity to principles. (Applause.)

> "*Man has been inclined to make woman his slave, or his plaything and his toy* ..."

The education of women was of concern, including university education:[23]

Archbishop Mannix, who presided, on Monday, formally declared open the girls' hostel provided by the guild in Gore-street, Fitzroy, and expressed the hope that it would only be the forerunner of many such hostels. (Applause.) Commenting on the papers discussed, and the resolutions passed, Dr. Mannix said he agreed that many women worked under inferior and unhealthy conditions, and for a very inadequate wage. In respect of education, women had not been catered for in the same manner as had the men, and he thought they should be. (Applause.) The £1000 that he had received from a leading Catholic in Melbourne was given to him as a protest against the malicious and unprovoked attacks made upon him by various people in different grades of society. Thus the attacks in question had not been without some good effect. (Laughter and applause.) He proposed to hand this £1000 over to the Catholic University College committee for the benefit of Catholic women's education, to be used in the form of scholarships, or in another form the committee and himself might decide. If scholarships were decided upon, he would suggest that they should be called the 'Argus' scholarships. (Loud laughter and applause.)

The "Demon drink"

As he had done at Maynooth, Mannix continued to condemn the evils of drink.[24]

In Australia, as in other lands, the present war has turned a strong light upon the evils of which the abuse of intoxicating drink is the cause. Reckless, appalling expenditure in drink, at a time when the people are told that the last shilling may be needed for national defence; shortage of war munitions, owing to drink, at a time when every shell counts; the degradation of drink, and the deterioration of our soldiers at a time when we are told that it is every man's duty to give his best for the defence of his country - these things are opening our eyes to the tragic reality and extent of the drink evil, here and elsewhere. We should not have needed so drastic a lesson. The degradation and wastage were going on under our eyes before the war began, and when the war is over they will still go on, if we relapse into apathy or listen to those who counsel remedies that are futile.

Colonialism and Aborigines

In 1922, Mannix addressed colonialism and the fate of the indigenous inhabitants of colonial possessions:[25]

Some nations boast of their great civilising influences in the outposts of the world. How did some of these nations acquire their colonial possessions and what use have they made of them? What has been the lot of the original inhabitants, the previous owners of these colonial possessions? In many cases these races of people were civilised out of existence. Indeed we do not have to go far from Australia for an example.

> *"How did some of these nations acquire their colonial possessions and what use have they made of them? What has been the lot of the original inhabitants . . .?"*

In 1933, Mannix joined protests against the proposed sending of an expedition to Arnhem Land in search of the "Caledon Bay blacks" who had murdered some whites. The expedition appeared to have the character of a punitive expedition to conduct reprisals, though the government denied that was the case.[26] The *West Australian* reported:[2]

OBJECTION TO PUNITIVE FORCE: CHURCH AND TRADES HALL OPINIONS.

The Roman Catholic Archbishop of Melbourne (Dr. Mannix) has sent the following telegram [sent on 5 September 1933] to the Prime Minister (Mr. Lyons) concerning the Caledon Bay blacks.

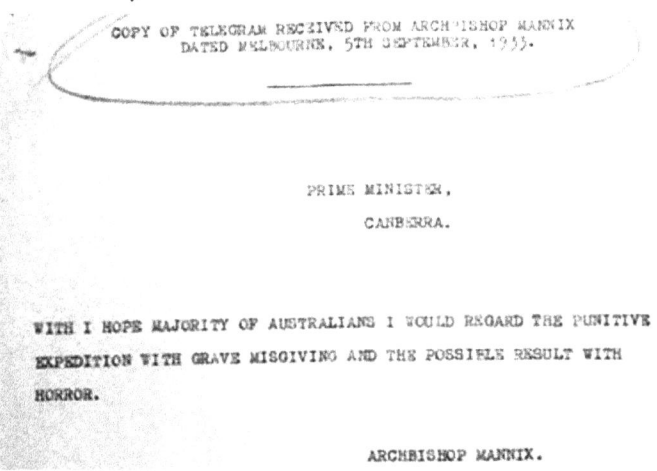

"With, as I hope, the majority of Australians, I would regard the proposed punitive expedition with grave misgiving and its possible results with horror."

> *"... I would regard the proposed punitive expedition with grave misgiving and its possible results with horror"*

The protests, which came from many sources, were successful and the expedition was not sent.

In 1940, Mannix took the opportunity on Social Justice Sunday to remind Catholics that justice applied to Aboriginal Australians too:[28]

I wonder if anybody else . . . thought that we owed something in the matter of social justice to the Aborigines of Australia. I believe in social justice, but I believe in it all round. I do know that the Aborigines of Australia would be able to furnish a very strong indictment against the present rulers and inhabitants of Australia and those who have gone before us. I hope that if social justice ever comes, that it will reach them as it reaches the rest of us . . .

ARCHBISHOP FEARS FOR SAFETY OF ABORIGINES

The fear that bomb experiments might harm aborigines in the Kimberley areas was expressed by Archbishop Mannix when he opened a fete at the Pallottine Missionary College, Kew, on Saturday.

The aborigines were not likely to take kindly to the destruction of their old haunts, he said. The Government should be careful with the experiments, and not remove natives from their old roaming ground, where apparently they found happiness and contentment.

Aborigines were afflicted with original sin; they were not the only ones:[29]

"White people in Australia had committed the original sin against the aborigines," Archbishop Mannix said at a fete in the Pallottine College grounds Kew on Saturday afternoon. The original sin he was afraid had not yet been blotted out. The Pallottine Fathers were doing their part to bring redemption to us from our original sin which had brought suffering to the black people. The Pallottine Fathers needed support in their missionary work at Kimberley (WA).

In 1946, concerns began about bomb tests in the remote outback and their effect on the inhabitants:[30]

JEWS

In March 1939, Mannix appealed on behalf of Jewish refugees fleeing Hitler's tyranny:[31]

The unfortunate Jews were hunted post and pillar out of every country of Europe. Many of them were coming here, although some people did not seem to offer them a welcome.

These people should ask themselves, what was to become of those unfortunate wanderers? It was not the Christian spirit to have distrust and an inborn hatred of the Jews. The founder of the Christian religion Himself was a Jew, and His Mother was a Jewish maiden. People

"It was not the Christian spirit to have distrust and an inborn hatred of the Jews . . ."

should remember these things when they were inclined to be hard upon the Jews, and when, perhaps, they were not as sympathetic with them in their sufferings as they ought to be as Christians. All of them were children of the One Eternal Father, whether they were Jews or Christians, Catholics or Protestants. There was no distinction. They should all give a helping hand to those who were afflicted and those who were heavily burdened. This was their duty as Christians.

Communism

The political issue that came to define the older Mannix was anti-Communism. In the mid-century, Catholics in Australia were known for the implacability of their hostility to Communism. Where many on the left preferred to ignore the news from Russia of famines and show trials, and others were apathetic about such a distant country, Catholics had an international network of information about Stalinist horrors. Mannix was in the lead from an early stage. Typical is his 1931 address at the annual Communion breakfast of the Catholic Young Men's Society:[32]

COMMUNISM AND SLAVERY.
EXAMPLE OF RUSSIA.
ADDRESS BY DR. MANNIX.

The Catholic Church was conservative in everything that was good, Dr Mannix said, but it is progressive and had always thrown its influence on the side of the working man. While the Church stood for the rights and progress of the workmen of Australia it was fundamentally and necessarily opposed to many of the doctrines that were being preached not so much by Australians as by aliens coming into the country. If those people should succeed it would not be good for Australia and if they were to be defeated it would be by the Catholic men. He knew that those preaching revolutionary doctrines in Australia formed a real hotbed of communism and Communistic ideas. The failures of capitalism had been great but the failures of communism would be infinitely worse. Centuries ago slavery was practically abolished but the worst slavery the world ever saw was in Russia today. A system to be successful must increase the production of the world's resources, and should distribute them to the benefit of humanity. Production of the world had increased under the capitalistic system, which, however, had failed to distribute the wealth to the benefit of humanity. There was more unemployment in the world now than had ever existed before, and people were worse off than when slavery existed. Slave-owners fed, clothed and housed their slaves and looked after them, but how many people who called themselves freemen had scarcely anybody to look after them. Until unemployment problems were solved the world would never be at rest. He did not think it would be solved along communistic or socialistic lines. The Federal and State Governments deserved credit for their efforts to steer a middle course between the different parties. He sincerely trusted that members of the society would give generous aid and intellectual support to those who were trying to do the best for Australia. They should not be led away by foolish propaganda. Archbishop Mannix said that he trusted that the society would extend its good work and its beneficence over the whole Commonwealth.

THE INTERVIEW

Archbishop Mannix was interviewed on 29 December 1961 in his study at *Raheen* by Gerald Lyons.[33]

Gerald Lyons: When did you first become aware of the danger of Communism in Australia?

Archbishop Mannix: In the 'forties. Of course, it was public knowledge that Communism was winning all round the world, and that without firing a shot. They were piling up great armaments but they didn't have to use them. Just by infiltration and propaganda they were succeeding all round the world. They conquered a great part of Europe. They were invading Asia, Africa and, later on, even South America, and all round the world they seemed to me to be achieving all that they wanted without going to war.

GL: Did you see this onward march of Communism in the world and Communist influence in politics and trade unions in this country, in particular, as more serious than the issue of conscription and Irish independence?

AM: The most serious problem that I had to face in 100 years of my long life.

GL: There's a Catholic organization which was set up in 1941, I understand, to fight Communism in the Australian Labour Party, in the Trade Unions, which I'll call "The Movement". Now was the idea of "The Movement" originally yours?

AM: No, I don't claim that it was originally mine, but when it originated I was in favour of it because in Australia the labour unions are very important. They really control the Labour Party. They may be in opposition now but next day they may be in power. In Australia, therefore, the activities of Communism are extremely important because they were so successful in winning to their cause the labour unions, and by winning the labour unions they were on the way to winning the Australian Government some time.

The Spanish Civil War, 1936

Mannix, like most Catholics, was an enthusiastic supporter of Franco. An address in Adelaide on 7 November, 1936 explains why.[34]

'We are all shocked at the events that have happened in the Old World. In Spain there is to-day a stand-up fight between God and Satan, between Communism and Christianity. In times like ours, the mettle of young men is being tested. We doubt if these things can happen here, but we do not know. Twenty years ago, an Archbishop could have stood up in Spain and declared that the things that happened in Mexico and Russia would not disgrace the fair name of Spain. But the arm of Russia was long. It reached to every corner of Europe. In Russia it was prophesied that Spain would be the first to follow Russia's example. But when the issues were knit in Spain, we found that the press of Australia and of the British Empire, with some notable exceptions, took the side of Satan and Communism in Spain, and endeavoured to poison your minds and my mind. But the Christian Brothers' teaching was not in vain and you, gentlemen, had the intelligence to know from the beginning what everyone knows now.

'God be thanked for it, things are coming right in Spain. In spite of the press of Australia, the Catholic people have sound views. Their hearts beat always in sympathy with the Catholic people of Spain. If the so-called rebels in Spain had not said to the Communists:

"Thus far shalt thou go and no farther," the Catholic Faith would have been wiped out in Spain. And if Spain had been captured by the Communists, I should not have liked to depend upon France. Nor could we have depended on Britain. We are proud of our achievements in the British Empire, but in Britain there are Communist cells. If Spain goes down, then God help Europe. But God stands by His own, and the Church that was founded on the Rock of Peter is not going to be shattered in Spain.'

Immorality of the Atomic Bomb

Speaking to the Holy Name Society in South Melbourne on 8 September 1945, a month after the atomic bombs on Hiroshima and Nagasaki, Archbishop Mannix condemned in general the atrocities of the war, but reserved a special word of condemnation for the use of atomic warfare:[35]

We are hearing a great deal of the horrors perpetrated in the German and Japanese concentration camps, where cruelty and ruthlessness, almost unbelievable, are reported to have occurred. But the Allies ended the war with the Atomic Bomb.

When all is said and done, there is nothing more ruthless, or nothing more indefen-

> "... there is nothing more ruthless, or nothing more indefensible than the Atomic Bomb directed against non-combatants, women and children"

sible than the Atomic Bomb directed against non-combatants, women and children. People are discussing whether or not it was lawful to make use of the Atomic Bomb. But surely the question is not new. The very same problem we had to face all through the war. First it was Germany bombing the women and children in Coventry, and then there was the bombing by the Allies of similar places in Germany. It was the same problem of indiscriminate bombing all through. All such bombing, no matter by whom, is indefensible and immoral. For me, the Atomic Bomb does not raise any new moral problems. It merely means that the immorality that was already practised on a small scale has assumed colossal proportions in the use of the Atomic Bomb. The only hope is that those who have the secret of the bomb may be able to keep their secret. I do not think they can. Let us hope, therefore that some means may be discovered by which war, or at least the Atomic Bomb, would be outlawed for the future ...

In the midst of the euphoria at the end of the War, Mannix shared with other anti-Communists grave fears at the advance of Stalin's empire in Eastern Europe and potentially in East Asia:

We went into the awful, colossal world conflict for the purpose of freeing a little nation, and now there are more little nations under the heel of a dominant power than there were when the war began. The whole of Eastern Europe and I do not know how much of Asia, are under foreign domination. The worst of it is that, after all our sacrifices, America, England, and the Dominions, do not seem to be able to stay the domination now threatening. We went into the war because appeasement had failed. For too long we were appeasing Germany. But the end of the war finds us appeasing, not Germany, but another power that is perhaps more powerful, more threatening, and, maybe more ruthless than Germany would have been ...

> "... the end of the war finds us appeasing, not Germany, but another power that is perhaps more powerful, more threatening, and, maybe more ruthless than Germany ..."

THEORY OF DEMOCRACY

In 1946 Archbishop Mannix wrote a foreword to *Democracy in Australia: an essay in organic reconstruction*, by Fr James Murtagh. Mannix was concerned about maintaining the balance between the authority of the rulers and the liberty of the subjects.[36]

The author of this slender, but worth-while, book sets out to try and reconcile man's liberty with State authority, especially with a view to Australian conditions. There has been so much talk about democracy in this totalitarian age, and so much patriotic praise lavished upon it, that many of us, perhaps, are ready to believe without question that the world-wide and immediate growth of democracy is the solution, and the only solution, of all the world's problems. Some of us may even hold that democracy, or that form of it that appeals to us, should be forced upon unwilling and unready nations, for their own good, of course, and the good of mankind.

Now, anyone who takes up this book expecting to find in it an attempt to prove that democracy, as Australia knows it, is the best of all forms of government and that, because it suits Australia, it should be good enough for all other nations, whatever their temperament, traditions, education or culture, will be disappointed. The author is much more temperate and modest. He assumes that for good or ill – and he thinks it is for good – Australia is committed to the democratic form of government that is, the government of the people, by the people, and for the people. Not being an anarchist, he takes it for granted that men living in society must submit to authority and that, if authority is to be logically defensible and stable, it must ultimately come from God. He then goes on to give an adequate account of the origin and development of civil authority in the democratic State and of how, in his view, it might be best exercised in existing Australian conditions.

Of course, God could have done in mundane affairs what He has done in the spiritual order. He might have given us an unerring guide in politics, in economics, in all the sciences, including the science of government. That would have settled many problems that have vexed the politicians and the statesmen of the world. But even then, I suppose, there would have been rebels or revolutionaries or reformers. At all events, outside of religion, God has given us no such reliable guidance. Questions of finance or of economics may be of vital importance, but we are left to solve them as best we can. And so, in the science of government, men have to work out their problems by study and effort and trial and error. Different ages and different nations have tackled the problems of government in different ways. But everywhere and always the task of reconciling authority and liberty had to be faced and we are still looking for a perfect balance. To put this vital problem in its proper perspective in relation to Australia and to help in its solution is the aim of this book. The author, of course, insists that the promotion of the common good, temporal and eternal, is really the sole reason for the existence of all governments, democratic or other, and should therefore be the dominant motive in every exercise of their authority. He gives much needed warning that governments should not trench upon the rights of the family or the Church, nor take away from subordinate bodies those activities that can be efficiently looked after by them.

> "... the recognition of functional groups as the best means of relieving the central government of a mass of detailed work with which it is incompetent to deal..."

He makes a strong plea – and this will prove the most interesting part of his book – for the recognition of functional groups as the best means of relieving the central government of a mass of detailed work with which it is incompetent to deal; of promoting the common good of the citizens: and of maintaining the balance between the authority of the rulers and the liberty of the subjects.

The author is deeply interested in what he fittingly calls the "floating vote," which is the nightmare of politicians in every election campaign. He suggests that, if the political parties were more expert, they should be able to capture this floating vote and use it for their own political purposes. But, for my part, I trust it will always remain the riddle that it is. For I am a democrat; and I believe that this perplexing, vexatious vote is and should remain the safety valve of democracy.

† D. MANNIX

St. Patrick's Cathedral

THE AUSTRALIAN COMMONWEALTH AND STATES RIGHTS

In May, 1954, an article appeared under Mannix's name on the separation of powers between the states and the commonwealth. It purports to deduce the answer – favouring the states – from the social justice principles of the papal encyclicals, in particular the anti-centralist principle of "subsidiarity" according to which decisions should be taken by the lowest, most local body possible.

The doubtful validity of deducing such a detailed political matter from such general principles lay behind the circumstances of the article's appearance. It had been intended as the bishops' annual social justice statement and was drafted as usual by B. A. Santamaria in consultation with Mannix. But enough bishops objected and it was never published as such. Mannix allowed his name to appear as author.[37] We print some extracts:[38]

The Australian Commonwealth and The States
THE MOST REV. D. MANNIX

FOR obvious reasons the rival parties in the present Federal election will not concern themselves with the division of power between the Commonwealth and the States. And yet that is more fundamental and, in the long view, more important than any of the questions so hotly debated in the policy speeches and at the election platforms. The principle underlying the relations between the Commonwealth and the States was treated at length by Pope Pius XI in his Encyclical, Quadragesimo Anno, in which he teaches that what he calls the principle of "subsidiary function" cannot be safely set aside.

In the same Encyclical, the principle of *"subsidiary function" was defined in the following words:*

> Just as it is gravely wrong to take from individuals what they can accomplish by their own initiative and industry, so also *it is an injustice and at the same time a great evil and disturbance of right order to assign to a greater and higher association what lesser and subordinate associations can do.*

The principle of "subsidiary function" in relation to Australia can be thus briefly described:

The central government has duties of its own which no other body can perform. Outside the range of these duties, its function is simply to help lesser bodies, to co-ordinate their efforts for the common good, but never to dominate or absorb them. To destroy lesser authorities is of the essence of totalitarianism, whether the central government is a dictatorship or nominally democratic.

The importance of treating this subject today is emphasized by the faulty machinery of administration which has developed with the gradual breakdown of the federal system of government and which prevents sound policies being transformed into reality by legislative action.

The Commonwealth, by its overall control of the principal source of revenue available to the States, increasingly fetters the liberty of the States to make their own policy decisions …

In this situation, all sense of freedom and responsibility tends to be enfeebled or destroyed. Is it any wonder that we have performed so indifferently in recent years in the vital fields of migration, primary production, land settlement and national development on which the future of this country depends?

The issue which faces Australia in this field is therefore very clear. Shall we drift on to complete political centralisation, as some would wish, placing all power in the hands of the Commonwealth and reducing the States to the status of local governments with

> *"Shall we drift on to complete political centralisation ... placing all power in the hands of the Commonwealth and reducing the States to the status of local governments with delegated powers?"*

delegated powers? Or shall we restore the original balance of the Constitution and re-allot effective powers both to the States and to the Commonwealth, providing for both adequate and independent sources of revenue?

The decision to which we are led by the principles of natural law and of the Christian Faith should not be in doubt. It was most cogently expressed by the late Holy Father, Pope Pius XI, in the following words:

"It is true that on account of changed conditions many things which were done by small associations in former times cannot be done now save by large associations.

"Still, that most weighty principle which cannot be set aside or changed, remains fixed and unshaken in social philosophy: Just as it is gravely wrong to take from individuals what they can accomplish by their own initiative and industry and give it to the community, so also it is an injustice and at the same time a grave evil and disturbance of right order to assign to a greater and higher association what lesser and subordinate organisations can do ...

"Therefore, those in power should be sure that the more perfect a graduated order is kept among the various associations, in observance of the principle of "subsidiary function" the stronger social authority and effectiveness will be and the happier and more prosperous the condition of the State."

The Pontiff deals here directly with the relations between a State and its subordinate authorities. But his reasoning, of course, applies with equal or greater force, to the relations between a central Federal Government and its constituent States ...

It is because it is firmly committed to this principle of natural law that the Catholic Church has always defended the right of the family to fulfil all the functions of which it is capable – the care and education of the young, the proper provision of all physical, educational and other needs of its members, and finally the protection of the old.

The first and most effective unit of government and authority is the family. The functions which it can fulfil are the most vital of all. Hence the Church has never wearied of demanding for the family both adequate family income and a measure of productive property which would assure its economic independence. The most generous system of social services is no substitute for these.

> *"... the Church has never wearied of demanding for the family both adequate family income and a measure of productive property which would assure its economic independence. The most generous system of social services is no substitute ..."*

It is because of this principle that Catholic thinkers have maintained the right of municipalities and local governments to carry out the functions proper to them – "the provision of roads, water, lighting, drainage, clinics, cemeteries, public baths, libraries and many other services."

Vietnam

During the 1950s, there was strong support in Australian Catholic circles for the Catholic-dominated regime of Ngo Dinh Diem in South Vietnam, at a time when most Australians took little interest in that country. The support came not only from the strongest anti-Communists like Mannix and Santamaria, but from a broader range, including Cardinal Gilroy, who had been a classmate in Rome of Diem's brother, the Archbishop of Huế.

Archbishop Mannix with South Vietnamese President Ngo Dinh Diem during Diem's visit to Australia in September 1957.[39]

On Anzac Day 1963, with the Australian military commitment to Vietnam just beginning, Mannix issued a statement which asked for prayers for world peace and for the souls of Australia's dead servicemen. After emphasising the importance of the American alliance, he took note of the conflict in Vietnam and the emergence of newly independent Third World nations:[40]

Our thoughts go to the small band of Australian soldiers who are serving in Vietnam, helping the people of that country to defend their freedom against a brutal and often murderous aggressor. The independence of small nations has always been dear to us. Like the Pope, we rejoice in the dawn of an age which has witnessed the birth of freedom for so many nations in Asia and Africa.

The US Government lost confidence in Diem's ability to control South Vietnam and he was killed in a CIA-backed coup on 2 November 1963, a few days before Mannix's own death. Discussing the news with Mannix, Santamaria wondered whether his outspoken remarks had done more harm than good. Mannix replied:[41]

The greatest harm you could ever do would be not to stand by your friends, especially when they're dead, and the rest of the world condemns them.

That remark is a significant one. It explains the loyalty to the bitter end that he gave to the two men he was most personally committed to, Eamonn de Valera and B.A. Santamaria.

1. http://www.abc.net.au/news/2007-09-12/health-minister-tony-abbott-says-that-whenever-the/696326
2. Bruce Duncan, *The Church's Social Teaching: From Rerum Novarum to 1931*, Collins Dove, North Blackburn, 1991.
3. Kevin Blackburn, The living wage in Australia: a secularization of Catholic ethics on wages, 1891-1907, *Journal of Religious History* 20 (1996), 93-113.
4. Paul Kelly, *The End of Certainty: Power, politics, and business in Australia*, 2nd ed, Allen & Unwin, St Leonards, 1994, introduction; Geoffrey Stokes, The 'Australian settlement' and Australian political thought, *Australian Journal of Political Science* 39 (2004), 5-22.
5. Rick Kuhn, Lenin on the ALP: The career of 600 words, *Australian Journal of Politics & History* 35 (1989), 29-49.
6. A.E. Cahill, Catholicism and socialism: The 1905 controversy in Australia, *Journal of Religious History* 1 (2) (1960), 88-101.
7. Duncan, *Crusade or Conspiracy? Catholics and the Anti-Communist Struggles in Australia*, University of New South Wales Press, 2001, p. 120.
8. Celia Hamilton, Irish-Catholics of New South Wales and the Labor Party, 1890–1910, *Historical Studies* 8 (1958), 254-67, section VI; Judith Brett, Class, religion and the foundation of the Australian party system: A revisionist interpretation, *Australian Journal of Political Science* 37 (2002), 39-56.
9. Michael Hogan, *Australian Catholics: The social justice tradition*, Collins Dove, Melbourne, 1993.
10. James Franklin, Regulated capitalism, market socialism, *Dissent* no. 5 (2001), 1113.
11. Recent developments in James Franklin, ed, *Life to the Full: Rights and social justice in Australia*, Connor Court, Ballan, 2007; *Solidarity: The Journal of Catholic Social Thought and Secular Ethics*.
12. J.N. Moody, The dechristianization of the French working class, *Review of Politics* 20 (1958), 46-69.
13. *Advocate*, 3 November 1917, pp. 6-7.
14. *Advertiser* (Adelaide), 29 January 1917, p. 7.
15. Frank Murphy, *Daniel Mannix: Archbishop of Melbourne 1917-1963*, Polding Press, Melbourne, 1972, 63-64, quoted in Race Mathews, Socio-political aspects of the Mannix Episcopate 1913-1931 Part I, *Australasian Catholic Record*, 88 (2011), at pp. 5-6.
16. As quoted in E. J. Brady, *Dr Mannix: Archbishop of Melbourne*, Library of National Biography, Melbourne: 1934, pp. 129-130, quoted in Mathews, Socio-political Aspects of the Mannix Episcopate, p. 6.
17. Original image supplied by Michael Gilchrist.
18. As quoted in Brady, *Dr Mannix*, pp. 244-5, quoted in Mathews, Socio-political Aspects of the Mannix Episcopate, p. 6.
19. Speech of 4 June 1933, Gilchrist, *Portrait of Archbishop Mannix*, p. 45.
20. *Maitland Daily Mercury*, 17 February 1938, p. 8.
21. Michael Gilchrist, 1983-84, *A Portrait of Archbishop Mannix: Religious Leader in a Pluralist Society*, manuscript of records of speeches, p. 11-12.
22. *Advocate*, 3 November 1917, p. 6.
23. *Catholic Press* (Sydney), 12 April 1917, p. 15.
24. Daniel Mannix, foreword to W.J. Lockington, *Personal Prohibition Needed – Not National*,

Melbourne, 1915, quoted in P. O'Farrell, *Documents in Australian Catholic History*, Geoffrey Chapman, London, 1969, vol. 2 pp. 263-4.

[25] Gilchrist, *A Portrait of Archbishop Mannix*, p. 41.

[26] *Sydney Morning Herald*, 6 September 1933, p. 13, http://trove.nla.gov.au/ndp/del/article/17004771

[27] *West Australian*, 8 September 1933, p. 19, http://trove.nla.gov.au/ndp/del/article/33325805

[28] Gilchrist, *A Portrait of Archbishop Mannix*, p. 30.

[29] *Argus*, 17 November 1941, p. 6, http://trove.nla.gov.au/ndp/del/article/22398488

[30] *Argus*, 9 December 1946, p. 3, http://trove.nla.gov.au/ndp/del/article/22398488

[31] *Freeman's Journal*, 6 Apr 1939, p. 18, http://trove.nla.gov.au/ndp/del/article/146383596

[32] *Argus*, 26 October 1931, p. 6.

[33] Frank Murphy, *Daniel Mannix: Archbishop of Melbourne 1917-1963*, Polding Press, Melbourne, 1972, pp. 255-6.

[34] Patrick O'Farrell, ed, *Documents in Australian Catholic History*, vol. 2 pp: 437-8; discussion in Griffin, Daniel Mannix, pp. 286-7.

[35] Gilchrist, *A Portrait of Archbishop Mannix*, pp. 69-70.

[36] James G. Murtagh, *Democracy in Australia: an essay in organic reconstruction*, Catholic Social Guild, Melbourne, 1946.

[37] Gerard Henderson, *Mr Santamaria and the Bishops*, 1982, pp. 85-8; Griffin, *Daniel Mannix*, 218-9.

[38] "Daniel Mannix", The Australian Commonwealth and the States, pamphlet, Advocate Press, Melbourne, 1954.

[39] Image from Bev Roberts, Raheen: a house and its people, Pola Nominees Pty Ltd, Melbourne, 2007, p. 36.

[40] *Advocate*, 2 May 1963, reproduced in Michael Gilchrist, *Daniel Mannix: Wit and Wisdom*, Freedom Publishing, 2nd edition, North Melbourne, 2004, pp. 263-264, fn. 87.

[41] Television program: *Point of View* (B.A. Santamaria), 10 November 1963, reproduced in Gilchrist, *Daniel Mannix*, p. 266, fn 100.

Chapter 10: Race suicide and immigration

Issues of population and immigration are especially important, because it was the area where Mannix's views did not stay in the realm of theory but were translated into action. Thanks to the political success of Arthur Calwell, immigration followed the lines called for years earlier by Mannix and his associates. Australia was transformed.

Catholicism has a strong natalist tendency – contrary to advocates of "zero population growth", it takes a positive attitude to birth and family life as good in themselves (if conditions are favourable for the upbringing of children). To that tendency was added, between the wars, alarm at the great falls in birthrate since 1900, which threatened "race suicide", as it was put then. In the 1890s, the birth rate was about 30 per thousand population, but in the 1930s had fallen to about 17. The slogan "populate or perish" pointed to the dangers of trying to defend an empty continent with a stagnant population.

Mannix felt strongly about these issues. While he was not often found preaching on "morals" issues in general, he was disgusted by contraception. He spoke a number of times on the theme of "race suicide" through low population growth, and advocated child endowment and similar schemes to make it more possible for those on low incomes to have children. Though doubtful about increased immigration during the Depression, since like many Labor men he feared it might increase unemployment, he became a strong proponent of it during the War years.

The Australian bishops' 1943 recommendations for postwar policies, *Pattern for Peace* – drafted by a committee headed by Santamaria and presented by Mannix to Ben Chifley, the Minister for Postwar Reconstruction – put on the national agenda the idea of attracting migrants from Southern and Eastern Europe, which became the mainstay of the multicultural immigration program of the late 1940s, 50s and 60s.

Federal child endowment was introduced by the Menzies government in 1941.

Empty cradles

Mannix's 'Catholic principles' speech of 1917 included a heartfelt section on children and "race suicide".[1]

The Church, being the Church of the weak, does not neglect the child. (Applause.) Her interest in the child does not begin when it is born – she looks after the child before its birth, at its birth, after its birth, (Applause.) You will not find the Catholic church giving any countenance to birth control; you will not find the Catholic Church or her ministers dumb when instruments of destruction are openly sold over the counter in chemists' shops. (Applause.) Her ministers will not be dumb when it is well known that the slaughter of the innocents is going on every day around us; her ministers abhor and denounce outrages whenever and wherever they are perpetrated. With them, what is outrage or murder in France or in Belgium does not become a trivial offence when the deed is done in Melbourne. (Applause.) The Church takes a firm stand against race suicide, and she does not mince her words. She teaches us with her long experience that, apart from the awful crime against God, race suicide viewed from a temporal and worldly point of view, is opposed to the best interests of this and every other nation. (Applause.) When a nation begins to sterilise itself voluntarily, the writing for that nation is already upon the wall. It may be soon, or it may be late, but ruin is in view. (Applause.) We know, unfortunately, what has happened in France.

"The empty cradles of France and her lack of men supplied the temptation for Germany, whose power was in the full cradles of the Fatherland"

The empty cradles of France and her lack of men supplied the temptation for Germany, whose power was in the full cradles of the Fatherland.

Empty cradles in Australia

In Australia, our history is all before us. (Applause.) We are a young nation, and ought to be virile and vigorous. Birth control cannot be justified or countenanced anywhere but, even from a worldly point of view, least of all in Australia. (Applause.) Other nations might excuse themselves – a vain excuse, of course – on the ground of surplus population, or because they had run their allotted course. Australia is an infant nation; an empty country. Yet, unfortunately, as empty as our country is, it is not as empty as our cradles. (Applause.) And yet, in the face of what is going on, if I raise my voice, as I have done before now, against this cancer in the community, I am attacked by hypocritical people in Melbourne, and denounced by people who know much more about race suicide than I know. (Applause.) They turn up the whites of their eyes as if they had never dreamt of these shocking things, and in their most charitable mood, they suggest that, as a newcomer to this country, I do not know what I am talking about. (Laughter and applause.) Some, whose virtuous indignation knew no bounds, urged that doctors and chemists should take legal action against me. (Laughter.) No action was taken, and no action is likely to be taken. (Applause.) And while the murder of Australia's babes goes on, no silly threats will silence me. If I cannot stop the murder, I can denounce the murderers. (Applause.) How comes it that the Catholic Church is alone – or almost alone – in denouncing this vice? Why is it that the press makes little or no comment?

When medical experts discussed birth control in favourable terms in 1935, Mannix urged the banning of the manufacture, import and sale of contraceptives.²

BIRTH CONTROL.

References by Dr. Mannix.

At a meeting of the Catholic Truth Society last night, Archbishop Mannix said that distinguished people were visiting Melbourne in connection with the B.M.A. Congress, and most likely references would be made by some of the visitors to the question of birth control. They should keep their eyes open. Catholic medical men should make themselves heard and felt if certain doctrines were propagated by any of the visitors which were not consonant with sound morality. Australia certainly would be greatly benefited if they could cut out root and branch all the literature connected with the detestable practice of birth control. If he were the Mussolini or the Hitler of Australia, he would prevent not merely the sale and the advertising and the rest, but also the manufacture of any of the so-called contraceptive appliances. He would not be satisfied with that, but he would prevent their importation as well. Efforts were made to keep out certain drugs, which were supposed to be injurious, but there was nothing coming into Australia that was doing more harm than the manufacture here and the importation from abroad of these appliances. If in countries having expanding populations something might be said if the people yielded to the temptation. It would be regrettable if they did, but at any rate it could be understood to a degree. However, Australia, which was as large as Europe, had a population of 6,000,000 only, and it was said to possess great potentialities. Surely then the Commonwealth should be the last place in the world to sanction such abominable practices. Looking at the good of Australia, even apart from religion, he thought everything should be done to ban contraceptive appliances. He was certain before the B.M.A. meetings ended that people would be found in violent disagreement with him. No doubt they would carry their way because they were in the majority, and majority rule was likely to prevail. However, it would be at the expense of Australia, which was really practically empty when its size was considered. It would be fatal for the country to go back in population, and then to set about getting people from other parts to settle here. He hoped that Australia would see the folly of the position in time.

On the more positive side of encouraging more children, child endowment was a favoured policy:[3]

It would be regrettable if anything happened to the child endowment scheme comparable to the case of the national insurance plan Archbishop Mannix said in an address in the Cathedral hall yesterday.

The state of things in which we were living was simply atrocious, he said. People with large families were expected to live upon wages that were intended to support and were scarcely able to support, a man, his wife and one or two children.

Rural virtue

Catholic thought had a tendency to see virtue in rural life, taking the opposite position to the Communist view that the force of history lay with the industrial proletariat. Life on the land, it was thought, promoted stability, respect for family and local community values, and more children. The idea of rural virtue has a long history in Australia, with many sources including Latin literature,[4] and many manifestations, including Banjo Patterson's 'Clancy of the Overflow' and the disastrous Soldier Settlement schemes of the 1920s.[5] Mannix, as we saw, brought from Ireland an interest in the "land question". He called for land redistribution in his 'Catholic principles' speech of 1917, in terms similar to his "land question" paper of 1901:[6]

[Those calling for higher production] are most anxious to "speed up" the workmen, and to get the last foot-pound of energy out of them, but they take no special pains to "speed up" in other directions. [Applause] There are men holding many thousands of fertile acres in Australia, and we never hear the great advocates of efficiency telling them to "speed up". [Applause] The land is certainly not producing as much wealth as it should produce. What a pity it is that no Government has produced some sort of Taylor card system* for big landholders who are locking up the wealth of Australia. [Applause] If statesmen or politicians are really anxious to increase production, then the first thing to do is to split up a great deal of the unused land, to settle upon it those who would endeavour to use it to advantage.

---

* The American Frederick Winslow Taylor was a leader of the "Efficiency Movement" for rationalising the fine detail of industrial workers' job tasks.

In 1940, Mannix made a rare visit to the country to urge those living there not to move to the big city.[7]

STAY IN THE COUNTRY
ARCHBISHOP MANNIX'S ADVICE

A plea for the welfare and development of country life which is vital to Australia was made by the Archbishop of Melbourne (Most Rev. D. Mannix, D.D.) in addressing a large country gathering in Victoria. His Grace said it was consoling to know that all the Catholic people were not confined to the city, but that a considerable sprinkling of them was to be found in the country. Families in the city after two or three generations seemed to die out; they did not seem to last long for one reason or another.[†] He hoped none of those residing in the district to which he was talking would think of going to the city. People should remain in the country as long as they could make a living. Australia was dependent upon the country and upon those who raised the primary produce ... those who were now there should stick to their holdings. Large tracts of land were not vitally necessary; the main thing was to have a sufficiency to make a decent living. Those who got a decent living should not be anxious to turn their backs on the country for the lights, cinemas and other so-called attractions of city life.

"Families in the city after two or three generations seemed to die out..."

The reconstruction of rural life was to be one of the issues closest to Santamaria's heart. His National Catholic Rural Movement took a great deal of his energy in the 1940s and was a substantial organisation up to 1960, though it achieved no great success.[8] When Santamaria eventually became a public figure after the Labor Split, he was sometimes caricatured in the wider community as wanting to settle Australia with peasants given three acres and a cow[9] – although the NCRM's organ, *Rural Life*, had actually said "Independent [of the market] does NOT mean that we all have to go back to THREE ACRES AND A COW."[10] [‡]

An official bishops' statement, entitled *Catholic Action in Australia*,[11] was issued in 1950 and clearly reflected the Santamaria-Mannix position. It warned against Australian Catholic Action following "too slavishly" French and Belgian models ... The bishops asked a series of rhetorical questions:[12]

[†] Lower fertility in urban than in rural areas has been a long-term and international phenomenon, see e.g. G. Hugo, What is really happening in rural and regional populations?, in *The Future of Australia's Country Towns*, ed. M.F. Rogers and Y.M.J. Collins, La Trobe University, Bendigo, 2001.

[‡] *Raheen* itself had three acres and four cows.

Today a beginning has been made on the work of diverting the Snowy River into the Murray or the Murrumbidgee. Great hydro-electric schemes, great irrigation projects will follow in the wake of this diversion. There will be vast industrial development in the Valleys. There will be great agricultural development. But will this development be on the lines of big industry and big agriculture, or small industry and small agriculture? For the Catholics of the Valleys, this is the real question of the hour. Should the former alternative be realised, the result will be slums, insecurity, class warfare and the threat of Communism. Should the latter alternative be chosen, there will be established the social framework of personal freedom, family life and social peace.

The 1955 Social Justice Statement, which came to be called *Big Cities*, was directed to the discussion of "the idea of decentralisation as applied to the size of the great city". As with the issue of Commonwealth and States rights, a dispute arose between Sydney and Melbourne bishops on the attempt to derive such detailed and technical matters of controversial political policy from the abstract principles of social justice. The draft was watered down but still quoted Pius XII condemning "the crowding of people into great cities".[13]

IMMIGRATION: 1930S DOUBTS

Like many on the Labor side of politics between the Wars, Mannix doubted the wisdom of immigration as a solution to the population crisis when there were so many Australians out of work.[14]

ST. AUGUSTINE'S ORPHANAGE
DR. MANNIX ON MIGRATION
GEELONG, SUNDAY.

Addressing a large gathering at Highton to-day Archbishop Mannix said that he doubted the wisdom of the reintroduction of migration to Australia.

The occasion was the ceremony of blessing the foundation-stone of the new St. Augustine's Orphanage in course of erection.

Archbishop Mannix said that in respect to the reintroduction of the policy of migration between Great Britain and Australia it had been said that the migrants would be of excellent quality, and that they would not displace Australians in industry. If these two conditions were observed he would be satisfied, but he doubted if it would be so. Australia's empty spaces could best be filled with young Australians. Boys leaving orphanages such as St. Augustine's and similar institutions should be given their opportunity. In the orphanages the boys and girls were being trained for citizenship, and they had a right to be considered. Australia was already afflicted with race suicide, such as was bringing European countries down, yet the Government was doing practically nothing. The post-office was open for the postage of shameful circulars, and shops were open for the display of those things which Christian people should be ashamed to look upon, let alone use. Things would be different if the people kept the Ten Commandments and the Government gave its help.

Foreword to *Exit Australia*

By 1943, however, Mannix had added immigration to the mix of policies to increase population. He wrote an enthusiastic preface to Charles Mayne's[§] alarmist book *Exit Australia: the future of Australia's population*:[15]

This booklet sounds an alert for Australia. Without any formal declaration of war, the enemy is already on the way. If Australia were even moderately alive to its own interests and its peril, this pamphlet need not have been written. But, apparently, public opinion is so dull and listless and complacent that the writing of it may prove to be a well-meant but wasted effort.

We are weary of hearing that Australia must "populate or perish"; as if the war in the Pacific left any doubt about that? If we give a thought to Australia's peril at all, we all agree, shake our heads ponderously, helplessly, unanimously; and then, like the weather, nothing is done about it. We just sit down to await the catastrophe, hoping that some stroke of luck, or a miracle, will save us; or, at the worst, that the crash, if it has to come, may not come in our time. Let the future take care of itself.

Meantime, immigration and the natural increase of population are subjects to be avoided or left to the wordy warfare of the debating societies; a rare politician, wiser or more outspoken than his kind, gravely warns us that Australia, for want of population, is facing disaster and death, but mere warnings will not fill cradles or immigrant ships; we arrogantly select the nations whose immigrants we will condescend to receive, and we flatter ourselves that the immigrants we wish for are straining at the leash to come, in spite of the churlish reception often given to those who have already come; our economic laws make for the postponement of marriage and for small families; increasing divorce is breaking up family life, and yet people agitate for easier divorce; the mother of a "large" family – that is a family of more than one or

". . . Australia, for want of population, is facing disaster and death, but mere warnings will not fill cradles or immigrant ships . . ."

[§] Fr Charles Mayne, Irish Jesuit, later Rector of Corpus Christi Seminary, Werribee and opponent of the Movement.

two – is too often made an object of pity, even of contempt and derision; birth-prevention clinics are thought to be a sign that we are progressive and up-to-date; contraceptives are openly sold and manufactured in Australia and imported from abroad; even in war time there must be no rationing in that department, the supply must be ample for civilians as well as for the fighting forces; the sparse population that we have is shifting from the countryside to our big cities, with their slum areas, so that we are losing our best hope of a large and healthy natural increase of population; and so, according to the prophets of evil, Australia with unheeding steps is tottering towards national decline and then to suicidal destruction.

"... we arrogantly select the nations whose immigrants we will condescend to receive"

Truly it is a gloomy picture. But, Father Mayne is buoyant and optimistic enough to hope that, even at this late hour, Australia may wake up to her peril and save herself by turning to the keeping of God's laws and by listening to the dictates of plain commonsense. At all events, he has given us a clear and painstaking diagnosis of the disease from which we suffer and most valuable suggestions for its cure. I hope that his warning will be widely read, and I pray that the results may justify his labour and his hopes.

The book *Exit Australia* itself is interesting for its recommendation at the early date of 1943, before there were any realistic plans for postwar immigration, that the solution would lie in Southern and Eastern European immigration – as in fact it was to prove in Calwell's and Menzies' immigration programs:

REMEDIES

Yet, due to the coming decline in population, large-scale immigration from Northern and Western Europe is very unlikely.

"Our principal source, then, will be Southern and Eastern Europe"

Our principal source, then, will be Southern and Eastern Europe. But unless we make conditions very attractive, emigrants from these regions are more likely to go to South or North America. To draw them here will require considerable planning – shipping, housing, employment, land settlement, etc., and Australian Immigration Stations will have to be set up in European cities. Preference should be given to young people of good character. That done, every effort should be made to absorb them into the social structure by suitable instruction and education. It has been found in other countries that when the alien is made to feel that he is an undesired and inferior intruder, and if opprobrious epithets are applied to him, the process of assimilation takes a long time. We are in dire need, and common sense as well as charity should cause us to do all we can to make newcomers feel at home. If we do not, this country will not be ours for long. We should remember, too, that immigrants often have something to give us. An American expert declared that the U.S.A. would be the losers if foreigners in their midst were to disappear. Their presence had enriched the national life by giving it variety, and he declared that present-day Americans must widen their outlook and appreciation of the contributions that other nations and races have made to the national life. Contrast this with the remark of Professor Carr-Saunders, who said that "the trouble which Australians experience with aliens is not unconnected with their attitude towards foreigners, which cannot be regarded as welcoming or encouraging. France, whose tolerance is well-known, has little difficulty. The same was true of Americans until recently." ...

Mr. Forsyth, in his book , "The Myth of Open Spaces,"[16] after a careful analysis, declares that "It is unlikely that British people will be available in significant numbers; the prejudice against immigrants from Southern and Eastern Europe will have to be overcome by careful selection, by education, by investigating the causes of friction." But after examining the prospects of future immigration, his final conclusion is that "the principal population problem of Australia is not immigration but fertility."

WHITE AUSTRALIA

Mannix disagreed with most Australians, including Calwell and other policymakers in immigration, on the White Australia policy. He argued in 1945 for a relaxation:[17]

The war has brought us more closely in touch with the coloured people. We have been brought to realise, in our contact with the native races, that we have much to learn from them . . .

It is unfortunate that by a crude insistence on our White Australia policy in its present form we have given them cause for resentment. It would not be good for us or for them if there were an uncontrolled rush of coloured races to Australia. But, by admitting a reasonable quota, we could surely make it plain to our coloured friends that there is no colour bar in Australia and that, as children of the Father, we recognise our brotherhood with all men, irrespective of race, or culture, or colour . . .

". . . we could surely make it plain to our coloured friends that there is no colour bar in Australia and that, as children of the Father, we recognise our brotherhood with all men . . ."

In 1958, Mannix issued a letter to coincide with the National Convention of the National Catholic Rural Movement (NCRM) which included:[18]

. . . that the total exclusion of Asians from Australia should be abandoned and that we should admit a sufficient number of the different races to dispel forever the myth of racial superiority inherent in the so-called White Australia Policy.

B.A. Santamaria also had a few words to say on the matter:

"The Kingdom of Heaven Has No White Australia Policy".[19]

---

1. *Advocate*, 3 November 1917, p. 7; similar in speech to Annual Communion Breakfast of the Hibernian Catholic Benefit Society, Catholic Press, 15 Mar 1917, quoted in P O'Farrell, *Documents in Australian Catholic History*, Geoffrey Chapman, London, 1969, vol 2, p. 278; and again in Walter A Ebsworth, *Archbishop Mannix*, H. H. Stephenson, Armadale, 1977, p. 201; P. O'Farrell, *The Catholic Church and Community in Australia*, Melbourne, 1977, p. 320.

2. *Age*, 12 September 1935, p. 7: http://news.google.com/newspapers?nid=1300&dat=19350912&id =FexjAAAAIBAJ&sjid=yZUDAAAAIBAJ&pg=4794,1069582

3. *Argus*, 17 March 1941, p. 5. http://trove.nla.gov.au/ndp/del/article/8158872#pstart610824

4. James Franklin, *Corrupting the Youth: A history of philosophy in Australia*, Macleay Press, Sydney, 2003, pp. 238-44; David Stove, A hero not of our time, in *Cricket versus Republicanism and Other Essays*, Quakers Hill Press, Sydney, 1995, ch. 2.

5. Ken Fry, Soldier settlement and the Australian agrarian myth after the First World War, *Labour History* 48 (1985), 29-43.

6. *Advocate*, 3 November 1917, p. 7.

7. 'Stay in the country: Archbishop Mannix's advice', Bunyip (Gawler), 24/5/40: http://trove.nla.gov.au/ndp/del/article/96698982

8. B.A. Santamaria, *The Fight for the Land : the program and objectives of the National Catholic Rural Movement* (pamphlet), Renown Press, Carnegie Vic, 1942, http://handle.slv.vic.gov.au/10381/120634; Duncan, *Crusade or Conspiracy?*, pp. 30-32, 88-9 Richard Doig, Historical Feature: Rural movement has message for today, *News Weekly*, 25/8/2001: http://newsweekly.com.au/article.php?id=411; Tony Ayers, Cottage Catholicism: Young Santamaria and the lure of the pastoral, *Arena Magazine* 34 (1998), 20-23; Kevin Peoples, *Santamaria's Salesman: Working for the National Catholic Rural Movement 1959-1961*, John Garratt Publishing, Melbourne, 2012.

9. John Douglas Pringle, *Australian Accent*, Chatto & Windus, London, 1958, p. 84; the text actually says 'six acres', no doubt updated for Australian conditions.

10. Duncan, *Crusade or Conspiracy? Catholics and the Anti-Communist Struggles in Australia*, University of New South Wales Press, 2001, p. 31. The slogan "three acres and a cow" goes back to the 19th century and was used by G.K. Chesterton.

11. *Catholic Action in Australia: Official Statement of the Archbishops and Bishops of Australia Associated in the National Organisation of Catholic Action*, 39 page pamphlet, issued 1950.

12. Geard Henderson, *Mr Santamaria and the Bishops*, Sydney, 1982, p. 33.

13. Henderson, pp. 92-4.

14. *Argus*, 31 January 1938, p. 4: http://trove.nla.gov.au/ndp/del/article/11144809

15. *Exit Australia: the future of Australia's population*, C Mayne, 3rd rev. ed. Melbourne: Australian National Secretariat of Catholic Action, 1943; Mr Santamaria and the Bishops, p. 52.
16. W.D. Forsyth, *The Myth of Open Spaces*, Melbourne University Press, Melbourne, 1942.
17. *A portrait of Archbishop Mannix: religious leader in a pluralist society*, M.T. Gilchrist, manuscript, 1983-1984, p. 30; comment in Anthony Cappello, Immigration: The end of the White Australia Policy, *News Weekly*, 27 January, 2001: http://newsweekly.com.au/article.php?id=498
18. *Enemy Aliens: The Internment of Italian Migrants in Australia During the Second World War*, Anthony Cappello et al, Preface by James Franklin, Connor Court Publishing, 2005, p. 56
19. *Advocate,* 4 October 1962, p.22.

CHAPTER 11: THE REAL MANNIX AT HOME

Raheen *from the air, taken c1930, photographer, Charles Daniel Pratt, Airspy collection of aerial photographs.*[1]

The real Mannix . . . there is no "real" Mannix left to see – no private diaries, no intimate letters, no personal memoirs by confidants. Instead there is rumour, anecdote, theatre.

Archbishop Carr had lived in a few simple rooms in the presbytery beside the Cathedral. When Mannix succeeded Carr, the Catholic Trusts Corporation at once bought for him the magnificent mansion *Raheen* in what was then semi-rural Studley Park. Mannix moved into *Raheen* in 1918 and died there in 1963.

The house was built on approximately 15,000 square metres of land. The two storeyed *loggia* and the four storeyed tower in one corner, in an Italianate style, dominate the view from the street.[2]

The aim of this extravagant purchase was not to live magnificently. On the contrary, Mannix's tastes and way of life were ascetic: he only used a telephone twice in his life, never flew in an aeroplane, never owned a car.[3] He had little interest in food and slept on an iron bed in a plain bedroom. The only major alteration made to *Raheen* was the conversion of the existing ballroom to a library.

The purpose of *Raheen* was instead to exhibit the apex of the Melbourne Catholic community as on a par with the finest the Establishment could offer. It was a theatrical prop, a stage for the Mannix performance as tribal leader.

In speaking of the "real" Mannix, one must remember that the real Mannix was an expert showman. Patrick O'Farrell writes of Mannix as actor – an actor with a purpose:[4]

The extent to which Mannix was theatre is a perception lost in the overlay of serious religious issues . . .

Daniel Mannix had all the marks of a consummate actor. He carried onto the stage, wherever it was, the commanding presence of an aristocratic self-image which he projected with all the aid of his poised physical bearing, superbly crafted lines deliberately underplayed, and a range of props: top-hat, biretta, even a cape in the Victorian thespian tradition . . . His enormous audience relished his performance, enjoying it because of its studied excellence as a role, and because it was constructed from, and deeply relevant to, real Catholic life. Here was leadership, not merely as directional encouragement, but in projecting effortless superiority. The money given away in the legendary private walks was aristocratic largesse, distributed in royal progress. The polite and polished insults to the secular authorities came from a source patently above them with no care for their regard.

> "*. . . the commanding presence of an aristocratic self-image . . .*"

A Maynooth student's view

When Mannix was first named as coadjutor Archbishop, Catholics in Melbourne wondered what manner of man they might expect. A former student of his at Maynooth who had come to Victoria was persuaded to set down his impressions. He paints a memorable portrait:[5]

My first impressions of the Bishop-elect were gained at a temperance lecture . . . He entered the pulpit, and for about three-quarters of an hour held our attention uninterruptedly from beginning to end . . . Mgr. Mannix uses no flamboyant rhetoric or histrionic gesticulations, nor does he aim at picturesque language. His style is vigorous, incisive, sometimes electric, and always dignified. His words are well-chosen, chiselled off by a distinct articulation, and one feels that there is behind them a master-mind, with a thorough grip on his subject, one who certainly impresses his auditors with a feeling of great reserve power, of intense conviction, and immense earnestness . . .

Mgr. Mannix is a singularly undemonstrative man. As Cardinal Logue remarked, "he is as silent as a ghost" on occasions where others might indulge in flattery. Once, however, it was not hard to detect a note of elation in his voice as he told of the congratulations he received for the unique record attained by one class when, out of seventy-three candidates for the B.A. degree, there was not a single failure.

Mgr. Mannix was certainly a strict disciplinarian. He seemed to look upon Maynooth as the West Point of Ireland, the military academy in which were trained the officers for the army of Christ, and to consider that one who proved unable or unwilling to submit to its regulations could not be safely permitted to bind himself irrevocably to the life-long discipline of obedience and self-denial of the priesthood . . . I have heard him, as President, refer very slightingly to [popularity]. As a past pupil of his tells me, "cheap popularity he heartily despised."

It could scarcely be said of him that he is gifted with the art of diplomacy, except his reticence and power of inspiring confidence be accounted such. He is too straightforward to hide his views if there be a call to express them; too much an enemy of subterfuge to employ the language that conceals thought . . .

He was not prompt to rebuke in person, but when he did it was short, sharp, and effective, clothed sometimes in a dry humour, or tinged with a quiet sarcasm that was still more successful. In one of such a reserved temperament, the more kindly side of his nature could not often be in evidence . . . Those who have had occasion to approach him know they may always count on a courteous reception, and a request would be sure of a fair hearing, and, if it did not always prove acceptable or practicable, his refusal would at least leave no sting. A suggestion would be considered on its merits, and he was not beyond adopting it if it recommended itself to his judgment. He was one of the last men it would occur to you to bluff or wheedle into a proposal. Diplomacy was useless in presence of those eyes, that seemed to read one through . . .

> *"Among his intimate friends and acquaintances he is said to unbend somewhat . . ."*

Among his intimate friends and acquaintances he is said to unbend somewhat and give play to a quiet humour and gentle raillery, but as students we seldom saw other than the sterner side of his character. A restrained laugh would occasionally appear, but oftener a smile would hover about the compressed lips. Once, though, we witnessed him in uncontrollable laughter, as from the stage of the Aula Maxima, a venerable Irish scholar and raconteur held an audience convulsed with merriment for nearly two hours at a wholly delightful mixture of sparkling wit and the sublimest egotism . . .

Of his inner life and spiritual characteristics I cannot speak. Outwardly, he was an example of regularity, said his daily Mass devoutly, and with such a grace and attention to rubrical accuracy that a student who paid particular attention to these matters used to refer to him and another as models in this respect. He always emphasised the religious note when addressing us on temperance during his professorial days, and on discipline when he became President. One saw too that he felt every word when he spoke of the example of the Christ who, as a youth, surrendered His will to his earthly guardians, and "went down to Nazareth and was subject to them."

Rumour of firearms stored at Raheen

Raheen, like Mannix himself, attracted rumours and anecdotes, which were part of the projected image. The first *Raheen* rumour was that its purchase had been funded by John Wren. (There is no evidence that it was.)

In 1918 a new rumour hit the street: that someone had seen firearms stored in a tunnel linking *Raheen* with John Wren's house across the road. The intelligence services were quickly on the case and tracked down the truth. The results of their investigations can be seen in the colour section of this book.[6]

Dinner at *Raheen*

Raheen served official purposes. Mannix rarely went out except to church events – no cinema, no sporting events, very rarely home visitations except a few of condolence in early years. When the Anglican archbishop wished to see him, he simply replied, "I never pay social visits or return them."[7] One came to him.

From the early 1920s onwards there were many important ecclesiastical meetings and other formal gatherings held at *Raheen*, as well as the frequent informal meetings that Mannix held in his library or study, and around his dining table. Though he was personally abstemious, he was a generous host, as one cleric has recalled:[8]

[Dr Mannix] gave many a pleasant clerical dinner party at *Raheen* to mark the visit of some distinguished cleric, and used to invite a wide circle of his senior priests to his table. Almost to the end of his days he entertained the Cathedral staff at Christmas dinner at *Raheen*. On great occasions, among them the consecration of any of the priests of his diocese to the episcopate . . . he was always happy to play host to a dinner for more than two hundred of the clergy both local and visiting.[9]

> "*. . . always happy to play host to a dinner for more than two hundred of the clergy . . .*"

One of Mannix's successors as Archbishop, Frank Little, recalled the dinners at a later period:[10]

The meals were good, thanks to the Virgona sisters. Always a three-course dinner starting with a grapefruit cocktail, so good that Little was sure it was laced with alcohol, so he went into the kitchen and checked, and of course it was. 'And there was Dan with his Pioneer Total Abstinence badge like a beacon.'

The sumptuous dinners were always accompanied by a variety of wines and selected liqueurs which were always on the table. Dr Mannix never drank, so often his guests wouldn't drink either. Some of the clergy who would drink as private guests would not touch the wine and liqueurs at banquets if no-one else started. Eventually Jean went around the table and poured the liqueurs into their glasses or coffee to save any embarrassment

One of the Bishops who had taken the pledge not to drink, once noticed that Jean had put a little more wine in the soup and made the remark that he didn't think Dr Mannix would take spirits, to which Mannix retorted: *'I never question what the cook puts into the meal.'*

> "*I never question what the cook puts into the meal*"

A niece of the Virgona sisters describes the menu:

The special dinners were major productions involving all the family. There were six or seven courses: antipasto, entre, soup, a fish course, a meat course, a sweet followed by petits fours, coffee and liqueur. Our parents and sometimes the cousins lent a hand. Preparations would begin well in advance and Jean wrote out a plan coordinating each stage of the operation. I remember peering into the dining room when the table was set.

There was a whole regiment of cutlery lined up at each setting, a pair of carved crystal wine glasses and a flower floating in each individual finger bowl. Dr Mannix sat at the head of the table. Protocol required that he begin eating first. On one occasion he never started and the whole course had to be returned to the kitchen.[11]

THE DAILY WALKS; MAUREEN

Adverting to his famous walks, the Archbishop confessed:[12]

I still did not expect to live to a great age in those days. And as I did not play tennis or cricket or football I decided that I would walk every day until I was 90, if I lived to be 90. And so I walked every day from *Raheen* to St Patrick's, the better part of four miles in and four miles out. It did me good.

All sorts of people might be met on the walks. Mr Menzies, for example, as we saw. Or the Eyres, who established a greengrocery business in Victoria Parade on the route of the walks; he frequently called at their shop. The Eyres' only child, Maureen, recalls the Archbishop:[13]

My first impression was standing outside St Patrick's Cathedral, East Melbourne, and looking up at him and 'thinking'. (He always treated me as his equal and never spoke down to me.) Anyway, he said:

Maureen, what are you thinking?

I answered: 'I was wondering if you put up your hand, could you touch the sky?' He said he did not know, but he tried and then smiled and said no, he could not.

Maureen enrolled at Catholic Ladies College in 1938 and soon excelled at the piano. Later that year, she wrote proudly of her work to Dr Mannix – she was now seven – and received a friendly handwritten reply:[14]

You are just wonderful! How did you get 91 marks out of 100 at your music examination?

I am sure that I never got as good marks at any examination that I sat for. And at the piano I should not get any marks at all. I am glad to know that you are to make your first Holy Communion soon and I shall gladly remember you often in my prayers in the meantime. Kindly give my best wishes to father and mother; and keep a big share for yourself.

By the age of 25, Maureen was a concert pianist with the Australian Broadcasting Commission. She brought her fiancée several times to see Dr Mannix. On the day of the wedding, 9 June 1956, a special picture was taken of the couple with the Archbishop at *Raheen*. Dr Mannix asked that the picture be taken so that a portrait of his mother on the wall appeared in the photo and as the picture was about to be taken, remarked:[15]

I'm still very handsome. They'll have trouble telling who's the bridegroom!

That brought smiles for the camera. The Archbishop then presented the couple with a large Bible containing a message on the inside cover:

To John and Maureen with every blessing for their wedding day and for the years to come.

A few months later, when Maureen learned she was expecting a child, she informed Dr Mannix personally of the news. He asked when the baby was due and Maureen gave the date as 4 March, Daniel Mannix's own birthday. This was a white lie, as she did not know the precise date, and it was given only to please him. But 4 March it was.

In later years, Maureen sometimes looked after *Raheen* during the day to give the Virgona sisters a break. On these occasions, her children had the run of the place, bringing delight to the old Archbishop.

Banter with Fr Hackett, "court jester"

Some brief glimpses of Mannix *en famille* (to the extent that that phrase makes sense) can be gleaned from the papers of Father Hackett, perhaps the closest Mannix had to a personal friend – although it is believed not on first name terms.[16]

In 1922, at the height of Ireland's tragic civil war, William Philip Hackett (1878-1954), Irish Jesuit, teacher and propagandist, was transferred to Australia by his order. That was possibly because of his over-close involvement in the Civil War. He knew well both de Valera and Michael Collins and had tried to arrange a meeting of the two, by then enemies, immediately before Collins' assassination by the Republicans. Collins' note to Hackett is believed to be the last letter he wrote.[17]

The last known letter of Michael Collins, written to Fr William Hackett, 21 August 1922, the night before his assassination. Hackett visited Collins' headquarters hoping to arrange a meeting between leaders, Collins and de Valera, in the civil war.[18]

In Australia Fr Hackett was Rector of Xavier College and founded the Catholic Central Library, a major effort to provide intellectual stimulation for the laity. He entertained Mannix on Monday evenings and accompanied him on his annual vacations at Portsea. The two certainly got on well, but Hackett's letters show from time to time a dislike of being "a quasi-episcopal hanger-on". A man of "gasps, grunts and angular gestures", he was the object of Mannix's friendly if sharp jibes.[19] The role could be trying:[20]

In a discussion of counties of origin, after a pointed tilt of disparagement at Cork, Fr. Hackett – butt of much byplay like the old time court jester, a role he loved – in self-defence replied,

"I was born in Cork, but crossed to Kilkenny to be civilised".

"And failed", said D.M.

At the dinner table one time an interstate guest provoked a laugh by pointing out that some of the cutlery was labelled, Made in Sheffield. When the merriment had subsided, Dr. Mannix observed,

"That is not the only thing English here".

"What else, your Grace?"

"Father Hackett's Oxford accent".[21]

Following Mannix around to functions was not always enjoyable:[22]

Easter Sunday dinner for 18 members of the Cathedral staff ('I loathe long meals') and two open air functions 20 miles apart, on Easter Monday, provoke Hackett to angry self-reflection: 'The poodle goes with him'.

RAHEEN UNDER THE VIRGONA SISTERS

For 20 years from 1944 – the year Mannix turned 80 – apart from two devoted sisters, Misses Jean and Angelina Virgona, who acted as his housekeepers, Mannix was the solitary resident of the large house, much of which was unused.

The sisters, then in their thirties, were introduced to the Archbishop by the chaplain to the Italian community, Fr Modotti SJ. Jean recalled:[23]

The first and only time I had seen Dr Mannix was in 1927 for an interview; 17 years later I found myself, with my sister, at *Raheen*, to fill a vacancy, supposedly for a few weeks. When His Grace died, 20 years later, we felt the bottom had fallen from our world, just as we had felt when our father and when our mother died.

Why so, seeing that we made repeated attempts to retire from the work? There was something about Dr Mannix that inspired more than loyalty to duty from those around him; or it could have been that we happened to fill a void, for he had once said to Fr Modotti shortly after we arrived at *Raheen*: 'I was a hermit until Jean and Lena came.' It seemed natural to hear our relatives speak of Dr Mannix, affectionately, as '*il nonno*' [grandfather].

He was our life during those years . . .

They did not wish to be paid, and when money was pressed on them they donated it to the education of priests. As there was no refrigerator, they brought one.[24] The normal household was only the Archbishop and the two sisters (not counting "Old Pat", the Irishman who looked after the cows and vegetable garden out the back). The Archbishop had no secretary, chaplain, or personal assistant. The sisters kept his clothes clean, but every aspect of his domestic life was completely private. He even cut his own hair. Not very well many would say; nor often.[25]

A long interview with another of Jean Virgona's nieces contains detailed information about life at *Raheen* from the inside:[26]

For the Virgonas "Raheen" came first. They rarely had any time off. The job was

Jean Virgona at the door of Raheen. *Courtesy of Crina Virgona*

full time, three hundred and sixty-five days. The only chance of some leisure or rest was in the summer when His Grace would go to Portsea for a month. They would go to their own home in East Malvern but not for long, having to return to give "Raheen" a spring clean, especially the huge library. This was a nightmare. Apart from the time it took to dust each book, people often borrowed books and didn't return them or there would be books returned and left on top of each other gathering dust. Summer was the only time they could cope with it because there were no visitors to interrupt the exercise. So much for their summer holiday!

However one day in the middle of this operation the door bell rang. They hesitated. Would they answer it or not? Their conscience won and they opened the door. Just as well, because it was a special relation, a very strict and distinguished gentleman Salvatore Favaloro and family down from Bendigo.

They were caught there and then up ladders, dressed in their old work clothes, certainly not exactly dressed for such visitors. He said: "Jean, you're doing this work! You can tell me it isn't my business but for the respect I had for your parents this isn't the sort of work you've got to do". Jean replied that it had to be done sometime. It was just as well that Uncle Salv didn't know what the daily routine amounted to.

It was amazing what the two girls fitted in each day. Jean was a natural gourmet cook so she did most of the cooking in between making appointments for Dr Mannix and taking messages and Lena looked after the housework in between answering the door bell. They would keep as much as possible to a daily routine. This meant that they would have to be up by 6.00am at least in order to be ready to answer Dr Mannix's Mass at 7.00am and to have prepared the breakfast ready by 8 o'clock and to have as much as possible of the essential daily routine cleaning done before Mass. This meant cleaning carpets, washing and polishing basins before the appointments began or any number of unexpected visitors . . .

. . . A lot of Jean's time was taken up making appointments for visitors to see Dr Mannix at "Raheen". There were the frequent ones that I knew of such as Father Ugo Modotti, Chaplain for the Italian Community; Bob Santamaria and Mr and Mrs Arthur Calwell. I have to include my mother Mrs Santospirito who was given the title of 'La Mamma degli Italiani' by a visiting journalist from America for the work she did for the Italians during the war.[*] She could not have done it without the help of Dr Mannix and Arthur Calwell, both dear friends. Through them the Italians were permitted to gather

---

[*] Lena Santospirito, leader of work for Italians in Melbourne in World War II and after, as member of the Archbishop's committee for Italian relief; see Cate Elkner and James Gobbo, 'Santospirito, Louisa Angelina (Lena) (1895-1983),' *Australian Dictionary of Biography*, vol. 18 (2012).

at the St George's Hall in Carlton and it was possible for her to place the children of internees into boarding schools. Moreover, His Grace was always sympathetic in the fifties when there was an influx of Italian immigrants needing jobs.

Jean Virgona saw Mannix's daily routine close up:[27]

The Archbishop offered his Mass each morning at 7.30. That occupied about three-quarters of an hour, and was marked by an extraordinary appreciation of the Divine Presence in its reverent attention to the rubrical actions. Then followed two hours of thanksgiving, for he never appeared for his meagre breakfast before 10.15.

His supper was taken at 10.30, a glass of hot milk and a biscuit, and often she would see the light on in his chapel well after midnight.

She remembered, ... the surprise expressed by strangers wandering around his enormous library to find a shelf of P. G. Wodehouse, whose perennial sense of humour was so akin to his own.

"... P.G. Wodehouse whose perennial sense of humour was so akin to his own"

Handling unexpected visitors was part of the job:[28]

The local police were constantly complaining of "undesirables" haunting his residence for the inevitable hand-out, insisted on by him, even in his absence.

Early one morning Jean Virgona was carrying breakfast to the Archbishop's study. She heard the front door-bell ring.[29] Although it was a long walk to the front door, Jean put down the tray and walked to the door. But when she opened it, there was no-one to be seen. So back she went to get the tray when the door-bell rang again; the same thing happened, but this time Jean walked down the drive-way to investigate. There, she found a small boy aged about six.

'What do you want?' she asked.

'I want to see the Archbishop; I want to make my First Communion.' was the reply.

Jean then went to the Archbishop and told him of the visitor.

'Well, bring him in,' he said.

So he was brought in, introduced, and remained with Dr Mannix while he had breakfast. About 20 minutes later, he brought the boy to the door to say good-bye and when he had departed, Jean asked:

'Did you give him what he wanted?'

'What did he want?' inquired Dr Mannix.

The boy had not raised the matter which was troubling him, so Jean was sent to fetch him back. When he had been recalled, the Archbishop asked what it was he desired of him.

'The priest said I was too young for receiving Communion and had to get the Archbishop's permission,' came the answer. So Dr Mannix asked him: "Whom do you receive in Communion?" "God," came the prompt response. "You know as much as I do," declared the Archbishop, who subsequently contacted the boy's parish priest and arranged for his First Holy Communion.

WHAT AFL TEAM DID MANNIX SUPPORT?

On the subject of television, Dr Mannix admitted that he watched very little apart from the news; but Bob Santamaria, a one-eyed Carlton supporter, reminded him that he watched the football replays:[30]

Ah, yes, the football. But I find it hard to distinguish which side is which. You know, I'm supposed to be a barracker for Collingwood. I suppose because Collingwood is in the vicinity. But the truth of it is that I have never seen a football match in my life.

TV COMES TO *RAHEEN*

When Mannix was 97, in late 1961, the bulky television cameras of the day moved into *Raheen* for Gerald Lyons' TV interview.[31]

With all the technicians and Mr Santamaria, who insisted on being present, the numbers there were around sixteen. Expected to last less than an hour, it began in mid-morning and finished well into the afternoon. [Jean Virgona] was constantly dashing in with tea and coffee and iced drinks and sandwiches, and all the Archbishop had was a cup of water, his endurance and patience an unforgettable wonder. Indeed, for the food he took each day one could put it all on a dinner plate.

Extracts from the interview have been printed in other chapters. They show excellent memory and clarity of mind.

---

1. Link to photograph at the State Library of Victoria: http://handle.slv.vic.gov.au/10381/177668
2. City of Kew Urban Conservation Study: Volume 2, p. 85; James Griffin, *Daniel Mannix: Beyond the Myths*, Garratt Publishing, Mulgrave, Vic., 2012, pp. 220-2.
3. Griffin, *Daniel Mannix*, p. 348.
4. Patrick O'Farrell, *Vanished Kingdoms: The Irish in Australia and New Zealand: A Personal Excursion.* Kensington, NAW: University of New South Wales Press, 1990, p. 246.
5. "G. Brendáin", Memories of Monsignor Mannix, *Austral Light* 13 (1912), pp. 707-19. Thanks to Patrick Morgan for supplying this article.
6. NAA, A8911, 240: Reverend Dr D Mannix (Anti-Conscription and Anti-British Utterances: Sinn Feiner): pp: 66-72.
7. Mannix to Archbishop Head, 30/12/1929, in D. Schütz, "May I write to you...?": The correspondence between Catholic Archbishop of Melbourne Daniel Mannix (1864-1963) and Anglican Archbishop of Melbourne F.W. (Frederick Waldegrave) Head (1974-1941) concerning the Eucharistic Procession Controversy, Part 1: Letters 1-11, 1929-1933), *Footprints* 28 (2) (2013), 8-48.

[8] Bev Roberts, *Raheen*, Pola Nominees, Melbourne, 2007, p. 34.
[9] Rev. Bernard O'Connell, memoir, 1965, in *Raheen*, p. 86, n. 20.
[10] Brenda Niall, *The Riddle of Father Hackett*, p. 262.
[11] Crina Virgona, Jean and Lena Virgona, housekeepers to Dr Mannix 1944-1963: a memoir, *Footprints* 28 (1) (2013), 4-10.
[12] Michael Gilchrist, *Daniel Mannix: Wit and Wisdom*, p. 253, n. 65, quoted from R. Hastings, 'And I Never Owned a Motor Car', *Bulletin*, 16 November 1963.
[13] Gilchrist, Daniel *Mannix*, p. 143, n. 30, quoted from an interview with Maureen Landy, Red Hill, ACT, June 1981.
[14] Gilchrist, *Daniel Mannix*, pp. 162-3, n. 99, quoted from a letter from Mannix to Maureen Eyre, 21 September 1938: copy in M. Gilchrist's possession.
[15] Gilchrist, *Daniel Mannix*, p. 237, n. 23, interview with Maureen Landy, Red Hill, ACT, June 1981.
[16] Griffin, *Daniel Mannix*, p. 348.
[17] Brenda Niall, *The Riddle of Father Hackett: A life in Ireland and Australia*, National Library of Australia, Canberra, 2009: pp: 97-105; James Griffin, 'Hackett, William Philip' (1878-1954), *Australian Dictionary of Biography*, vol. 9, 1983.
[18] Image and caption reproduced from *The Riddle of Father Hackett*: page before p. 97: from Michael Collins to William Hackett, 21 August 1922, Hackett Papers, Archives of the Society of Jesus, Australia (ASJASL).
[19] Griffin, 'Hackett'.
[20] Walter A. Ebsworth, *Archbishop Mannix*, H. H. Stephenson, Armadale, 1977, p. 431; recollections of Hackett's successor as Portsea holiday companion in Leo Clarke, Archbishop Mannix: what was he like? *Footprints* 20 (1) (2003), 28-48.
[21] Ebsworth, *Archbishop Mannix*, p. 431.
[22] *The Riddle of Father Hackett*, p. 249, n. 7: WPH to Florence Hackett. 19 April 1954. Hackett Papers, ASJASL.
[23] Gilchrist, *Mannix: Wit and Wisdom*, p. 236, n. 21, recalled by Jean Virgona in letter to M Gilchrist, 15 February 1982.
[24] Virgona, Jean and Lena Virgona.
[25] Niall Brennan, *Dr Mannix*, Rigby Limited, Adelaide, 1964, p. 308.
[26] Maria Santospirito Triaea, Jean Virgona: Archbishop Mannix's Italian housekeeper, Australia Early Years, *IHS Journal*0017, p. 17: downloaded from: http://ebookbrowsee.net/gdoc.php?id=311576464&url=685e7d73627612bb83b93be0558c78de
[27] Ebsworth, *Archbishop Mannix*, p. 432.
[28] Ebsworth, *Archbishop Mannix*, p. 431.
[29] Gilchrist, *Daniel Mannix*, p. 236-7, n. 22, recalled by Jean Virgona in letter to M Gilchrist, 15 February 1982.
[30] Gilchrist, *Daniel Mannix*, p. 253, n. 65, quoted from R. Hastings, 'And I Never Owned a Motor Car', *Bulletin*, 16 November 1963.
[31] Ebsworth, *Archbishop Mannix*, p. 432.
[32] Curator's notes: http://aso.gov.au/titles/tv/interview-archbishop-mannix/notes/

Chapter 12: Arthur Calwell, Mannix's man

Arthur Calwell transformed Australia into a multicultural nation. In the late 1940s, his immigration program brought to Australia 180,000 Eastern European refugees from the Red Army (a majority of them Catholic).[1] These "New Australians", followed by the Italians, Greeks and others brought by the Menzies' government, broke the mould of the old Anglophone Australia forever. Without Calwell's drive and determination it would not have happened and Australia would have remained, in Calwell's words, "a dull inbred country of predominantly British stock."[2]

Calwell's ideals were Mannix's ideals. In the fifty years from the day Calwell saw the new coadjutor Archbishop arrive at Spencer Street Station to the day he wept at his deathbed at *Raheen*, Calwell idolised – Santamaria's word, and not too strong – Mannix, even in the dark years of the Labor Split when Mannix supported Santamaria's forces opposing Calwell.

Calwell's Catholicism was very public and flamboyant in expression, like Mannix's. That contrasts with the religion of the Australian Prime Ministers, which has in general been somewhat private and theologically imprecise, though genuine.[3] He was created a papal knight in 1964.

Support for Ireland was an early enthusiasm, and like others pursued with great thoroughness. Calwell learned Irish Gaelic – something Mannix never attempted – and addressed part of the great Richmond Racecourse meeting of 1917. In 1918 he was arrested and interrogated by security forces for his role in the Young Ireland Society,* suspected of sympathy with Sinn Fein. He and his wife in 1933 launched the *Irish Review* as the official organ of the Victorian Irish Association.

Like Scullin, his personal relationship with Mannix between the Wars was based on shared commitments to the ideals of Labor and the relief of the ills of the working classes.

His maiden speech in the Federal Parliament, when he was finally elected in 1940, was on another of Mannix's favourites themes, population and child endowment. His immigration program of 1947-50 then realised the proposals that Mannix and his supporters had put forward in *Pattern for Peace* in 1943: mass immigration including from Southern and Eastern Europe.

On certain issues, Calwell did disagree with Mannix. Like Scullin, he believed that any attempt to include state aid for church schools in Labor's electoral platform would be electoral poison, and as opposition leader in the early 1960s he avoided the issue. He was blindsided in the 1963 election when the "simple Presbyterian" Menzies made the first offer of small amounts of state aid. He disagreed with Mannix also on the White Australia policy. Calwell believed that any large influx of non-Caucasians would risk Australia importing the race problems of the US and South Africa, and that any token small quota, as Mannix wished, would be a meaningless and insulting sop to public opinion.

The main issue of disagreement, though, came over Mannix's support of Santamaria's secret Movement, which in the mid-1950s led to the Split of the Labor Party. Although an early supporter of secret action, by the late 1940s Calwell came to regard the Movement as out of control and misguided. Though it was not strictly true, as often claimed, that Calwell was refused communion after the Split, he did experience difficulties with church opinion that portrayed a vote for Labor as a vote for Communism.

At the end of his life Calwell dictated from his hospital bed his autobiography, characteristically titled *Be Just and Fear Not*. Here he recalls the broad lines of his long relationship with Mannix.[4]

---

* The security services did uncover a genuine though small revolutionary organisation, the Irish Republican Brotherhood, complete with Gaelic messages written in invisible ink. Mannix led the protests when seven members were interned. See Garrath O'Keefe, Australia's Irish Republican Brotherhood, *Journal of the Royal Australian Historical Society* 83 (2) (1997), 136-52.

Calwell reminisces

I was a boy of sixteen when I saw Dr Mannix arrive in Melbourne. I walked from our home in West Melbourne to the Spencer Street railway station, where about 300 people were present to see the new coadjutor greeted, as he stepped from the Adelaide express, by Archbishop Thomas Joseph Carr under whom he was to serve. I saw Archbishop Carr walk along the platform and greet Mr Andrew Fisher, who was then Prime Minister. Mr Fisher was apparently waiting to meet somebody from the same express. Dr Carr introduced Dr Mannix to Mr Fisher. I later saw Dr Mannix installed at St Mary's church in West Melbourne.

I saw Archbishop Daniel Mannix arrive in Melbourne on Easter Sunday, 1913. I saw him dying on November 6, 1963, four months short of his hundredth birthday. I left his room twenty minutes before he breathed his last, and I wept unashamedly. During most of that span of half a century, my relations with Dr Mannix were very good.

> *"I consulted with [Mannix] often and I was always only too anxious to help"*

I consulted with him often and I was always only too anxious to help him. I have letters from him thanking me for my help. I believe he was pleased when I became the Federal MHR for Melbourne in 1940 because he trusted me. Without abusing any of his prerogatives or using the pulpit in my favour or in favour of the Australian Labor Party, his friendship was real and continuing. It was not until he grew very old and the Labor Party and the church were split in 1955 after the Petrov case, that my relations with him deteriorated very badly. But, although he did not approve of what I had done, he did not go out of his way at any time to be publicly hostile to me.

Young Calwell picked up by Security

Having become secretary of a Labor Party branch, Calwell received a considerable amount of literature from various union and socialist groups as well as some pamphlets about the Irish troubles. Calwell was picked up and interviewed by security in 1918 as a possible Sinn Fein activist. He reports on the incident:[5]

Then [at the age of 22] they picked me up at a CMF refresher course in 1918 and took me home, where they examined the literature I had in my possession. All the literature had come to me by virtue of my secretaryship of the Melbourne branch of the Australian Labor Party, a position which I took over at the age of eighteen. There were letters which I had received from the Industrial Workers of the World, there were letters from various socialist groups, and there was a pile of anti-conscription letters and literature and some pamphlets about the Irish troubles. The detectives took all these documents away with them, and I had to attend the Victoria Barracks next day. I was questioned there for an hour and a half, but nothing further happened.

I saw nothing wrong, at that time, in warning people connected with the Young Ireland Society that they were likely to be raided, because I knew that there would be nothing found on their properties that would incriminate them. They were emotional people and they were reacting as people are reacting in Northern Ireland today. They were reacting to the tragedies of Easter Week and to the subsequent internments and executions. I passed the word around to those who were likely to be raided. The raids took place on the following Monday night according to plan, but nothing was taken from any of the members of the society.

Below is a facsimile of the letter sent to Detective H. E. Jones[§] by the Director of Military Intelligence on 26 March 1918.[6]

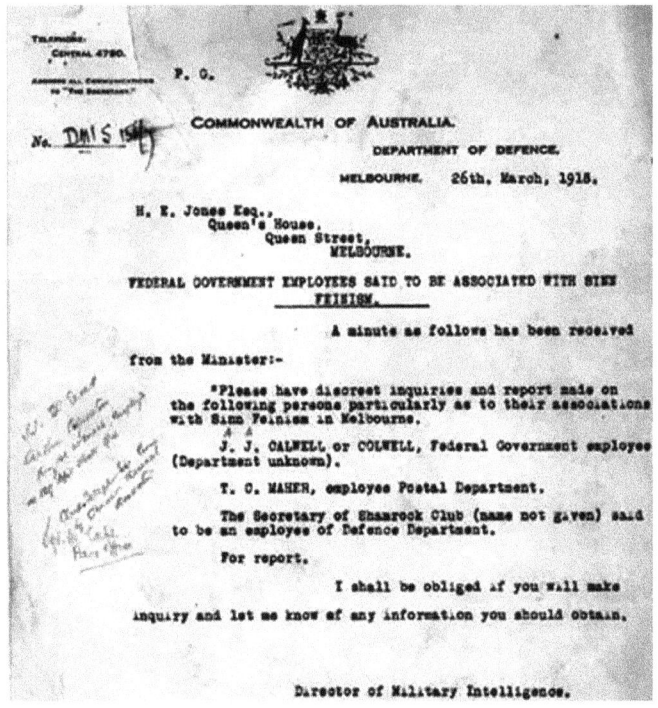

[§] Harold Edward Jones of the Special Intelligence Bureau, later Director of the Commonwealth Investigation Branch, the forerunner of ASIO; see Jacqueline Templeton, 'Jones, Harold Edward (1878–1965)', *Australian Dictionary of Biography*, vol. 9 (1983).

This was followed by several letters between Detective Jones and Military Intelligence as well as intradepartmental memos until Calwell was finally able to make the response pictured below on 11 September 1918. There was no further action.

```
                              C o p y
  EI

  Arthur  Augustus  CALWELL

           States:-
                      I am a public servant at the Department
  of Agriculture, and I am an Officer (Lieutenant) in the
  Citizen Forces, 64th. Infantry, - and I live with my
  parents at 391. King St., West Melbourne.

                     I was born on 28th. August, 1896.  I
  was educated at Christian Brothers College, North
  Melbourne, where I gained Junior and Senior Public, and
  at the age of 17 I entered the Public Service.
  I am a Catholic, and I have held office in the Catholic
  Federation Catholic Young Men's Society and the Past
  Pupils' Association, North Melbourne, Secretary to the
  Melbourne Branch, Australian Labor Party, a member of
  the Young Ireland Society since October, 1917, to which
  I was elected a member of the Committee, but I have only
  attended 2 meetings of the Committee, the last meeting
  being in April 1918, also the Young Ireland Party which
  was composed of a few of the male members of the Young
  Ireland Society, this party was formed in April, 1918,
  and I was styled secretary until June 1918, when I
  ceased to take an active interest.    During the period
  the activities of the Young Ireland Party were concerned
  with lectures on prominent Irishmen during the 18th.
  and 19th. Centuries, Daniel O'CONNELL, Thomas DAVIS,
  and Sir Charles Gavan DUFFY, etc.,      I was never a
  member of the Irish National Association.

                      During my office as Secretary to the
  Australian Labor Party, I received as secretary, a large
  quantity of circulars from various bodies, consisting
  of the No-Conscription Fellowship, Australian Freedom
  League, and the Australian Peace Alliance, - which the
  exhibits produced are portion thereof.

                      I moved on all occasions that this
  correspondence be received and no further action was taken

                      When the Irish were interned in Melbourne
  a meeting of all Irish Societies were called to discuss
  the question and define the real position.   I was
  requested to become a delegate, which after demur I did,
  and I attended several committee meetings and was present
  at Richmond when that general open-air meeting was
  called.    Since then I have taken no further interest
  in the matter.

                      This statement has been read over by
  me and is true and correct.

                                     (Sgd.) A. A. CALWELL

  11.9.'18
```

Calwell on social justice

Calwell, like Mannix and Scullin, was an enthusiast for the Church's social teaching as laid down in *Rerum Novarum* and subsequently, and made it clear that those ideas gave direction to his political activity. He wrote:[7]

> *"Many anti-Labor Catholics appear to me as status-seeking, half-educated, pietistically minded introverts"*

Many anti-Labor Catholics appear to me as status-seeking, half-educated, pietistically minded introverts. It might do some of them good to read the Papal encyclical *Rerum Novarum*, issued by Pope Leo XIII in 1891, which was an arraignment of capitalism while also pointing to the deficiencies of Marxism. Then there was the 12,000-word encyclical issued by Pope Pius XI in 1937,[†] in which he also condemned the evils of both communism and capitalism.

Pius XI wrote:

> Towards the close of the nineteenth century the new economic methods and the new development of industry had sprung into being in almost all civilized nations, and had made such headway that human society appeared more and more divided into classes. The first, small in numbers, enjoyed practically all the comforts so plentifully supplied by modern invention; the second class, comprising the immense multitude of working men, was made up of those who, oppressed by dire poverty, struggled in vain to escape from the straits which encompassed them.
>
> This state of things was quite satisfactory to the wealthy, who looked upon it as the consequence of inevitable and natural economic laws, and who, therefore, were content to abandon to charity alone the full care of relieving the unfortunate, as though it were the task of charity to make amends for the open violation of justice . . .
>
> Unfortunately, many Catholics have either ignored, forgotten or failed to read those encyclicals. They have developed a tradition of subservience to wealthy interests and a desire to create an impression of respectability for Catholic church leaders and those associated with them. The Catholic church in Australia from its beginnings has always consisted of people of Irish or part-Irish decent. There are a growing number of other nationalities on the church rolls in all Catholic parishes, including Italians and Maltese, but I believe that most of the bitter experiences I feel bound to relate can be attributed largely to those of Celtic strain. All Celts are bitter people . . .

[†] Sic, for 1931 in the encyclical *Quadragesimo Anno*. The Pope did condemn Communism in 1937 in *Divini Redemptoris*.

Maiden speech on the population problem

Arthur Calwell's maiden speech, when he was finally elected to Federal Parliament in 1940, was on one of Mannix's favourite themes, the population problem. His solutions are those promoted by Mannix.[8]

The Right Honorable R. G. Casey, introducing into this Parliament a bill to establish national insurance, recited a dismal tale in respect of the future of this country. He said that, according to figures that had been supplied to him by the Commonwealth Statistician and by actuaries who had worked upon them, the population of Australia would become stationary by 1955, and by 1970 would have begun to decline. That kind of dirge was preached in anticipation of the death of the white race in the Pacific area.

Although we are but 150 years old as a nation, apparently we are slowly bleeding to death, and within a 200 year period this outpost of white civilization in the Pacific will have almost entirely disappeared. Yet this Government, which is acquainted with the facts, neither does nor suggests anything, but resists every attempt that we make on humanitarian and national grounds to establish a scheme of child endowment or family allowance, because under such a scheme those of their friends who benefited from the work of the community would have to pay. The Government is neither courageous nor wise enough to take time by the forelock and do what should be done. It would appear that only one honorable gentleman opposite has interested himself in this problem; he is the septuagenarian Minister for the Navy (Mr. Hughes). He is the only one who has told this country that it must either populate or perish.[‡] We may learn something from our enemies in this connexion. In fact, we shall be foolish if we do not learn from them anything worthwhile that they can teach us. A good deal of attention has been given in Europe to the encouragement of family life and the increase of the birth-rate. Family allowances were introduced by private enterprise in certain European countries in the nineties of the last century. Strangely enough, the practice was adopted almost simultaneously in countries with such divergent policies as Germany and France, and it proved to be successful in serving the ends for which it was designed. It was only a very few years ago, however, that the Governments of Germany, Italy, France and Russia tackled the problem in a statesmanlike way, and commenced to do what was required to be done in the interests of their women and children.

> "... we are slowly bleeding to death, and within a 200 year period this outpost of white civilization in the Pacific will have almost entirely disappeared"

[‡] The phrase was introduced into public debate by (Sir) Joseph Cook http://trove.nla.gov.au/ndp/del/article/50693113. It was to be popularised by Calwell in his promotion of immigration. "Mr Hughes" is Billy Hughes, still Minister in the Menzies government although nearing 80 years of age.

It was my fortune three years ago to be associated with a select committee of the Legislative Assembly of Victoria on child endowment. A questionnaire submitted in 1938 to the Consuls of various nations during the investigation that was made by that committee resulted in the gathering of some most interesting information. Professor A. Lodewyckx, of the University of Melbourne,[§] also furnished information to the committee through an article in the Economic Record which indicated some important trends. He pointed out that one of the chief preoccupations of National-Socialist Germany was population. The decline of the German birth rate from the beginning of this century until 1933 had been catastrophic. Professor Lodewyckx made the following observations on the subject:-

> However, soon after the National Socialist party took office early in 1933, energetic measures were adopted in an endeavour to stop the downward trend. These measures may be summed up under the following four headings:
>
> (1) Direct financial advantages to large families and to newly-married couples.
>
> (2) Reduction of unemployment.
>
> (3) Intensive propaganda aiming at a new outlook on population problems amongst the whole people.
>
> (4) Stricter enforcement of the law prohibiting the practice of abortion.
>
> The result has been a substantial increase in the birth-rate. The numbers of births registered for the years 1933 to 1937 are as follows:

Year.	Births.
1933	971,000
1934	1,198,000
1935	1,204,000
1936	1,297,000
1937	1,276,000

". . . 300,000 more children are born in Germany to-day than during the last few years before the National Socialist party took over the reins . . ."

It will be seen that about 300,000 more children are born in Germany to-day than during the last few years before the National Socialist party took over the reins of government. So that, assuming that the figures for 1938 are about the same as those for 1936 and 1937, during the five years 1934-38 German mothers have given the

---

[§] Augustin Lodewyckx, Associate Professor of Germanic Languages at Melbourne University, father-in-law of Manning Clark.

Fatherland 1,500,000 more children than would have been the case if conditions as prevailed before 1933 had continued.

The record of Australia in relation to the birth-rate is such as to demand serious consideration. Our birth-rate fell from 4.3 per 1,000 of the population in 1862 to 1.7 per 1,000 in 1937. The effect can be expressed in another way: In 1911, when Australia had a population of roughly 4,500,000, more children were born than in 1938, when our population was approaching 7,000,000. This problem cannot be ignored, and we cannot procrastinate in dealing with it if we wish to continue to progress as a white nation. Several State Governments and, I am glad to say, also some municipalities, have done something to cope with the position. As the honorable member for Henty (Mr. Coles) well knows, the Melbourne City Council has done a great deal of good work in this connexion, although only 10 of its 33 members belong to the Labor Party. The council has improved the conditions of mothers and children by establishing a number of public health centres and kindergartens throughout the areas under its control. I am sure that what has already been accomplished in this regard will be an inspiration to the council to do more in the future. With the help of the Commonwealth Government, the council has established a child welfare centre in my constituency of Melbourne, and good results have been achieved by it. It is also subsidizing many denominational kindergartens. But a great deal more must be done in this way if the nation is to prosper. Surely it is not too much to ask that steps should be taken to do for Australian women and children at least as much as was being done before the war for the German women and children. [Leave to continue given.] I thank honorable members for their courtesy.

Family endowment allowances need to be supplemented. I favour, as a complementary measure, the granting of marriage loans. The young people of this country cannot marry at as early an age as is desirable from a national point of view unless they be granted some financial assistance. In 1939 action was taken in France to give financial aid to young married people, but, unfortunately for that country, it was too late to be of much value. Long before the outbreak of war schemes had been put into operation in Germany and Italy to assist newly married couples. Arrangements were made in those countries for interest-free loans of from £100 to £200 to be made to young married couples . . .

> *"Family endowment allowances need to be supplemented. I favour, as a complementary measure, the granting of marriage loans"*

Mannix and Calwell in support of Italian internees

During the War, Italians in Australia were in many cases interned as enemy aliens and many injustices occurred. Mannix and Calwell cooperated to alleviate the problem. Working with the Italian Jesuit Fr Ugo Modotti, they made representations and organised charity work on behalf of the Italians.[9] (Indeed, early in the War Modotti himself needed saving: when the security forces arrived to arrest him, he drove instead to *Raheen* and Mannix contacted the Minister for the Army for assurances he would be left alone.[10] On 13 September 1943, Archbishop Mannix wrote to Prime Minister John Curtin, to ask for his support in rectifying the many iniquities the internees were suffering.

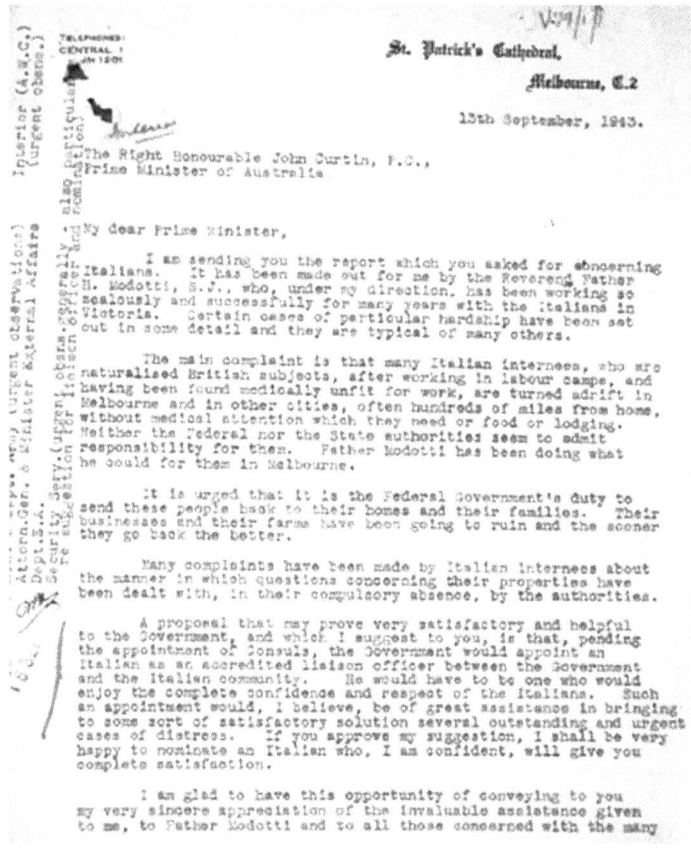

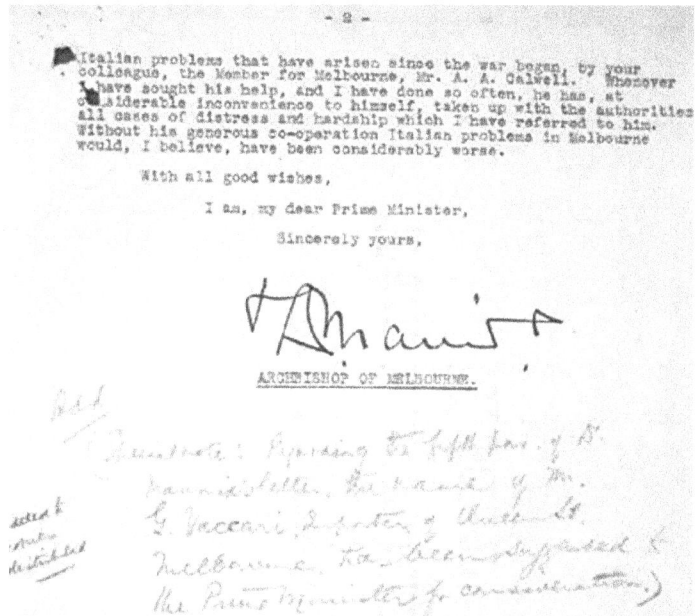

Mannix was the sort of figure who could expect an immediate reply from the Prime Minister. Curtin replied the next day:

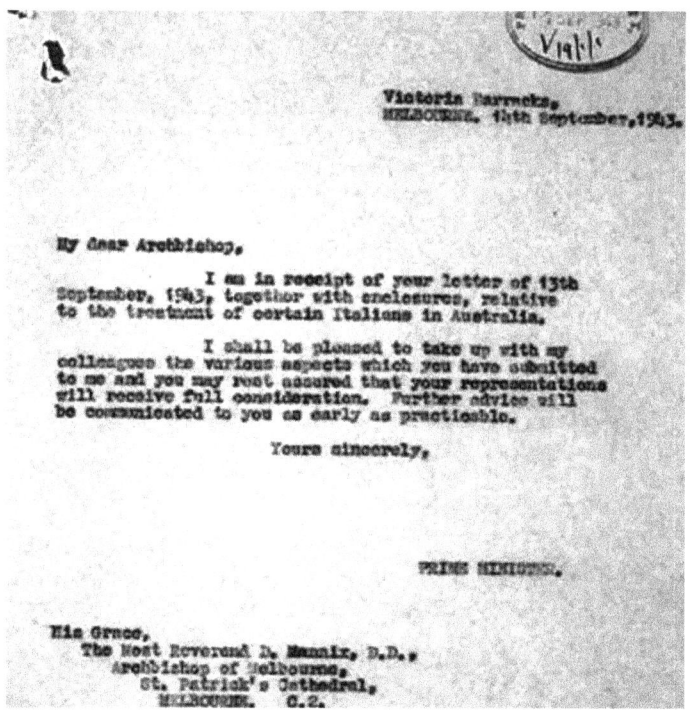

Gilroy's reception of the red hat

In 1945 Australian Catholics rejoiced in the appointment of Archbishop Gilroy as cardinal, the first of that rank in Australia since the death of Cardinal Moran in 1911. Or most of them rejoiced. Mannix's supporters were dismayed at his being passed over, and none more so than his devoted follower Arthur Calwell. Despite the expectations that a minister of the Crown should speak diplomatically, Calwell determined to say exactly what he thought. He spoke to the press directly:[11]

On December 24, 1945, I became the first Catholic layman in the English-speaking world to challenge a Papal appointment. My action brought me a lot of trouble. It happened when I heard on the radio of the appointment of Archbishop Norman Gilroy, of Sydney, to the College of Cardinals. Having gone home at lunch time, I prepared a statement and issued it to the press.

The statement was made at a time when I was Minister for Information and Immigration in the Chifley Government. Emphasizing that I was speaking as a Catholic layman only, I said:

> The news that Archbishop Gilroy has been created a Cardinal will be received with very mixed feelings by Australian Catholics. While there will be congratulations for the new Cardinal, widespread consternation and bitter resentment will be felt that the honour which rightly belongs to the Archbishop of Melbourne, Dr Mannix, should have gone elsewhere, and to quite a comparatively junior member of the Australian hierarchy. It has been the hope of Australian Catholics in the past twenty-five years that when the Vatican decided to confer this very long overdue distinction on Australia, it would select for the honour its greatest ecclesiast, the Archbishop of Melbourne, whose magnificent intellect has shed lustre on his church, and dominated its councils, for the thirty-three years he has been in Australia.
>
> Unfortunately, during the war years, the Vatican has had to depend on a representative whose limited ability and equally limited knowledge of Australia and Australians has ill-fitted him to influence the destinies of the Australian church.

"... bitter resentment will be felt that the honour which rightly belongs to the Archbishop of Melbourne, Dr Mannix, should have gone elsewhere..."

If the Catholic Church in this country has come of age to the extent that she can now claim an Australian-born Cardinal, the time is surely ripe when she should have an Australian-born Apostolic Delegate. For reasons which appear to me to be valid, I hope that Archbishop Panico's[¶] influence in Australian church politics, and in Australian affairs generally, will cease with his early return to Rome. I hope also that his successor will be one who will adequately voice Australian thought and sentiment on church appointments and other matters.

My statement was given considerable prominence in the press and on radio. I later rang Monsignor Arthur Fox at St Patrick's Cathedral in Melbourne and asked him if he had heard it. He said he had, and asked why I had not consulted the cathedral authorities first. I replied, 'If I had consulted you, you would have urged me not to make the statement. And I was determined to make it.' During the next few days, I was on the receiving end of an avalanche of mail commenting on my statement. Some of it was complimentary and the rest highly abusive. I was rebuked in a telegram dated December 27, 1945, from the then Bishop of Ballarat, Dr James O'Collins:[**]

GREATLY RESENT YOUR UNWARRANTED ATTACK ON HOLY FATHERS ACTION IN ELECTION OF CARDINAL GILROY YOUR UNDIGNIFIED AND UNJUSTIFIABLE OUTBURST AGAINST THE APOSTOLIC DELEGATE AND AS IT APPEARS TO ME YOUR UNDUE PUBLIC HUMILIATION OF DR MANNIX.

I replied immediately to Bishop O'Collins:

YOU EXPRESS RESENTMENT OF MY OBSERVATIONS ON APPOINTMENT OF NEW CARDINAL I EQUALLY RESENT NATURE AND TONE OF YOUR TELEGRAM STOP YOUR CHARGE THAT I MADE ATTACK ON HOLY FATHERS ACTION IS ENTIRELY WITHOUT FOUNDATION MY CRITICISM BEING DIRECTED TOWARDS ADVICE TENDERED HIM BY DR PANICO WHOSE PRESENCE IN AUSTRALIA HAS BEEN AN EMBARRASSMENT TO THIS COUNTRY STOP I AM CONVINCED THAT YOUR VIEWS ON MY STATEMENTS ARE NOT SUPPORTED BY GREAT MAJORITY OF CATHOLIC LAITY STOP THERE HAS BEEN NO INDICATION THAT YOUR CONCERN ABOUT HUMILIATION OF DR MANNIX IS SHARED BY HIM STOP I REGARD DR MANNIX AS THE GREATEST GIFT OF THE IRISH CHURCH TO AUSTRALIA AND THE GREATEST CHURCHMAN THE COUNTRY HAS KNOWN

[¶] Archbishop Giovanni ("Panicky Jack") Panico, Apostolic Delegate 1935-48, pursued a policy of favouring Australians over Irish in episcopal appointments.
[**] (Sir) James O'Collins, Bishop of Ballarat 1942-71, supporter of Santamaria's Movement, mentor of George Pell, accused of inaction over sexual abuse cases.

OR WILL KNOW FOR GENERATIONS TO COME STOP I AM PROUD OF MY ACTION AND MY AUSTRALIANISM.

"If I had ever wanted to be a Cardinal, I would certainly have charted my life differently"

I did not see Archbishop Mannix until a few weeks later, when I visited him at Queenscliff in Victoria where he was on holidays. When I entered his room, he was standing in front of the fireplace. He certainly did not rebuke me. He smiled at me rather benignly and said, among other things, 'If you had consulted me, I would have advised you not to say it.' Later, he said: 'If I had ever wanted to be a Cardinal, I would certainly have charted my life differently.'

Dr Mannix knew then that he never would be a Cardinal, because he was an Irish-born cleric who had not been educated in Rome.

Calwell either ignores or does not know more pressing reasons why Mannix was unlikely to become a cardinal, such as his gross levels of disobedience to Rome.

Melbourne's first opportunity to welcome the new Cardinal in person came on Sunday, 26 May 1946, with the celebration of a Pontifical High Mass in the Cathedral, followed by a Liturgical Welcome. Mannix welcomed the new cardinal in terms that were certainly cordial. But the more suspicious minds in the audience wondered if the remarks were a touch double-edged, especially when it came to the relation of Cardinal Gilroy's own qualities to his appointment:[12]

The Archbishop began his address with the observation that it might have seemed strange that Australia, with its relatively few Catholics, should merit a Cardinal. But it was now the Vatican's policy to distribute Red Hats to all parts of the world and to all races. Sydney's previous Cardinal, Dr Moran, had been "a distinguished Irishman who just happened at the moment to be living in Australia", and his elevation was not any recognition that Australia deserved a Red Hat. Now, the honour came "to an Australian who happens to live in the right place in Australia", observed Dr Mannix with more than a suggestion of irony. The elevation of Cardinal Gilroy, he continued, was "a signal honour bestowed on Australia".

I am old enough, and observant enough to have watched his [Cardinal Gilroy's] career since he first put his foot upon the first rung of the ecclesiastical Jacob's ladder that has brought him to his present exalted position. God looked after him. He protected him on the shell-raked shores of Gallipoli;[††] He called him to the Sanctuary and guided him to Propaganda College, that nursing mother of many prelates. For years, the future

---

[††] Before ordination Gilroy had served as a junior wireless operator on a ship off Gallipoli.

Cardinal was buried in the silent catacombs of the Delegation and, no doubt, that too was providential. But there was a resurrection when he went as Bishop to Port Augusta. Perhaps people thought it was not a milestone on his way to the Sacred College. But God has His own way of working out His designs. Dr Gilroy soon went to Sydney, and if there was to be an Australian Cardinal, his selection was inevitable . . .

I have just been reading a beautiful tribute to Cardinal Newman and could not fail to be struck by the contrasts and the likenesses of the two Cardinals. The one was old and enfeebled by the weight of years and sufferings. The other is young and full of energy and vigour. The one was all his life a student, the other has been a man of action which left little time for academic leisure. The one was 80 years before the cloud of suspicion and calumny was lifted and he was created a Cardinal; the other has reached the same goal by pleasant ways and easy stages.

Immigration succeeds with Eastern Europeans

Calwell was appointed Australia's first Minister for Immigration in 1945. He addressed himself with immense vigour and competence to the cause which he and Mannix had been promoting for so long, of finding more people for Australia. It was not just numbers Calwell sought, but diversity. He had written confidentially to Chifley in 1944 of his

. . . determination to develop a heterogeneous society: a society where Irishness and Roman Catholicism would be as acceptable as Englishness and Protestantism; where an Italian background would be as acceptable as a Greek, a Dutch or any other.[13]

". . . a society where Irishness and Roman Catholicism would be as acceptable as Englishness and Protestantism . . ."

Until 1947, success eluded him despite his best efforts. Shipping was very scarce after the losses in the War, and despite the disturbed conditions in Britain and Europe, few immigrants were able to come. Then a solution suddenly appeared. On 21 July 1947 Calwell signed an agreement with the International Relief Organization for the importation of 12,000 refugees. The IRO was a Western Cold War body set up to deal with the million Eastern European refugees from the Red Army who had refused to be shipped back east. The Truman administration provided old army transport ships to move them to any countries willing to take them. With a remarkable feat of logistics, the first shipload, comprising 843 young, single Baltic refugees, many of them blonde, blue-eyed and Lutheran, left Bremerhaven on 30 October, to be met in Melbourne by Calwell and his publicity machine on 7 December.[14]

The number agreed to was soon changed to 20,000, and, when there were few complaints in Australia except from Communists and extreme Protestants, 200,000. Over the next three years, about 180,000 Eastern European "Displaced Persons", about 60% of them Catholic, were transformed into "New Australians". The old insular Anglophone Australia was gone forever. As Calwell said years later:[15]

Had we had an anti-immigration man as prime minister, or a lukewarm one, we would still be a dull inbred country of predominantly British stock.

In 1949, when the Displaced Persons immigration scheme was well under way, Calwell received a letter from Mgr Montini, Vatican Under-Secretary of State.‡‡ The letter begins by conveying the Pope's thanks for copies of Calwell's pamphlets *This is Australia* and *The Australian Scene*. It concludes:[17]

Arthur Calwell with newly arrived migrant children at Bonegilla Migrant Camp in 1949.[16]

---

‡‡ The title does not convey Montini's importance. The position of Secretary of State was vacant and Giovanni Battista Montini, later Pope Paul VI, was in charge of all political matters including the fight against Communism in Italy and support for refugees.

> *"His Holiness prays that Your Excellency's activity in the field of immigration may continue to open up new avenues of life"*

His Holiness prays that Your Excellency's activity in the field of immigration may continue to open up new avenues of life for the many thousands of people whose future at the moment seems bereft of hope, and, as a token of his paternal benevolence, He imparts to you His Apostolic Blessing.

It would be possible to regard this as no more than a piece of polite Italianate officialese. On the face of it, the language is far from effusive. That is not how Calwell read it. He wrote requesting a cleaner copy, and distributed copies to those in the Catholic Church who had most enthusiastically worked to promote immigration, including Mannix. His covering letter says that the Pope's words apply to "everyone who like yourself has given such willing and helpful co-operation in the implementation of the plans which have excited the interest and won the commendation of the Supreme Pontiff."[18] He replied to Montini:[19]

> I was deeply touched by the expression of the Supreme Pontiff's paternal regard when he bestowed His Apostolic Blessing on me and on the work in which I am engaged as Minister of State in the Commonwealth of Australia. It is most gratifying to know that the work of arranging for the settlement of an ever increasing number in Australia of Displaced Persons from European countries meets with such august approval and evokes such touching commendation . . . I ask you to accept the assurance that no letter which I have written in the six years in which I have been privileged to hold Ministerial office in this country has given me greater pleasure than this acknowledgement of the Holy Father's appreciation of my humble efforts in the cause of distressed humanity.

THE WHITE AUSTRALIA POLICY

One matter on which Mannix and Calwell disagreed was the White Australia Policy. It was Calwell's commitment to strict Labor principles of support for the workers and White Australia that gave him the credibility to overcome Labor suspicions that immigration would undermine conditions for Australian workers. But Calwell's support for the White Australia policy was also principled, as he explained in 1949. He replied to the suggestion of Mannix and others of a small quota for non-whites:[20]

Can Be No Half-Measures About White Australia
By the Hon. ARTHUR A. CALWELL, Minister for Immigration

PROFESSOR Macmahon Ball[§§] in an article in *The Argus* of October 17 expresses the belief that the introduction of a quota for Asian migrants to Australia would be a wise step.

It is a step, the wisdom of which I would strongly challenge; and I am confident that I would have the overwhelming majority of Australians behind me in that challenge.

Introduction of a quota would simply be a form of appeasement – and appeasement has never solved any problem. There can be no half-measures in a matter such as the maintenance of the White Australia policy, on which Australians hold such emphatic views.

The ideal that this country, which was settled and developed by Europeans, should remain predominantly European was sponsored by our forefathers, and has had the unwavering support of all good Australians ever since. Establishment of a quota system for Asians would be an undermining of that Australian ideal which, I am sure, Australians would not tolerate.

If it is necessary to repeat it again – and I would have thought everybody knew it by now – I will repeat: Underlying the White Australia policy is no suggestion of racial superiority. It began as a positive aspiration, and from it has resulted a positive achievement.

This achievement is a united race of freedom-loving Australians who can intermarry and associate without the disadvantages that inevitably result from the fusion of dissimilar races; a united people who share the same loyalties, the same outlook, and the same traditions.

Evils Elsewhere

We will avoid the evils that plague America, that distress South Africa, that embitter Malaya, and that worry Fiji.

[§§] William Macmahon ("Mac") Ball, diplomat, broadcaster and Professor of Political Science at Melbourne University; see Peter Ryan, *William Macmahon Ball: A Memoir*, Melbourne University Press, Carlton, 1990.

Ingredients of an explosive character are inherent in the conditions existing in all those countries, and when the explosion occurs, as it did in Durban recently,¶ there is civil war. The evils of miscegenation always result in rioting and bloodshed. We have avoided them in this country, thanks to the foresight of our forebears and our own innate common sense.

We will continue to avoid them, if we are wise – and if we have the affection that parents ought to have for their children and their children's children. We are heirs of a glorious past. We are also trustees for what can be an even more glorious future.

'What the Popes have said on capitalism' and Mannix on Nationalisation

A major issue in the Federal election campaign of 1949 was the Chifley government's failed attempt to nationalise the banks. Many right-leaning Catholics, including Archbishop Duhig of Brisbane, argued that nationalisation conflicted with Catholic principles of respect for private property and advised voting against Labor.[21] Calwell replied with a pamphlet, 'What the Popes have said on capitalism and the employing class, the wage system, trades unions'. It quoted the pro-worker statements of the Papal encyclicals, and also a recent speech of Mannix:[22]

Labor policy and Catholic bishops not in conflict

His Grace Archbishop Mannix addressing members of the Irish National Foresters on October 16, 1949, spoke of the conscientious difficulties of two Catholics who had recently sought his counsel.

Dr. Mannix said:[23]

"One asked me whether, in view of the policy of the Liberal Country Party, he could continue to support it. He pointed out that he had conscientious difficulties, and that the Party was so attached to private enterprise and to capitalism of the old style that it seemed to him to be opposed to the best interests of Australia and to the teaching of the Pope.

"The other writer, a Labour supporter, asked if he could continue to support the Labour Party, which seemed to him to have too rigid a socialistic policy.

"My answer to both correspondents will be that they can dismiss their scruples.

"No doubt there are some diehards in every political party, but the Liberal Country Party, as such, does not stand for unrestricted, uncontrolled capitalism, I am sure.

¶ In January 1949, 142 Indians in Durban were killed by Zulus.

"There are die-hards in the Labour Party, too, who would socialise everything. Their policy, however, is not the policy of the Labour Party.

"Some twelve months ago I said that if the Blackburn interpretation really expressed the policy of the Labour Party there was no conflict in principle between the statement of the Australian Bishops and the policy of the Labour Party.

"I am glad to see that in recent times we had statements from the Labour Party, the Prime Minister, Mr. Calwell and Senator McKenna and others stating that the Blackburn interpretation of the Labour policy is and has been the policy of the Labour Party.

"I see no reason to change the statement that I made some twelve months ago. The Labour Party says it wants to nationalize such public utilities as cannot safely be left in the hands of private individuals. I think this is perfectly right and a consistent attitude to take, though, of course, there may well be wide differences of opinion when we come to determine what and how many public utilities there are which cannot, or should not, be left in private hands."

SANTAMARIA AND CALWELL FALL OUT

Calwell supported for some time the anti-Communist efforts of the Movement in the unions. As late as 1949 he admitted in Parliament to asking for a telephone connection for an anti-Communist organiser in the Communist-controlled Clerks Union.[24] But relations between him and Santamaria soured, as he came to see Santamaria's secret manoevrings as a threat to the Labor party – and also, possibly for more personal reasons, at least in Santamaria's opinion:[25]

RH (Interviewer): . . . what was Arthur Calwell's relationship to the Movement?

Bob Santamaria: Well in the very early stages when the Movement was formed at the beginning of the forties, Arthur Calwell was one of the people who wanted to bring it into existence and I would say that from 1941 to 1944 I thought I was on a very friendly and confidential basis with him [...] Around about '44 his attitude changed.

RH: Did you ever reconcile with him?

BS: I wanted to, but he didn't want to. I have told this story before, that I found it quite a shattering thing really. He hadn't spoken to me for a number of years, and he was quite hostile and I understood that because he gradually became opposed to the Industrial Groups and he adopted an opposition line to us, within the Labor Party, which is perfectly legitimate. He had a different idea. But although we had not spoken for a number of years, he had a young son, and whether he was nine or eleven of age I forget, but this young boy got leukaemia and died, and not long after that I ran into Arthur Calwell in Robertson & Mullins bookshop, and I knew it was taking a risk, and I went up to him and I said, 'I know that you don't want to talk to me, but I want to say to you that I understand what you're going through and I really am sorry', because I had my own children. And I was amazed. He said, 'I don't want sympathy from you', and I knew how deep it was. And it was just like that. I think about him, it was a great misfortune, because in many ways he was a very considerable man. He would have made a good prime minister.

RH: Do you think that it was difficult for him having decided to be against the Movement, and being himself a Catholic, that he was perhaps torn internally . . .

BS: Yes, I think he . . . I think he was.

RH: . . . and he projected that feeling on to you?

BS: I think so. I think that there was another aspect to it and I'm not sure about this.

He had been, during . . . He was older than I was. During the conscription period he had been a very loyal supporter of Dr Mannix, and I think he idolised Dr Mannix and I think that as he went into public life and got into the Curtin . . . or the Chifley Cabinet, and he was away, and as I got to know Dr Mannix better, and became quite close to him, not consciously – it just happened – I think he resented that. But I may be wrong, but I think it's right.

"I think [Calwell] idolised Dr Mannix . . ."

". . . as I got to know Dr Mannix better, and became quite close to him, not consciously – it just happened – I think [Calwell] resented that"

CALWELL "HURT" BY MANNIX

During the Split of 1955 and after, Calwell was widely reviled by the followers of the Movement and his motives for staying with Labor questioned. Mannix himself did not explicitly condemn Calwell in personal terms. But Calwell recalled the one time that he felt hurt by Mannix:[26]

The one time when Archbishop Mannix hurt me, and hurt me deeply, was after the 1955 Labor Party split. He addressed a conference of his clergy and laid down the guidelines for functions to which he was to be invited, whether they followed church services or not. He said the priests could invite whatever public figures they liked, but he added: 'I will not appear with any of those who have been false to their principles.' Of course, it followed naturally and inevitably that every Catholic politician, Federal or

State, who refused to join the DLP was excluded from church functions. The order affected me directly and greatly.

A function was arranged in connection with a church opening. I had been asked by a nun who taught at the local school to present a tabernacle to the church, and I promised to do so in memory of my son, Arthur Andrew, who died of leukaemia in 1948 at the age of 16. But there was a delay in arrangements because another church was being blessed and there was no tabernacle available. So the one for which I had paid 100 pounds was transferred to the other church. The parish priest concerned spoke to me and said that the parish would pay half the price of the next one, which was to cost 200 pounds. But I said that as my wife and I had promised to install the tabernacle, we would pay the full cost. In the meantime, Archbishop Mannix had made his pronouncement, and within a day or so the same priest visited me at my office. I invited him in and immediately put him at ease by saying that I had already heard the story he wished to tell me and I would not embarrass him. The priest said to me: 'As a matter of fact, Dr Mannix will not be blessing the church because he is not well enough.' He said: 'Archbishop Simonds will perform the ceremony.' I replied: 'Well, if Archbishop Mannix were well enough, he would not want me present. And I have no intention of taking advantage of his illness. I know I would be welcomed by Archbishop Simonds, but if I can't enter the church by the front door, I am not coming in the back way.' The priest said: 'Well, you and your wife could have breakfast with me one morning and then inspect the tabernacle.' I said: 'No. Under no circumstances will I ever go near the church. I don't ever expect to see that tabernacle.' I have never seen it or the church.

In 1964, a brown paper parcel arrived at Calwell's office. It proved to contain a document from Rome in Latin, of obscure meaning. When translated some time later, it revealed that Calwell was now Knight Commander of the Order of St Gregory the Great with the Grand Silver Star. Though it had no detailed citation, he later heard it was awarded in honour of his general devotion to the Church, the possibility (by then remote) of becoming Prime Minister, and his work on post-war immigration. It was well deserved.[27]

1. J. Franklin, Calwell, Catholicism and the origins of multicultural Australia, *Proceedings of the Australian Catholic Historical Society 2009 Conference*, 42-54, http://web.maths.unsw.edu.au/~jim/calwellACHSconf09.pdf.
2. Calwell in *Auckland Star* 26/1/65, quoted in C. Kiernan, *Calwell: A Political and Personal Biography*, Thomas Nelson, West Melbourne, 1978, p. 119.
3. Roy Williams, *In God They Trust: The Religious Beliefs of Australia's Prime Ministers 1901-2013*, Bible Society, 2013.
4. Arthur A. Calwell, *Be Just and Fear Not*, Lloyd O'Neil Pty Ltd, in association with Rigby Ltd, 1972, pp. 147-148.
5. Arthur A. Calwell, *Be Just and Fear Not*, pp. 36 and 37
6. Arthur Augustus CALWELL, T C MAHER and William McCABE (Alleged Sinn Feiners), item NAA: A8911, 244: http://recordsearch.naa.gov.au/SearchNRetrieve/Interface/DetailsReports/ItemDetail.aspx?Barcode=821871
7. Calwell, *Be Just and Fear Not*, pp: 137-138.
8. House of Representatives Hansard, 27 November 1940: http://parlinfo.aph.gov.au/parlInfo/search/display/display.w3p;query=Id%3A%22hansard80%2Fhansardr80%2F1940-11-27%2F0227%22
9. Anthony Cappello, Archbishop Mannix and Italian relief, in A. Cappello, ed., *Enemy Aliens: The Internment of Italian Migrants in Australia*, Connor Court, Ballan, 2005; Anthony Cappello, Mannix, Modotti and the Italian POWs, *Quadrant*, 48 (7/8), (Jul/Aug 2004): 38-41.
10. Anthony S. Cappello, To be or not to be an Italian: BA Santamaria, culture, descent and the social exclusion of Italian-Australians, PhD thesis, Victoria University, 2009, ch. 5.
11. Calwell, *Be Just and Fear Not*, pp: 128-130.
12. *Tribune*, 30 May 1946, quoted in Michael Gilchrist, *Daniel Mannix: Wit and Wisdom*, Freedom Publishing, 2nd edition 2004, ch. 8, pp. 189-192.
13. Quoted in J. Zubrzycki, *Arthur Calwell and the Origin of Post-War Immigration*, Canberra, 1995, p. 3.
14. Franklin, Calwell, Catholicism and the origins of multicultural Australia; Mary Elizabeth Calwell, *I Am Bound To Be True: The Life and Legacy of Arthur Calwell*, Mosaic Press, Preston, 2012, pp. 65-7.
15. Calwell in *Auckland Star* 26/1/65, quoted in Colm Kiernan, *Calwell: A Political and Personal Biography*, Thomas Nelson, West Melbourne, 1978, p. 119.
16. *Border Morning Mail*, 2 July 1949; http://www.bonegilla.org.au/block19/visitorbook.asp.
17. Montini to Calwell, 4/4/49, in Calwell papers, National Library of Australia, Box 62; M. E. Calwell, *I Am Bound To Be True*, pp. 85-6.
18. Letters of 30/5/49.
19. Calwell to Montini, 30/6/49.
20. *Argus*, 24 October 1949, p. 2: http://trove.nla.gov.au/ndp/del/article/22787419
21. Duncan, *Crusade or Conspiracy?* p. 144.
22. Arthur A. Calwell, *What the Popes have said on capitalism and the employing class, the wage system, trades unions*, Melbourne, 1949, http://handle.slv.vic.gov.au/10381/123190; M. E. Calwell, *I Am Bound To Be True*, p. 79
23. *Argus*, 26 November 1949, p. 2.

24 House of Representatives Hansard, 21/9/1949. The organiser, W. T. ("Diver") Dobson, was not what he seemed: Philip Deery, Labor, communism and the cold war: The case of 'Diver' Dobson, *Australian Historical Studies* 27 (1997), 66-87.

25 Santamaria interviews from a transcript of the complete original interview conducted for the Australian Biography project by Robin Hughes, Recorded: April 23, 24 and 25, 1997: Interview 2: http://www.australianbiography.gov.au/subjects/santamaria/interview2.html

26 Calwell, *Be Just and Fear Not*, pp: 141-2

27 Calwell, *Be Just and Fear Not*, pp. 159-61

Chapter 13: Santamaria and the Movement

No other country's Catholicism produced a figure quite like B.A. Santamaria. And if he had been destined to exist somewhere, Australia should have been the least likely place for him to fall to earth. The sceptical, secular, isolated Anglophone society of mid-twentieth-century Australia was surely stony ground for an ideologue with a European sensibility and a vast plan to reorder society according to a rational and divine moral order.

Bartholomew Augustine Santamaria was the son of a Brunswick greengrocer who had immigrated from the Aeolian Islands. He was dux of St Kevin's College, a school established in 1918, with Mannix's strong support, to promote high academic standards among boys completing Leaving. He graduated in arts and law and became committed to Catholic social theory, co-founding in 1936 the *Catholic Worker*, a journal dedicated to opposing both capitalism and communism from the perspective of Catholic social teaching as set out in *Rerum Novarum*. Then in 1937 Mannix called him in for a chat and to put a request which changed his life forever. Santamaria was to help lead a National Secretariat for Catholic Action, dedicated to advancing Catholic policies in the social, industrial and political sphere.

Catholics soon came to consider Communism a more urgent threat than capitalism. By the end of World War II, Australian Communist Party membership rose to 20,000 and the Party controlled a number of powerful unions. Overseas, Communist takeovers in Eastern Europe and East Asia threatened to deliver world domination to the Soviet Union. At a time of widespread naivety in Australia about the realities of Soviet repression, Catholics understood from news of Communist persecutions what a Soviet victory would mean. Santamaria led the formation of groups in the unions aimed at countering Communist influence.

By the early 1950s, "The Movement", whose existence was still unknown to the public, had had great success in breaking Communist control of the unions and was widely influential in the Labor Party. Santamaria began to hope that the (mostly Catholic) parliamentarians associated with the Movement might gain control of a Labor government and implement a Catholic vision of the political good.[1]

In 1954, the Labor opposition leader, Dr Evatt, denounced the influence of the Movement in the Labor Party. Santamaria, hitherto a man of power without glory, became suddenly a public figure. A bitter split of the Labor Party ensued, with the result that Labor remained in the political wilderness federally for another seventeen years. A largely Catholic right-of-centre minor party, the Democratic Labor Party had little success in its own right except for winning a few Senate seats, but its preferences excluded Labor from electoral success.

Santamaria always retained the strong support of the aged Mannix for his endeavours. Other elements in the Church, especially the leadership in Sydney and the Vatican, feared that the Movement had wrongly embroiled the Church's spiritual mission in party politics. In 1957 the Papal Secretary of State, Archbishop Tardini, sent a secret condemnation of the too close relationship between elements of the Australian Church and political action. Mannix, as he had done decades earlier over Irish republicanism, took virtually no notice.[2]

Throughout these campaigns Santamaria, a tireless organiser and an intellectual capable of absorbing vast amounts of information on a huge range of topics, wrote many articles on such topics as Communism, economics, geopolitics, immigration and population policy, rural affairs. They appeared in his organ *News Weekly* and sometimes as social justice statements of the Australian Catholic bishops.[3] They are all in line with Mannix's earlier statements on those topics.

Mannix makes an offer

Santamaria met Mannix for the first time when discussing the foundation of the *Catholic Worker*. The first issue of the *Catholic Worker*, almost entirely written by Santamaria, appeared on 2 February 1936. It was filled with such Mannix themes as an aggressive stance to men "who believe Birth-Control is a boon, Communism a possibility, sterilization and race suicide as advantages, and in materialism as an ultimate standard." Circulation reached 27,000 by August.[4]

Then in 1937:[5]

... one day – it was on the day that I signed the solicitor's roll, having just got my law degree – I got a phone call to go up to the cathedral to meet Archbishop Mannix, which I did, and he asked me if I'd take the second job [with the Secretariat]. I'd never dreamt, so I said ... I said,

> *"I said 'Yes', because I would have said yes to anything that he said"*

'Yes', because I would have said yes to anything that he said. And then, as I walked downstairs I had the terrible thought that I had to go home and tell my father, whose great ambition was his son should be a lawyer, so I thought of the speech I'd make, and I pointed out that it was only for two years and then I discovered that my father was enthusiastic, because he would do anything Archbishop Mannix wanted, so he caused no difficulty at all. But unfortunately the two years were extended. That would have made it 1940, and this is 1997.

I met Daniel Mannix for the first time when he was seventy odd years of age and I was only twenty. I was not to know then that in the last fifteen years he was to become the closest friend I ever made; under God, the point of reference of my life. Whatever the future may bring, life has lost a certain flavour: and nothing can bring it back.

"... under God, the point of reference of my life"

B.A. Santamaria and Archbishop Matthew Beovich at Catholic Action youth rally, 1943.[7]

During the early 1940s, Calwell supported the anti-Communist efforts of the groups. The old network came together in 1941 and 1942 to protect Santamaria from call-up for war service, to preserve what was regarded as his essential work. At Mannix's request, Scullin sought a deferment for Santamaria and the cathedral organist. When new regulations made call-up more likely, Mannix wrote to the Minister for Labour and National Service, and Calwell phoned the Minister for the Army in support of Santamaria's exemption. They were successful.[6] (There is no evidence that Santamaria knew of these efforts on his behalf.)

THE COMMUNIST PARTY DISSOLUTION DEBATE

In 1951, with Australian troops in Korea, the Menzies government held a referendum which would have allowed it to ban the Communist Party. Although Communism had by this time little political support in Australia, there were doubts across the political spectrum about the wisdom and morality of suppressing civil liberties to the extent of banning the Party. Santamaria was one of those who believed the threat of Communism was pressing enough to need urgent action. Dr Evatt, leader of the Federal Labor opposition and a passionate opponent of the referendum, sent an envoy to see Mannix. Senator Nick McKenna explained to Mannix that in principle Menzies' proposed legislation might allow a bigoted or Masonic government to declare the Catholic Church a Communist organisation, in view of the near-socialist objectives such as free education that had been supported in the bishops' social justice statements.[8] Whether as a result of these representations or because of inherent doubts about government restrictions on the freedom of organisations, Mannix supported a No vote.

In the event, the referendum was narrowly defeated, achieving a majority yes vote in three states but failing in the other three, including Victoria.

In a covering letter to a memorandum to Cabinet in 1950, Mannix sets out his misgivings.[9]

Needless to say, I am glad that your Government proposes to give no quarter to Communists. For with me the Communist menace is no mere political matter; it threatens the Christian way of life.

Those who have drawn up the Memorandum are the same people who a few years ago, almost single-handed, tackled the Communists in their chosen battleground the industrial unions. I have been in close touch with this fight, and I venture to say that there has been a large measure of success. Indeed, anything that the late Government was

> "... with me the Communist menace is no mere political matter; it threatens the Christian way of life"

able to achieve against Communism was made possible because, by quiet but effective work, the mass of the unionists were gradually won over to sanity. A definite cleavage was made between them and the Communists.

Of course the battle is not over. The Communists will now try to undo what has been done, and set up a common front against your Government. Any unwise move would play into their hands.

Like the authors of the Memorandum, I have more faith in securing clean union elections than in banning the Communists, or making strikes illegal. Above all, I fear that any attempt to hamper unionists in the election of their officers might just be the one thing that would line up the mass of unionists in a common front with the Communists. At the moment certain repressive measures may be quite logical, but yet unwise.

You will pardon me for writing at such length. The Memorandum speaks for itself, and I shall be grateful if you can bring it before the Prime Minister and the Cabinet.

Faithfully yours,

† D. MANNIX

Santamaria describes the strange feeling of being in disagreement with Mannix:[10]

Mannix stated that he could not agree with our new position. He thereupon handed me two sheets of paper and asked me to read the text of a short address which he proposed to deliver some time before the vote. In essence, the view he proposed to state was that there was no such thing as a Catholic position on the referendum question which, or course, no one disputed. Catholics were free to vote either way, depending on their view as to whether priority should be given to the Communist question (the Government's view or to the danger to civil liberties, the Opposition's). There were other ways in which Communism could be fought (for example, in the unions themselves) but the question of how to vote was open. Although it was not stated, informed readers could deduce from his statement that the Archbishop himself would vote 'No'.

It was an unusual moment. I had not previously found myself in conflict with Mannix. Before I could say anything he cut across me with a terse comment: 'You have come to your own conclusion and if you change it simply to fall in with mine I will have no respect for you'.

This brief, indeed abrupt, statement was an illustration of the genuine liberalism which characteristically informed his attitude not merely towards the Movement but towards all Catholics, whether he regarded them as friend or foe.

Everyone was entitled to his own opinion. He would not attempt to direct them as to

"Everyone was entitled to his own opinion. He would not attempt to direct them as to what they should believe, say, or write on matters which were not directly issues of faith or morals"

what they should believe, say, or write on matters which were not directly issues of faith or morals. On the other hand, he was equally free to declare his opinions, even if they involved opposition to theirs. If the fact that he did so resulted in unfavourable consequences for those whose view he opposed, because of the influence of his voice on the Catholic public as a whole, that was something they would have to weigh. But just as he would not attempt to muzzle them, they should not expect to muzzle him.

Santamaria reports to Mannix on the Movement's aim to transform Australia

In the debate over the Split in 1955, an issue heatedly debated was whether the Movement was engaged merely in a fight against Communism in the unions, or whether it was a pressure group attempting to take over the Labor movement and direct it into its own ideological path. A crucial PERSONAL AND CONFIDENTIAL LETTER of Santamaria to Mannix 1952, makes it absolutely clear that in Santamaria's mind, at least, the latter was true. He had large ambitions to implement a Catholic political and social program through gaining control of the ALP. The only obstacle, in his view, was that the bishops might withdraw support for his political manoeuvrings and that less zealous Catholic laypeople might not follow his directions.[11]

In one sense, therefore, the Social Studies Movement has fulfilled its immediate task. Were it to resign its mandate in the immediate future there would, of course, be an immediate increase in the Communist pressure throughout the entire Labor Movement. A number of unions including some of the largest, would fall to the Communist Party. But the Australian industrial situation is such to-day that the country would only have itself to blame were it to allow the Communists to regain the grip which they had in 1945.

For the last three years, however, it has been recognised that the possibilities of the Social Studies Movement are far wider than those offered by the defensive battle against Communism. As a result of the fact that the Australian trade unions are affiliated with the Labor Party, and that the leading figures in each trade union become delegates to Labor Party Conferences, rising then to executive and parliamentary positions, it was inevitable that as our people obtained prominence in the unions, they would rise also in the political field. This has become a factor of very great importance. It has been

"... the possibilities of the Social Studies Movement are far wider than those offered by the defensive battle against Communism"

traditional in the Australian Labor Movement that Catholics should play a prominent part. However, in the past, through no fault of their own, very many of these Catholics have not realised the social and moral implications of their faith in the field of public affairs. The new generation now rising to political prominence as a result of their work in the Social Studies Movement have a far clearer realisation of these obligations and accordingly, despite human limitations, can achieve far more in terms of the national welfare.

Since Your Grace is well aware of the personalities whom we have been able to influence and organise within both State and Federal political circles, it is unnecessary to labour this particular point.

As a result of what has been achieved to date, and in the light of reasonable and conservative expectations for the future, there is no reason why the Social Studies Movement should not be able to do far more for the public welfare in the future than it has been able to achieve in the past. What it can reasonably be expected to achieve can be listed under the following heads:

> *"The Social Studies Movement should within a period of five or six years be able to completely transform the leadership of the Labor Movement . . ."*

(1) The Social Studies Movement should within a period of five or six years be able to completely transform the leadership of the Labor Movement, and to introduce into Federal and State spheres large numbers of members who possess a clear realisation of what Australia demands of them, and the will to carry it out. Without going into details, they should be able to implement a Christian social programme in both the State and Federal spheres, and above all, to achieve co-ordination between the different States in so doing. This is the first time that such a work has become possible in Australia and, as far as I can see, in the Anglo-Saxon world since the advent of Protestantism.

(2) It should be possible, within the next six years, as a result of the political forces thus organised, to solve the problem of financial aid to Catholic education. Whether the taxing powers remain with the Commonwealth, or whether they revert to the States, this result is equally feasible, in view of the condition of our organisation at Federal and State levels respectively.

(3) Again, it should be possible to execute large-scale plans of land settlement.

As a result, not only will Australia benefit by a continuation of the migration programme, but the Church will be able to gain great accessions of strength because of the religious composition of the migrant groups which would be thus absorbed into Australian life.

Large-scale plans of land settlement cannot be achieved without the full co-operation of State Governments in providing land at low cost. It has been possible to secure this co-operation from the Tasmanian Government already, because of our influence with the Premier and his Party. The same co-operation is likely to be obtained in New South Wales and Queensland, and now possibly also in Victoria.

> "... the Church will be able to gain great accessions of strength because of the religious composition of the migrant groups ..."

That was not to be. In 1954, Dr Evatt denounced the influence of the still-secret Movement and blamed them for the loss of the recent Federal election. Other Labor members began to criticise the influence of the secret Catholic bloc controlled by Santamaria. Mannix issued a statement denying that the Church had ever wished to control the ALP.[12]

"NO CHURCH AIM TO CONTROL LABOR" DR. MANNIX ANSWERS DR. EVATT

It is not my wish to concern myself in any way with the internal controversies of any political party. However, I note with regret that the name of the Catholic Church has been drawn into the controversy initiated during the past week by the leader of the Opposition.

> "... the Catholic Church has never aimed to control the Labor Party ..."

It is being suggested in various quarters that the real purpose of the leader of the Opposition's statement is to pinpoint what is alleged to be a policy of the Catholic Church – to control the Labor Party through Catholic Action. Needless to say, the Catholic Church has never aimed to control the Labor Party – or any other party. Nor does it aim to do so today.

If the Church has at different times expressed its viewpoint on public policy, it has done no more than the leaders of non-Catholic religious bodies.

The leader of the Opposition's attack seems to be concentrated on those men who have been most active in the fight against Communism in the trade unions and in the Labor Party.

Although many of these men are Catholics, many are of different religious beliefs. They have united, irrespective of creed, but as Australians, to defend their country against Communism. In this they deserve the support of all loyal Australians.

In so far as they have energised the Labor movement in its fight against Communism, it seems to me that they have strengthened rather than weakened the Labor cause.

We are in the midst of a period of grave national danger, when the united energies of the Australian people should be concentrated on the basic problem of national survival. It seems, therefore, a singularly ill-chosen moment to divide the nation along sectarian lines.

Does Calwell deserve absolution?

In Melbourne especially, there were extremely bitter feelings between Santamaria supporters who had been expelled from the ALP, sometimes at the cost of their jobs, and those such as Calwell who stayed with Labor. The atmosphere of the time and the way religion tangled with politics is caught in Santamaria's recollection of a difficult question he faced at a priests' conference: [13]

> At the next monthly conference of clergy, the two speakers were the same. Seated in the front row was my old antagonist, Father Lombard.* He prefaced his question by stating that it was addressed to me. Then he asked: 'Mr Santamaria, in view of all that has been said, if you were a priest and Mr Calwell came to confession to you, would you give him absolution?' Since the question was not political but theological, and therefore neither my business nor within my competence, I attempted to pass it over to the Archbishop. To my consternation, I saw that he was quivering with suppressed laughter. He simply nodded to me to take the question. Something made me answer: 'Father Lombard, as a layman my job is to receive absolution, not to give it'. The next day Mannix referred to the answer. 'There was a touch of the Delphic oracle about it'. I could only say: 'And about Your Grace's action, there was a touch of a captain refusing to throw a life belt to a sinking sailor.'

The Pope acts against Mannix and Santamaria

Catholic Labor men, especially in Victoria and Queensland, formed the Democratic Labor Party. It won few seats but took votes from Labor. Santamaria and Mannix had to fight not only on the political front against Evatt, Calwell and other Labor leaders, but against enemies in the Church. In Sydney, Cardinal Gilroy and Archbishop Carroll urged Labor supporters to "stay in and fight", and requested the Church authorities in Rome to speak against Mannix's directly involving the Church in political controversy.

The "Sydney line" gained Vatican support. Word came from Rome in 1957 directly contradicting the Mannix-Santamaria line that the Movement needed to become a body both political and explicitly Catholic in order to fight Communism. The Pope expressed his "profound grief" that the Australian bishops are publicly brawling over politics, "not without detriment to the respect which is owed by that same laity to their Bishops". The operative clause in this letter instructs:

---

* Fr Frank Lombard, who had fought since the mid-1940s to curtail Santamaria's influence.

. . . it is not deemed advisable that a Confessional Political Party be created, or that the Movement take a political character upon itself, and hence freedom should be left to Catholics to belong to other political parties, provided those parties do not act in contrast with the principles of the Church.[14]

Nothing could have been a clearer slap in the face for the hope of Mannix and Santamaria to support the DLP and condemn voting for Labor. Mannix, as usual, gave cheek. His reply to the Pope was:[15]

Holy Father,

With deep humility, and much confidence in your paternal care for all your children, I ask Your Holiness for guidance regarding the enclosed Instructions given to the Bishops of Australia.

The first, dated 27th May 1957, would I hope, have ended the unhappy controversy amongst the Bishops. It contained one instruction, number 3, which might possibly be construed as a direction to the Movement to withdraw from the Trade Union and political aspects of the struggle against Communism; but I discarded that interpretation as being inconsistent with the praise of the Movement's activities in the same letter of the 27th May. I therefore concluded that paragraph number 3 must be a gentle intimation, not to the Movement, but to the Bishops, that they, the Bishops, would do well to leave the purely industrial and political fields to the laymen. In that sense, I wholeheartedly and joyfully accepted the first letter as ending the controversy.

But the second letter of the 25th July suggests, to my surprise that my interpretation was erroneous, and that the lay Movement is really to cease operating in the industrial and political fields altogether. There are many things that I could say and that perhaps need saying about the whole controversy, but I deal with only one aspect of the matter.

At this stage, the controversy is not a matter of mere dispute between Bishops. That could be ended behind closed doors, as it were. The Catholic laymen who, I venture to say, are unsurpassed in their loyalty to the Church, and to the Holy See – these laymen, thousands of them in every state of Australia, must be informed without any assignable reason, that the anti-communist and antisocialistic activities, for which they have so often hitherto been commended by the Bishops, and even by the Holy See, must cease forthwith. They used to be assured, and rightly, that they were the only effective force fighting against Communism, for the protection of Church and State. Surely they will be bewildered at the sudden and unexplained change of front, and grieve to see all their best efforts frustrated by the stroke of a pen. The Communists too, will learn of the latest decision. They have recognised that the Movement is their most deadly and effective foe in Australia, they therefore set out to smash the Movement, and its Industrial

Groups. They failed. If the new interpretation of the Roman Instruction is upheld, the Communists will be in a position to boast that, while they failed to crush The Movement, their purpose has unexpectedly been achieved by other means.

> *"Holy Father, if I have spoken too strongly, I most humbly apologise"*

Holy Father, if I have spoken too strongly, I most humbly apologise, but I feel strongly, and I do appeal to Your Holiness to have these Instructions, or rather their interpretation further examined. I ask whether, under the said Instructions, rightly interpreted, loyal Catholic Australian laymen of The Movement are free, like the laymen of Italy and other nations, to engage even directly in the affairs of industrial and political unions or parties, in the course of their fight against Communism, provided:

1. The activities of The Movement are not in conflict with moral law, and

2. The Movement gives assurance publicly, if necessary, that the Church or the Bishops are in no way responsible for its policy or activities.

Signed, D. Mannix
Archbishop of Melbourne.

The Secretary of State replied that Mannix was absolutely wrong.[16]

Danial [sic] Mannix D.D., Archbishop of Melbourne.

Your Excellency,

The letter, which Your Excellency addressed to the Holy Father on August 22nd last, was transmitted without delay by the Apostolic Delegation in Australia, and placed in the august hands of His Holiness. The Sovereign Pontiff has deigned to take into consideration the contents of Your Excellency's letter, and I am now charged to inform you that the Instructions contained in the two letters of the Sacred Congregation of Propaganda Fide (N2909/57, N1975/57) must retain their full value. At the same time, in order to provide Your Excellency with some elements which might illustrate the aforesaid decisions, I am setting forth here below, a few remarks. These however, as Your Excellency will understand, cannot eventually be interpreted or quoted as modifying or attenuating in any way, the authoritative directives already communicated to the Hierarchy of Australia.

1. In the first place, I would like to recall the situation which Their Eminences, the Cardinals were charged to examine. Concerning the Catholic Social Movement and its Activities, there had arisen discussions and discordant views among the Bishops and amongst the Catholic laity of Australia. In fact, the division amongst the Hierarchy had

gone so far as to become notorious, to become the subject of public comment, and to be mentioned even in the press. All this had disturbed the consciences of Catholics and caused wonderment in wide circles of public opinion, with the consequent danger of bringing about a diminution of the prestige and authority of the hierarchy, and a weakening of cohesion and collaboration between Catholic forces. This was injurious to the life of the Church, to its evangelising activity, and in particular, to that struggle against atheistic Communism which the Catholic Social Movement fixed as one of the most important points in its programme. Their Eminences, the Cardinals therefore, not only did not underestimate the need and urgency for continuing that struggle, but precisely in view of it, they have been concerned with eliminating such motives and attitudes as might weaken it. [. . .]

Your Excellency pointed out that paragraph 3 of letter number 1975/57 from the Sacred Congregation of Propaganda Fide, under the date of May 22nd last (leaving aside all direct action), could be interpreted as "a gentle intimation, not to the Movement but to the Bishops, that they, namely the Bishops, would do well to leave the purely industrial and political fields to the laymen". This is an interpretation which, as Your Excellency later admits, cannot be maintained. It would be sufficient in fact, to note that the purpose of the above mentioned instruction was merely to indicate the aims and the limits of the Catholic Social Movement's activities, and that furthermore, it would be out of place to remind the Bishops to avoid interfering in unions and political parties, since there was never any question or doubt about this point. And now, having explained the criteria which inspired the decisions of the Holy See, I am to tell Your Excellency that it is the Holy Father's heartfelt wish that an effective and cordial unity of aims and purposes should be established as soon as possible between the members of the zealous Hierarchy of Australia. His Holiness furthermore, feels warmly confident that Your Excellency generously accepting these directives, will render your invaluable assistance enriched as it is by the long and very active pastoral experience, in order to bring about the reconstitution of the Catholic Social Movement in accordance with the new orientation laid down for it.

"it is the Holy Father's heartfelt wish ... to bring about the reconstitution of the Catholic Social Movement"

I take this occasion to assure Your Excellency of my high esteem and cordial regard,

I remain,

Yours sincerely in Christ,

Domenico Tardini[†].

[†] Cardinal Domenico Tardini, Vatican Secretary of State 1958-61, under John XXIII; effectively occupied that role for some years previously.

Mannix despondent

Santamaria recalled the "wake" at the receipt of the news.¹⁷

It was rare that Mannix fell victim to depression: he had seen too many things not to understand that few turns of fortune had any real finality. This was, however, a different situation. Never abashed by opposition from fellow bishops, or even from cardinals; undisposed to accept what he regarded as the pretensions of the Vatican bureaucracy, the Pope's word had always been final for him. The Pope had quite clearly spoken, and clearly he had supported those against whom Mannix had fought.

On the face of it there was nothing more to be done.

At the informal meeting at Raheen to which Mannix had invited his suffragan bishops, O'Collins of Ballarat, Stewart of Sandhurst, Lyons of Sale – and at which I was also asked to be present – the atmosphere was one of total despondency.

> "On the face of it there was nothing more to be done"

It would be quite untrue to say that I was not affected by the same general gloom as the others who were present. The emotion I experienced most strongly, however, was anger, not at the decision, but at the arguments used to sustain it. The rulings of the Vatican, especially now that the Pope himself had spoken, were rulings, and should be obeyed. The arguments used to sustain them, however, should stand or fall on their own merits. Too many conflicting arguments had been used and justified over the years to evoke superstitious awe.

How could one have any respect for the argument that the Australian bishops, in the course of the struggle against Communism, should steer clear of any political involvement, when the Pope himself had involved the entire Italian hierarchy and the Church in the Italian elections of 1948, when there was a real prospect of a victory by Togliatti and the Italian Communist Party?‡

Mannix and Evatt clash: the 1958 election

On 19 November 1958, three days before the federal election, Cardinal Gilroy said that he would take no action to prevent his name being used in advertisements by the ALP – that is, in support of the view that Catholics might vote Labor. Mannix took that as a licence to make his own statement:¹⁸

---

‡ Santamaria is correct that the Church took many and effective political actions to prevent the predicted Communist victory in the 1948 Italian elections. See Elisa A. Carrillo, The Italian Catholic Church and Communism, 1943-1963, *Catholic Historical Review* 77 (1991), 644-57. He omits to mention that the Communist Party was unlikely to be elected in Australia in 1958.

> *"Every Communist and every Communist sympathizer in Australia wants a victory for the Evatt party"*

Amid the turmoil of the election, one thing seems clear. Every Communist and every Communist sympathizer in Australia wants a victory for the Evatt party. That is alarming. It should be a significant warning for every Catholic, for every decent Australian. Hitherto, I have not deemed it necessary to sound a note of warning. The Communists have long been falsely suggesting that Cardinal Gilroy stands for comparatively neutral benevolence.

Of course, the Cardinal ignored their malevolent use of his name. But now that the Evatt party, forgetting all about sectarianism, is trying to shelter under his name in nationwide advertisements and in pamphlets distributed outside Catholic churches to congregations on Sundays, I deem it timely to recall the official attitude of the Cardinal and of all the Catholic Bishops of Australia.

Writing at a time when the menace of Communism was not as pressing as it is now, and writing, not in the pressure and heat of election time, but in the calm, restrained atmosphere of a national pastoral letter, the Cardinal wrote and all the Bishops signed the following words:

> At the moment there is one outstanding issue for the nation and the Church. It is the immediate Communist threat to the security of the people and to the freedom of religion in Australia.

The Cardinal, with the Bishops, went on almost prophetically to say:

> It is very regrettable that highly placed public men, including some Catholics, seem to have closed their eyes to the great issues involved in the present upheaval. They do not appear to realize that they are forwarding the interests of Communism.

It seems to me timely to recall these calm and weighty words. It is needless to add that the Democratic Labor Party, Protestant and Catholic alike, at heroic cost to themselves, have stood, and stand consistently for the principles espoused in that Pastoral Letter. Can the same be said of others?

Dr. Evatt, and the (Catholic) Leader of the Opposition in the Senate, Senator McKenna, in a joint statement, described the comments by Archbishop Mannix as,[19]

> ... an open entry into the field of party political activity as distinct from normal and regular exercise of episcopal functions ...

His views on many highly controversial national issues are well known since World War I.

> While we admire and respect his long service as chief pastor of his diocese charged

with the care of souls, his views on party politics can only be accepted as those of any other individual Australian churchman whatever his ecclesiastical status or denominational affiliation.

With the failure of the DLP, Santamaria and Mannix were in the political wilderness and increasingly out of temper with the times, although Santamaria's pronouncements, now he was a well-known figure, were a part of public debate.

Mannix continued to reciprocate Santamaria's high regard. In his 1961 television interview, Mannix was asked about his relations with Santamaria.[20]

> Archbishop Mannix: Well, friendly on my part. I don't know what he thinks, but on my side they are very friendly, and I regard him as the saviour of Australia at the present time because while other people say they are not Communists and say they hate Communism, they do not do anything about it. Communists don't bother whether they are hated or liked, as long as they are winning their way. But Mr. Santamaria is one man who has stood out all along. He was one, of course, among many, but he stands out in fighting Communism in the unions, in the political sphere, in fact, everywhere that he could exert influence, and so far he has had a large measure of success. It's for the Australian people to say in the end whether they want Communism or whether they want those who are opposed to Communism.

SANTAMARIA AT THE DEATH OF MANNIX

On Monday 3 November, 1963 Dr Mannix received nine visitors in his usual unhurried way. One of them was Bob Santamaria who stayed half an hour and discussed the proposed building of Mannix College at the recently established Monash University. Santamaria reported that Mannix said to him, "'I'd be grateful to you if you'd take these plans down to Sir Michael Chamberlain on your way home. If I die, that College will never be built.' And he just burst out laughing."[21]

It was only a few days later that Mannix died. Santamaria recalled:[22]

> Since with a few others I knelt and stood by his bedside over long hours and watched him die, the thought which has haunted my mind is not the things he did, but the kind of man he was.
>
> He was a man of infinite humour, tinged only with irony at the follies and pretences of the world. I remember sitting in his study one day several years ago, together with Bishop O'Collins and Bishop Lyons. Someone had remarked in the press that when the Archbishop died, his death would lead to great changes in the political situation in

Australia. There was a rather animated discussion about this, the Archbishop, whose death was the topic of conversation, saying never a word. I looked at him to see what he was thinking of this very strange discussion about his own death. Suddenly, Bishop O'Collins said emphatically: 'I say that Mannix dead will be more powerful than Mannix alive'. For the first time the Archbishop opened his mouth,

'That may console you' he said, 'but I don't see what it does for me!'

---

1. Bruce Duncan, *Crusade or Conspiracy: Catholics and the anti-Communist struggle in Australia*, UNSW Press, Sydney, 2001; Patrick Morgan, ed, *B.A. Santamaria: Running the Show: selected documents: 1939-1996*, Miegunyah Press, Carlton, 2008.
2. Duncan, *Crusade or Conspiracy*, pp. 344-7.
3. Michael Hogan, ed, *Justice now!: Social justice statements of the Australian Catholic Bishops. First series, 1940-1966,* Dept. of Government and Public Administration, University of Sydney, Sydney 1990.
4. Colin H. Jory, *The Campion Society and Catholic Militancy in Australia 1929-1939,* pp. 76-7; James G. Murtagh, *Australia, The Catholic Chapter*, Angus and Robertson, Sydney 1959, pp: 175-8.
5. From the transcript of interview 2 of the complete Santamaria interviews conducted for the Australian Biography project, interviewer: Robin Hughes, recorded: April 23, 24 and 25, 1997: http://www.australianbiography.gov.au/subjects/santamaria/interview2.html
6. Duncan, *Crusade or Conspiracy*, p. 45.
7. http://en.wikipedia.org/wiki/B._A._Santamaria#mediaviewer/File:Matthew_Beovich_and_B_A_Santamaria_1943.jpg
8. Clyde Cameron, Reflection: Clyde Cameron on Archbishop Mannix and Bob Santamaria, *News Weekly*, 30 November 2002, http://newsweekly.com.au/article.php?id=1077
9. Quoted in B.A. Santamaria, *Daniel Mannix: The quality of leadership*, Melbourne University Press, Melbourne, 1984, p. 211.
10. Santamaria, *Daniel Mannix*, pp: 212-3.
11. *Your most obedient servant: B A Santamaria letters, 1938–1996*, edited by Patrick Morgan, Miegunyah Press & the State Library of Victoria, pp 74-5.
12. *Argus*, 11 October 1954, p. 7. http://trove.nla.gov.au/ndp/del/article/23445017
13. Santamaria, *Daniel Mannix*, p. 222; Calwell's warning to Mannix in 1953 in M. E. Calwell, *I Am Bound To Be True*, p. 97.
14. Sacred Congregation of Propaganda Fide to Cardinal Gilroy, 27 May 1957, and 25 July 1957, in F. G. Clarke, *The Democratic Labor Party in Western Australia: Evolution and Early Development*, M.A. Thesis (W.A. 1969) (summarised in F. G. Clarke 'Labour and the Catholic Social Studies Movement', *Labour History*, No. 20 (May, 1971), pp. 46-59), Appendix 3.3, 4, p. 319.
15. Archbishop Mannix to Pope Pius XII, 21 August 1957, in Clarke, *The Democratic Labor Party in Western Australia*, Appendix 3.6, pp. 330-1.

16. Copy of Letter and Memorandum, Secretariat de stato sua di santita to Archbishop Mannix, 3 November 1957, in Clarke, *The Democratic Labor Party in Western Australia*, Appendix 3.4, pp. 323 and 325.
17. Santamaria, *Daniel Mannix*, p. 231.
18. Sydney *Daily Telegraph*, 21 November 1958, quoted in Santamaria, *Daniel Mannix*, p. 237.
19. *Canberra Times*, 21 November 1958: p. 1; other bishops condemn Evatt's "wild attack on Mannix: *Catholic Herald*, 28 November 1958, p. 5.
20. Frank Murphy, *Daniel Mannix: Archbishop of Melbourne 1917-1963*, Polding Press, Melbourne, 1972, pp. 256-7.
21. Michael Gilchrist, *Daniel Mannix: Wit and Wisdom*, Freedom Publishing, 2nd edition, North Melbourne, 2004, p. 266, n. 99: Interview with B.A. Santamaria, Hawthorn, 13 December 1976.
22. Morgan, *BA Santamaria: Running the Show*, p. 327.

Chapter 14: Death and Transformation into Legend

On Tuesday morning, 5 November, 1963, the Archbishop complained to his housekeeper of not feeling well but as the morning wore on, he said he was feeling better. However, after lunch, he suddenly collapsed and his personal physician, Dr John T. Cahill, was summoned and shortly after, Mgr Moran arrived to administer the last rites.[1]

It was soon evident that Daniel Mannix had not long to live, and as the news went out over the radio, a relay of visitors kept vigil at the bedside, including the Anglican Archbishop, Dr Frank Woods, Bob Santamaria, Arthur Calwell and Bishop Fox. The Archbishop seemed periodically to recognise people around him and nodded his head several times, but when he tried to speak, no sounds came out.

As Wednesday 6 November dawned, Dr Mannix was still hanging on to life and when Bishop Fox said he would celebrate Mass for him, Mannix nodded perceptibly and seemed to understand what was said. Sister M. Chrysostom from the nearby Caritas Christi Hospice tended the prelate almost continuously for the last 20 hours of his life, and as he finally lapsed into unconsciousness, he clasped the Sister's hand and would not let go.[2]

Finally, at 12.35pm on Wednesday, 6 November 1963, he breathed his last.

The nation's press, which had once castigated the Archbishop for his political views, was now lavish in its tributes. *The Age* extolled Dr Mannix's worldwide reputation, the international scope of his vision and his historical role in Australia:[3]

He was a reformer both within his own Church and in the broad fields outside it. In the first half of this century he was in the centre of fierce controversy on national and political questions and, while the passage of years brought a gentler temper to his reforming zeal, he was still in this past decade, a powerful voice with a political persuasion.

Archbishop Mannix lying dead in his bedroom at Raheen

He commanded loyalties and respect at all levels among clergymen and laymen. He was a great Irishman who served his communion in Australia – his adopted country – as faithfully as if it were on his native heath. He was a unique figure in the Australian story and one of historic proportions.

This assessment was shared by a wide range of public figures: the Prime Minister noted Dr Mannix's "power of persuasive speech which I have never known surpassed"; Mr Calwell linked Archbishop Mannix with Cardinal Moran as one of the two greatest figures in the history of the Church in Australia; Mr Henry Bolte, the State Premier, called him "one of the outstanding men of Australia" and Melbourne's Anglican Archbishop described Dr Mannix as "a legend in his own lifetime".[4]

To die at 99 is normally to outlive one's own legend. Not for Mannix. From the 1950s, the "image" of the old prelate has been kept alive and burnished by both enemies and devotees. "Mannicdotes" accumulate and proliferate in the dim world of after-dinner speeches, though no-one knows which of them are true.[5]

Unfortunately, the words of the Archbishop were never recorded, and all that was left were memories. A letter is extant in which he advised Archbishop Killian of Adelaide to destroy all personal correspondence before his death. He declared his determination not to be psycho-analysed after his own departure.*

---

* The destruction of Mannix's papers is itself the stuff of legend. The papers are not in existence, as far as anyone knows, but no-one has admitted to seeing the bonfire.

People file past Archbishop Mannix lying in state at Raheen

In the absence of the documented truth, the space is occupied by half-remembered anecdotes. Since the point of Mannix was to project a distinctive image, the anecdotes are part of what Mannix means and his story is incomplete without them.

Schoolgirls line the route of Mannix's funeral, on their knees (Fairfax images)

Mannicdotes

A typical anecdote is about Mannix's reluctance to appoint Monsignors. The reason may be that he did not wish to seek permission from Rome for their appointment, or again it may be that he wanted no barons with independent fiefdoms and rivalries to flourish. One monsignor got under his guard – Fr Hannan was made Monsignor with the rank of Domestic Prelate by the Apostolic Delegate. On one occasion Monsignor Hannan is said to have gunned his smart red sports car into the drive at Raheen and come to a screeching halt amid the smell of burning oil and flying gravel. Mannix observed:

'If that's a domestic prelate, I wouldn't like to see a wild one.'[6]

Five months after his arrival in Australia he was in Sydney to attend the second anniversary Mass for Cardinal Moran. Archbishop Kelly had spread himself as usual at considerable length, and was anxious to know how the young Archbishop [Mannix] appraised his panegyric. But all his hints were skilfully parried. Finally, he was compelled to ask straight out: "What did you think of my effort?" The answer was a masterpiece of ambiguity: "I envied the Cardinal."[7]

[Mannix] continued with this story about Archbishop Kelly, 'The only occasion that I got near to [a snake] was when Dr Kelly was down from Sydney, and he said he had never seen a snake. So someone arranged for both of us to go to the zoological gardens.' (He never abbreviated things). The two of them would have gone out there in their soutanes in the chauffeur-driven car. You can imagine what wonderment they caused out at the zoo. He continued, 'We did not see a snake. They told us that, as it was a dull day, the snakes stayed under rocks and dead trees, so we did not see one.' I said, 'So it was a waste of time?' 'Not exactly,' he replied, 'Dr Kelly had his zucchetto blown off into the monkey pit:' I said, 'Did he get it back?.' He said, 'After what the monkeys did with it, no sane man would have wanted it back.'[8]

Preaching the Sunday sermon he [Fr Hackett] almost invariably expounded the mystery of the Trinity, with all its relations, processions, missions, etc. Dr. Mannix once passed this comment: "I always knew the Trinity was a mystery, but had no idea of its magnitude until I heard Fr. Hackett explaining it."[9]

Often, the Archbishop brought back amusing tales to the Cathedral or *Raheen* meal tables about some character or incident encountered on one of his walks. On one occasion, Dr Mannix – a total abstainer – gave the usual donation to one individual with the advice, 'Now don't go spending it in that hotel across the road.' To which he responded, 'Which pub would you recommend, Your Grace?'[10]

An American visiting Australia to conduct research in the problems of old age interviewed the nonagenarian and produced a microphone to record the conversation. His first question was, "To what, Your Grace, do you attribute the fact that you have lived to your great age?" The answer came back, "Well, the basic reason is that I was born in 1864."[11]

Hardy's *Power without Glory*

Mannix's first transformation into myth, strictly so called, came at the hands of the Communist Party. The Party set its journalist member Frank Hardy to write a hatchet job on the evil capitalist John Wren. It was self-published in 1950 as a novel, *Power Without Glory*, with very lightly fictionalised characters – "John West" for Wren, "Daniel Malone" for Mannix, and so on. The fictionalised format allowed Hardy to include many allegations that suited leftist propaganda purposes, "West" himself being fitted up with a range of crimes from pigeon-race fixing to the murder of a detective.[12] Hardy was prosecuted for criminal libel in 1951 concerning the inclusion in the book of an affair by "West's" wife with a bricklayer, but won the case.

The paragraphs on "Malone" represent him as a sinister figure behind the scenes of Labor politics, defending such ideological outrages as the right to private property.

In Australia, the Church should turn to the Labor Party as the main basis of its political influence. It should cease to contest elections through the Catholic Federation, and should, for the time being, allow the agitation for Government grants for Catholic schools to fade into the background. Daniel Malone [Mannix] pointed out that he had already begun to implement this policy. His Holiness and his Cardinals were aware of this, he was told.

There was just one other little matter, the Cardinal intervened tactfully. Archbishop Malone must cease his open association with a certain notorious man named – what was his name? West, that was it, John West!

To accept West's money was quite in order, to use his political influence was laudable, but to associate his name with that of an Archbishop in public affairs was going too far. The Church could not afford to be particular about its allies, but must avoid scandal.

Though he had failed to get into Ireland to help implement Vatican policy it was now plain to him that the new Government under De Valera was successfully doing so.[13]

Though John West had been hoping to be recognised by the Vatican with a Papal knighthood, he suppressed his great disappointment and humiliation. No one else would know that the Vatican had more or less insulted him. Ever since he had emerged again into the public light he had realised that he must return to the shadows when his purpose was achieved. Power becomes more mighty and satisfying when exercised by remote control. He did not want glory, he wanted power – power without glory.[14]

"What financial reforms do you envisage?" Malone asked sharply. His hands were folded on his lap, his long face expressionless.

Summers [Prime Minister James Scullin] sighed wearily. "There are many plans. Ashton [Premier of NSW Jack Lang] and others want to nationalise the banks. Thurgood ["Red Ted" Theodore, the Labor Treasurer] has a plan for a fiduciary issue to stimulate production. I'm opposed to Ashton's plan, but if the tariff wall fails I will support Thurgood. But then we would need the Senate. As well, the Bank Board has suggested that Thurgood and I invite Sir Otto Niemeyer† to come from England to suggest economies. But there would be uproar in the Party and the Trade Unions if we did. Niemeyer would be sure to suggest pension and wage cuts."

"Perhaps economy is the only way out of this terrible depression," Malone replied. "And if Niemeyer came here, no one need know that you invited him."[15]

Malone [Mannix] referred to the *Rerum Novarum*, an encyclical that His Holiness Pope Leo XIII issued, stating the Church's attitude towards Socialism, poverty and private property.

"The most significant point in the pamphlet," Malone concluded, "especially now, is this one, '*The first and most fundamental principle, if one would undertake to alleviate the conditions of the masses, must be the inviolability of private property*' ".[16]

OAKLEY'S *THE FEET OF DANIEL MANNIX*

Mannix's fifty years as Catholic tribal leader in Melbourne have cast a long shadow in Catholic memory, in that city if not elsewhere. A generally affectionate tribute to Mannix's large place in Melbourne Catholic psychology is Barry Oakley's play, *The Feet of Daniel Mannix* (1971), a surreal and very funny run-through of Mannix's life story. Here, Oakley imagines what might have happened when Mannix met the Pope:[17]

---

† Sir Otto Niemeyer, Director of the Bank of England, did come to Australia by arrangement with the Commonwealth Bank of Australia and agreement by Prime Minister James Scullin and, when he warned that Australia had two years 'to get its house in order' before a tranche of external debt matured in 1932, his visit did cause an uproar.

The Pope's office, deep in the Vatican. POPE sits at a large desk which carries mountains of files. An attendant fans him with an ostrich feather.

POPE: Troubles in Latvia, troubles in Bavaria, Rumania, Lithuania, Prussia, Austria. Everywhere we got troubles! I tell you, who wants to be head of the Catholic Church? Boy, you can have it!

A knock

Yes, what is it?

VOICE: Doctor Daniel Manic of Mellerbrun.

POPE: Doctor Daniel Manic of Mellerbrun. And how do you like this awful Roman heat?

MANNIX: No worse than in my own city your holiness.

POPE: Hot in your home city? Mellerbrun, the southernmost city of New Zealand?

MANNIX: No holiness, Australia.

POPE: Well I was, how do you say, warm, was I not? Ha ha. Papal summer joke. Advise you to laugh if you wish to obtain rank of cardinal.

MANNIX: I find the cares of an archbishop are quite enough, holiness.

POPE: What, not interested in a red hat? I find that unusual […]

POPE: Dr Manic, that is the point you must grasp. Tradition first, utility second. Understand that and you understand the Vatican. There's quite a few papers on you, doctor. Quite a fat file. There would appear to be a number of complaints. Including one from the Prime Minister of your country, asking that you be replaced. He writes quite well for an aboriginal native. I note that my knowledge of your homeland surprises you, but that is my business. I note a letter here also that sings your praises. From Mr John Wren, Gentleman, of Kow-ling-wood. Somewhere in Hong Kong perhaps?

MANNIX: Your holiness, I was hoping to have a few words with you about Ireland.

POPE: Ireland? Why Ireland? Haven't we troubles enough in other countries? And the heat!

MANNIX: Ireland is my native land, and it is being torn apart by the British occupation forces, commonly known as the Black and Tans.

POPE: The British in Ireland? No one told me about this. How long have they been there?

MANNIX: About three hundred years. The people of Ireland are looking to the Vicar of Christ for relief. A statement, or a letter of encouragement. Something to show that he cares.

POPE: It's too hot for an encyclical. I'll do them a papal note.

MANNIX: You must encourage them, give them heart.

POPE: Yet not discourage the English. You see my problem?

MANNIX: Keep their spirits from flagging!

POPE: Without appearing to side with them. The Pope of the Universal Church must not offend anyone. That is the secret of the job. Balance, you must have balance. Now, where is the official style for papal notes? We must be quick; I've got the papal stocktaking to do in five minutes. Imagine! An inventory of all the goods and chattels! See, we have here standard forms of papal address to the faithful. Have the communists anything to do with it?

MANNIX: No, holy father.

POPE: Contraception? Birth control? Any suggestion of rubber goods or unnatural acts?

MANNIX: It's a simple matter of the British imperialists entering and refusing to withdraw.

POPE: Can't say that, can't say that. For a Pope, nothing is simple, please understand. There's the relationship of the Irish to the English, the English to the French, the French to the Germans, the Germans to the Italians, and so on. Ah! Here we are. Papal address number 48. Listen, "When we contemplate the faction and strife that still racks the world after the conclusion of so calamitous a war, our hearts fill with sorrow, and this especially is the case of dot-dot-dot (you fill in the country see) and this especially in the case of Ireland, one of the most precious jewels in the papal crown . . ."

MANNIX: Yes, but could we get to the point . . .

POPE: Dr Mannix, when the Vicar of Christ writes a letter there are certain formalities to be observed. One introduces oneself gradually to the matter. Otherwise, where would be the respect? If I can just continue without interruption—keep that fan going for the love of God—"How sad it is to see this great Catholic nation, small in size but big in spirit—beautifully put doctor, though I say so myself—at odds with another, whose conduct could be construed as somewhat less than neighbourly or fraternal . . ."

VOICE: Time for the stocktaking, holiness.

POPE: Yes, yes, I'll just round this off—"may we express the fervent hope that this less than fortunate conflict can be settled soon to the satisfaction of all parties". Signed: your loving Pope and stamped with the papal seal.

MANNIX: (aside) The papal seal has just done the greatest balancing act of all time.

POPE: Quickly now, an envelope. I have this appalling inventory to get through, to check who has stolen what in the last financial year. Here you are doctor. Now Vittorio, let's get this over with. Ready?

Cherubs, coated in gilt, one thousand.

Cherubs, solid gold throughout, eight hundred and fifty.

Damask for ecclesiastical hangings, four thousand yards.

Relics of bone, three hundred fragments.

Ostrich feathers for the cooling of the papal countenance, two hundred.

Busts of the papal fathers, three thousand seven hundred.

Parts of the true cross twenty seven …

THE NEXT GENERATIONS

Mannix's fourth successor as Archbishop of Melbourne, George Pell, recalls growing up with the legend and is happy to place himself in the tradition. In the foreword to *Daniel Mannix: Wit and Wisdom,*[18] he writes:

My personal memories of Archbishop Mannix are limited, although an aunt and a cousin listed "Mannix" among their Christian names and my grandparent's house, where I grew up, had the Archbishop's portrait in the dining room.

I visited him once at Raheen, as part of a group of three Victorian seminarians leaving in September 1963 to study at Propaganda Fide, Rome. He received us upstairs, with a rug over his knees and an Irish theological journal by his side. He rather deflated our self-importance by asking if we had been working in the garden!

I had heard him speak publicly on a couple of occasions, remembering particularly when he opened the Christian Brothers Training College at Bundoora in 1959. He received a long standing ovation and gave the best speech of the afternoon.

As Archbishop of Melbourne I wore one of his rings for my reception and regularly for the great feasts such as Christmas and Easter. I hoped something of his spirit would pass to me and I also wore his long lace surplice (or rochet) for blessing and opening ceremonies.

"His legacy endures. He was the most influential churchman in Australian history"

One cross-grained old Sydney priest, unaware of the surplice's origin, who was critical of what he imagined were my views on conscience, also felt that all that lace was conclusive evidence of my conservative mind-set!

It was my privilege to arrange for Nigel Boonham's magnificent sculpture of the Archbishop to be placed near the entrance to St Patrick's Cathedral in Melbourne and unveiled by Sir James Gobbo, the Governor, who had been a migrant school boy in Melbourne Catholic schools.

Archbishop Daniel Mannix was a father to his people and remains a model and an inspiration. His legacy endures. He was the most influential churchman in Australian history.

+ George Card. Pell

Archbishop of Sydney

13 January 2004

The second generation of Mannix followers, bringing us up to the present, is represented by Tony Abbott, who took as his mentor B.A. Santamaria several times during his early years in politics[19] and remained, in his own words, "under the Santamaria spell ever since."[20] "Santa was an idealist", Abbott says, and he was sometimes thought to "channel Santa" in Cabinet meetings, although he moved away from Santamaria's interventionist economic ideas.[21]

Here, Abbott tells a classic Mannicdote for the benefit of a couple probably not brought up to be Mannix admirers, Her Majesty Queen Elizabeth and the Duke of Edinburgh. During the Royal visit to Australia in October 2011, the Prime Minister, Julia Gillard, recalled Robert Menzies' cloying words of 1954, "I did but see her passing by", and updated it by declaring that the Queen, "far from passing by, [has] endured".[22]

The Opposition Leader,‡ Tony Abbott, went a step further, declaring that when he read this was expected to be the Queen's last Australian tour, he was reminded of an interview undertaken by Archbishop Mannix on his 96th birthday.

"At its close, the youthful reporter said that he hoped to do the same interview again next year. 'I don't see why not,' said the prelate, 'you look healthy enough to me,'" Mr Abbott chuckled, drawing a smile from both the Queen, 85, and the Duke of Edinburgh, 90."

---

‡ Prime Minister Abbott from November 2013.

1. Michael Gilchrist, *Daniel Mannix: Wit and Wisdom,* Freedom Publishing, 2nd edition, North Melbourne, 2004, p. 266, n. 101: Advocate, 14 November 1963.
2. Gilchrist, *Daniel Mannix*, p. 267, n. 102: Interview with Fr W.G. Smith SJ, Ballarat, October 1981.
3. Gilchrist, *Daniel Mannix*, p. 267, n. 103: *Age*, 7 November 1963.
4. Gilchrist, *Daniel Mannix*, p. 267, n. 104: *Age*, 7 November 1963.
5. Walter A. Ebsworth, *Archbishop Mannix*, H. H. Stephenson, Armadale, 1977, p. 429.
6. Patrick Morgan, Australian History: Archbishop Daniel Mannix's public roles, *News Weekly*, April 27, 2013: http://newsweekly.com.au/article.php?id=5552
7. Ebsworth, *Archbishop Mannix*, p. 430.
8. Leo M. Clarke, Archbishop Mannix: what was he like? *Footprints* 20 (1) (2003), 28-48.
9. Ebsworth, *Archbishop Mannix*, p. 64.
10. Gilchrist, *Daniel Mannix*, p. 143, n. 32.
11. Frank Murphy, *Daniel Mannix: Archbishop of Melbourne*, The Polding Press, Melbourne, 1972, p. 234.
12. Jenny Hocking, Research without glory, *Age*, 19 November 2005.
13. Frank Hardy, *Power without Glory*, Granada Publishing Limited, 1975, p. 388.
14. Hardy, *Power without Glory*, p. 390.
15. Hardy, *Power without Glory*, p. 498.
16. Hardy, *Power without Glory*, p. 500.
17. Barry Oakley, *The Feet of Daniel Mannix: A play*, Angus & Robertson, Sydney, 1975, pp. 20-24, reprinted with permission of Barry Oakley. Oakley was confirmed by Mannix in 1940.
18. Gilchrist, *Daniel Mannix*, Foreword, p. iii.
19. R. Fitzgerald and S. Holt, How Tony Abbott laboured over choice of party, *The Australian* 13/10/2012, http://www.theaustralian.com.au/national-affairs/how-tony-abbott-laboured-over-choice-of-party/story-fn59niix-1226494801586#
20. Tony Abbott, The legacy of B. A. Santamaria, *News Weekly* 17/2/2007, http://newsweekly.com.au/article.php?id=2943
21. A. Clark, Abbott's higher calling, *Australian Financial Review 27/4/2012,* http://www.afr.com/p/lifestyle/afrmagazine/tony_abbott_higher_calling_aNGk1uJKD26R4KQ6TWkbJJ; further in M. Duffy, *Latham and Abbott, Random House, Milsons Point, 2004.*
22. *Sydney Morning Herald*, 22 October 2011: http://www.smh.com.au/national/an-audience-with-her-majesty-takes-a-political-detour-20111021-1mcvc.html

Afterword: Back of house

Mannix occupied for fifty years the apex of the pyramid of Catholic Melbourne, a vast and powerful edifice which affected, sometimes controlled, the lives of thousands. At the base of society, certain of the powerless experienced grave evils. It would be unjust not to remember briefly the sufferings of these victims, even though Mannix cannot be accused of any direct responsibility for them or knowledge of them. The failures of the system of which he was head are one part of his story.

Near *Raheen*, just off Mannix's daily route to St Patrick's Cathedral, stands the huge complex of Abbotsford Convent. Now a heritage site, it is proud of its Bishop's Parlour, with fireplace elaborately decorated in poker wood.[1] Mannix frequently called and said mass.

Back of house in the mangle room, conditions were not so pleasant. One section of Abbotsford was the largest Australian example of the "Magdalen" laundries that have been a scandal in Ireland but were also found in all Australian capital cities. Teenage girls were confined in the laundries for reasons such as being prostitutes, unmarried mothers, intellectually retarded, without means of support, or unwanted by parents or step-parents. Hours were long, education poor and conditions shocking. It has to be remembered that the convent was offering shelter to women who had nowhere else to go. Nevertheless, memories of former inmates are almost uniformly negative. Protestant charges of "convent slave laundries" were not entirely false.[2]

Mannix defended Abbotsford against charges of commercial sharp dealing, claiming reasonably that the laundry used labour off the streets who were hard to train and that the laundry made a loss.[3] He did not discuss the conditions inside.

Orphanages too were scenes of dreadful conditions, as has been revealed by recent inquiries into institutions. Again, the context must be remembered. In the years before the Pill, there were thousands of unwanted children underfoot, many suffering from malnutrition and intellectual impairment. The Catholic Church provided shelter to great numbers of these "orphans", and did so under very difficult financial circumstances – state aid was as unavailable for orphanages as it was for schools, with minor exceptions. But orphanages such as St Augustine's, Geelong – its new buildings opened by Mannix in 1939 – and St Vincent's, South Melbourne were the scenes of extensive physical, mental, emotional and sexual abuse in Mannix's time and later.[4,5]

The clerical sexual abuse scandal is believed to have reached its height in the late 1960s and 1970s, but the beginnings go back to Mannix's time – although there are no known cases of abuse from Mannix's early years when he was genuinely in charge of the Archdiocese. His Corpus Christi Seminary opened in 1923 and trained generations of priests, most of whom performed their duties with credit. A few did not. Of the 378 graduates of Corpus Christi between 1940 and 1966, 18 were known child abusers.[6] Two Corpus Christi graduates, Kevin O'Donnell and John Day, were among the most notorious pedophile priests, and their careers of abuse began very early. O'Donnell's first known offence was against a boy aged 8 in 1946.[7] One victim and his scoutmaster reported the abuse in 1958-59 to the Melbourne Vicar-General (that is, the administrator in charge of the Archdiocese) and he was interviewed by Bishop Fox, but told to keep quiet.[8] O'Donnell was allowed to continue as parish priest, and in the 1980s repeatedly raped primary schoolgirls Emma and Katie Foster, leading to the death of one and the disablement of the other.

An earlier graduate of Corpus Christi was Monsignor John Day, who escaped prosecution for his decades of abuse with hundreds of victims in Mildura and elsewhere. The Catholic detective who pursued him unsuccessfully reported being approached in Melbourne in the early 1960s to join a group of Catholic police who "at the request of the Cathedral, look into instances where priests have been charged with offences to see if we can have these matters dropped or dismissed so the Church's good name will not be brought into disrepute."[9] He refused but saw many instances of priests being protected from the consequences of offences, from paedophilia down. That is the downside of tribalism.

Catholic political influence contributed to the conservative nature of legislation on "moral" questions like censorship, contraception and abortion. (Mannix, as we saw, had a horror of contraception, though he rarely mentioned censorship and only occasionally abortion.) No doubt there were benefits from that – indeed, a main purpose of strict moral views was to prevent people from producing the unwanted children who flooded orphanages.[10] But at the same time there were some now little-remembered victims. In the years between the wars, before antibiotics, Royal Women's Hospital in Melbourne had a ward dedicated to women who had had illegal abortions. Deaths from septicaemia were normal.[11] It may not be proved that there would have been fewer such victims if contraception and abortion had been more freely available. It is also true that many of the victims were married women unable to afford more children, and Mannix's campaigning for a reasonable minimum wage and child endowment was aimed at that problem. Nevertheless, in the actual world, those deaths were partly caused by legal prohibitions supported by Catholic influence.

There is no evidence that Mannix knew about what was happening in the underbelly of his jurisdiction. Given his "hands-off" approach to administration,[12] it is likely enough that he knew nothing. Like many bishops, he operated on the "general principle that when you give a man a job to do, you totally trust him"[13] – a sound principle when the subordinates are trustworthy, but not otherwise.

It is difficult to write about these matters, and doubly difficult to do so fairly. But they cannot in justice be ignored.

---

[1] http://www.abbotsfordconvent.com.au/venues-hire/venues/bishop%E2%80%99s-parlour

[2] James Franklin, Convent slave laundries? Magdalen asylums in Australia, *Journal of the Australian Catholic Historical Society* 34 (2013), 70-90.

[3] 'The Victorian Protestant Federation: An Attack on Convent Laundries', *Freeman's Journal* 12/9/1918, http://trove.nla.gov.au/ndp/del/article/116785928

[4] Christian Brothers apologise for abuse at an orphanage: http://brokenrites.org.au/drupal/node/205; Sex abuse at two Christian Brothers orphanages in Victoria – St Augustine's and St Vincent's: http://brokenrites.org.au/drupal/node/70; 'Dying orphan tells Royal Commission of church abuse in Geelong', *Geelong Advertiser*, 8/4/2014.

[5] The Senate Community Affairs References Committee: *Forgotten Australians, A report on Australians who experienced institutional or out-of-home care as children*, August 2004: http://www.aph.gov.au/Parliamentary_Business/Committees/Senate/Community_Affairs/Completed_inquiries/2004-07/inst_care/report/index

[6] 'One in twenty priests an abuser, inquiry told', *Age*, 23 October 2013.

[7] Chrissie Foster with Paul Kennedy, *Hell on the Way to Heaven*, Bantam, North Sydney, pp. 69-73.

[8] http://www.brokenrites.org.au/drupal/node/62; Foster, *Hell on the Way to Heaven*, pp. 314-8; another instance in http://brokenrites.org.au/drupal/node/59 .

[9] Denis Ryan and Peter Hoysted, *Unholy Trinity: The hunt for the pedophile priest Monsignor John Day*, Allen & Unwin, Crows Nest, 2013, pp. 36-8, 8-9, 15-20.

[10] Thomas Aquinas, *Summa Theologiae*, II-II q. 154 art. 2.

[11] Janet McCalman, *Sex and Suffering: Women's Health and a Women's Hospital: The Royal Women's Hospital, Melbourne 1856-1996*, Melbourne University Press, Carlton, 1998, pp. 215-21; Jo Wainer, ed, *Lost: Illegal Abortion Stories*, Melbourne University Press, Melbourne, 2006.

[12] Described in Leo M. Clarke, Archbishop Mannix: what was he like? *Footprints* 20 (1) (2003), 28-48.

[13] Fr N. Ryan, quoted in Gilchrist, *Daniel Mannix*, ch. 9.

INDEX

Abbott, Tony 269
aborigines 178-80
abortion 195
alcohol and temperance 178, 208
Anderson, F. 162
Argus 14, 29, 34, 91-2, 178
Armstrong, H.G. 55
atomic bomb 183-4
Australian Labor Party 68, 159, 164-7, 170, 221, 238, 256

Balfour, A. 18
Baltic 40, 55-64
Benedict XV 10, 36, 117, 128-30, 265
Bernardini, Archbishop P. 130
Bolte, H. 261
Bootle 73-6
British Empire 9, 11, 15, 18-21, 36, 68-9, 106-7

Cadogan, A. 125
Calwell, A. 143, 214, 219-40, 246, 251 260
canon law 90, 136-9
capitalism 172-5, 224, 237
Carr, Archbishop T. 3, 11, 139, 165, 221
Carroll, Archbishop J. 251
Catholic Federation 91, 159-60, 165
Catholic Worker 243-4
Cattaneo, Archbishop B. 120, 123, 130
Cecil, R. 123
Cerretti, Cardinal B. 118, 121
Chesterton, G.K. 67
Chifley, J.B. 137, 194, 233

child endowment 176, 227
Churchill, W. 130
Collins, M. 210-1
Communism 175, 181-3, 189, 224, 243-4, 246-8, 251, 264
conscription 11-12, 15-16
contraception 146, 193-4, 244, 267
Corder, F. 93
Corpus Christi College, Werribee 199, 272
Cosgrave, W.T. 80-4
cows 197
Curzon, G.N. 127, 129

D'Arcy, Archbishop E. 152-3
De Salis, J.F.C. 18, 119, 125-7, 130
De Valera, E. 39-50, 70, 78-80
democracy 113, 155, 184-6
Democratic Labor Party 156, 240, 244, 252, 256-7
Dunne, Bishop J. 26

Easter Rising 10, 24, 27-8, 53
Elizabeth II, Queen 269
Evatt, H.V. 244, 250, 256

Fitzgerald, S. 61
Fox, Bishop A.F. 231, 260, 272
Freemasonry 90-1, 246

Gasparri, Cardinal P. 121, 127-8, 138
Gasquet, Cardinal F.A. 124
Gilroy, Cardinal N. 189, 230-3, 251, 255-6

275

Hackett, Fr W. 135, 210-2, 263
Hardy, F. 264
Heydon, C. 104-8, 120
Holt, H. 156
Hughes, W.M. 9-11, 15-16, 18, 68-70, 91, 112-4, 123-4, 225

immigration 198-201, 219, 233-5, 249
imperialism 18, 85, 87, 179
influenza epidemic of 1919 98-101
Irish Civil War 72-3, 78-84, 210
Irish War of Independence 39, 72
Italian community 212-4, 227-9

Jeffs, H. 20
Jehovah's Witnesses 113
Jesus 144-5, 207
Jews 129, 180-1
Jones, H.E. 222-3

Kelly, Archbishop M. 34, 136, 263

Landy, *née* Eyre, M. 209-10
Leo XIII 170-2, 175-6, 224
Leslie, S. 66
Lodewyckx, A. 226
Lombard, Fr F. 251
Loyal Orange Lodge 28, 74, 90, 104-5, 166

MacSwiney, T. 72
Magdalen laundries 166, 271
Mannix, Daniel
  American tour 39-57
  Archbishop of Melbourne 143, 146-52, 205
  arrest by Royal Navy 63-4
  Australian nationalism 10, 18-19, 37
  coadjutor Archbishop 2, 160
  death 260-1
  Irish nationalism 3, 29-36, 41-54, 77-8, 85-7
  and lay initiative 150-4
  meeting with Pope 128-30
  pastoral work 146-8, 206, 215
  personal relationships 190, 208-12, 239, 257
  piety 145-6, 207
  political activities 118, 130-1, 159, 246, 255-6
  Rector of Maynooth 23, 27, 110, 136, 206-7
  rhetorical style xi-xii, 205
  self-image 23, 34, 77-8, 148
  social justice ideas 24, 155, 169-81
  theological ideas 141-5, 152-6
  and Vatican 118-33
  vision for Catholic Australia 3, 7, 36, 139-41
Mannix, Ellen (mother) 80
Mayne, Fr C. 199
McCarthy, M.J.F. 92-3
McKenna, N. 238, 246, 256
Menzies, R. 93-7, 156, 209, 246, 261
minimum wage 170-2, 176
Modotti, Fr U. 212, 228
Mole, E. 64-5
Moran, H. 108-11
Moran, Cardinal P. 232, 261, 263
  Movement, the 197, 244, 248, 251-4
Munro Ferguson, R. 17-18, 118
Murtagh, Fr J. 184

Newman, Cardinal J.H. 148-9
Newman College 135, 148-9

Oakley, B. 265
O'Collins, Bishop J. 231, 257-8
O'Duffy, E. 131
O'Farrell, P. 205
O'Reilly, M. 35-6, 79
orphans 198, 272

Panico, Archbishop G. 231
Parker, F.C. 93
Paul VI 234-5
Pell, Cardinal G. xii, 117, 268-9
Pius XI 131, 187, 224
Pius XII 198, 251-4
population problem 7, 193-5, 220, 225-7
Prince of Wales, later Edward VIII 70
Protestantism 9, 20-1, 28, 89-105, 111-2, 137

Raheen 110, 112, 197, 204-17, 224, 228, 255, 260-2, 268
Redmond, J. 23
Rentoul, L. 91-3
Rerum novarum 166-7, 170-2, 243, 265
rural virtue 196-8, 249
Ruth, T.E. 21
   Ryan, T.J. 10

St Kevin's College 135, 243
Santamaria, B.A. 150, 156, 176, 186, 197, 238-9, 243-260, 269
Scullin, J. 166-7, 246, 265
security services 10, 17, 110, 113, 207, 219-23
sex education 146, 152

sexual abuse scandal 272
Simonds, Archbishop J. 240
Sinn Fein 17-18, 33, 39, 70, 105, 221
social justice 169, 176, *see also Rerum Novarum*
Spanish Civil War 183
Split, Labor 220, 239-40, 244, 250
state aid for church schools 4, 89, 97, 156, 159-64, 220
states and federalism 186-9
Steward, G. 10, 16

Tardini, Cardinal D. 244, 254

universities 5, 34-5, 148-9, 162, 178, 257

Walsh, Archbishop W. 124
women 177-8

Van Rossum, W.M., Cardinal 120
Vatican II 152-3
Vaughan, Fr A. 62
Vietnam 189-90
Virgona sisters 208, 212-6

White Australia policy 19, 201-2, 220, 235-7
Wilhelm II, Kaiser 28, 70
Wilson, H. 76
Wilson, W. 43-4
Wodehouse, P.G. 215
World War I 9-10, 13, *see also* conscription
Worrall, Rev H. 14, 98
Wren, J. 103, 207, 264

www.ingramcontent.com/pod-product-compliance
Lightning Source LLC
Chambersburg PA
CBHW061128010526
44117CB00023B/2990